iAd Production
Beginner's Guide

Create motion-rich, beautiful iAd adverts for iOS devices and incorporate techniques to help boost revenue and brand awareness

Ben Collier

BIRMINGHAM - MUMBAI

iAd Production
Beginner's Guide

First published: February 2012

Production Reference: 1160212

Published by Packt Publishing Ltd.
Livery Place
35 Livery Street
Birmingham B3 2PB, UK.

ISBN 978-1-84969-132-1

www.packtpub.com

Cover Image by Asher Wishkerman (a.wishkerman@mpic.de)

Credits

Author

Ben Collier

Reviewers

Karl Norsen

Olivier Rabenschlag

Acquisition Editor

Sarah Cullington

Lead Technical Editor

Susmita Panda

Technical Editors

Apoorva Bolar

Naheed Shaikh

Copy Editor

Brandt D'Mello

Project Coordinator

Shubhanjan Chatterjee

Proofreader

Aaron Nash

Indexer

Monica Ajmera Mehta

Graphics

Manu Joseph

Production Coordinator

Prachali Bhiwandkar

Cover Work

Prachali Bhiwandkar

About the Author

Ben Collier is based in Brighton, UK and specializes in responsive HTML5 websites/cross-platform web-apps, and great native iOS apps on Apple's App Store. He enjoys the constraints and challenges of working with small-screen mobile devices, as it forces focus on the important content and functionality within an app. You can visit Ben's personal website at http://bencollier.net or follow him on Twitter at @ben_c.

Ben is a partner at Ocasta Studios, who make and manage mobile and small-screen apps across all the leading mobile platforms. Visit http://ocastastudios.com for more info.

I'd like to thank those key into making this book a reality; the countless cups of coffee, fresh olives, and episodes of Mad Men. My friends and family were incredibly patient through the late nights and long weekends during which they didn't get the attention they deserved, and for that I'm extremely grateful. The team at Packt Publishing did a fantastic job at keeping me on schedule and turning this book into a reality; working with them has been a pleasure.

About the Reviewer

Karl Norsen is a technology strategist, manager, and technical lead. He is passionate about leveraging new and emerging technologies in marketing and expanding on how businesses can use technology to further connect their brand with consumers. His background in both technology and advertising has given him a unique perspective on brand awareness, innovative digital media, and utilizing technology to facilitate lasting consumer connections. His future interests include further expanding the reach of a creative technical director and continuing to provide innovative solutions that build on the ever-increasing role of technology in brand and business success.

For more information, you can find his full profile on LinkedIn.

Olivier Rabenschlag's roots are back in the UK where he worked for a variety of advertising agencies as a creative director. He launched numerous Axe body spray campaigns for Unilever and took on digital duties for Sony Ericsson in Europe. In 2006 Olivier moved to Miami to work for Crispin Porter & Bogusky on clients including Burger King, Coke Zero, Sprite, and Volkswagen. After a year in New York following Crispin he eventually moved to Los Angeles where he's now the Group Creative Director of Media Arts at TBWA\CHIAT\DAY responsible for the agency's innovation and integration capabilities across emerging media platforms. Clients include Activision, The Grammys, Nissan, Infiniti, Pedigree and Visa. Olivier helped launch the world's first iAd for the Nissan Leaf that was also presented as a case study at Apple's worldwide developers conference in 2010 by Steve Jobs.

www.PacktPub.com

Support files, eBooks, discount offers and more

You might want to visit www.PacktPub.com for support files and downloads related to your book.

Did you know that Packt offers eBook versions of every book published, with PDF and ePub files available? You can upgrade to the eBook version at www.PacktPub.com and as a print book customer, you are entitled to a discount on the eBook copy. Get in touch with us at service@packtpub.com for more details.

At www.PacktPub.com, you can also read a collection of free technical articles, sign up for a range of free newsletters and receive exclusive discounts and offers on Packt books and eBooks.

http://PacktLib.PacktPub.com

Do you need instant solutions to your IT questions? PacktLib is Packt's online digital book library. Here, you can access, read and search across Packt's entire library of books.

Why Subscribe?

- ◆ Fully searchable across every book published by Packt
- ◆ Copy and paste, print and bookmark content
- ◆ On demand and accessible via web browser

Free Access for Packt account holders

If you have an account with Packt at www.PacktPub.com, you can use this to access PacktLib today and view nine entirely free books. Simply use your login credentials for immediate access.

Table of Contents

Preface

Think of an iAd as a micro-app contained within an app, on a user's iPhone or iPad, that they've downloaded from the App Store. When the user taps your advert's banner, it bursts into life, filling the entire screen of their device.

iAd Beginner's Guide takes you from start to finish of building rich, compelling, and interactive iAds. You will learn how to create beautiful multi-page ads with store finders, social sharing, 3D images, and video galleries.

You will create ads that utilize the powerful technologies in the iPhone to make your brand shine. Once you have engaged the user, you can carry out targeted advertising campaigns with location-based coupons, store finders, and social engagement. Using the iTunes Store, you will see how it's even possible to add one-click digital content purchasing, right within your ad. Learn how iAd producer manages all the HTML5, JavaScript, and CSS3 behind your iAd. You will be creating emotive, gripping, and effective mobile advertising campaigns in no time.

What this book covers

Chapter 1, Getting Started with iAd, introduces you to iAd, the immersive mobile advertising platform from Apple. We'll look at what an iAd is, why they're awesome, and the underlying technologies they're written in.

Chapter 2, Preparing Your Content, shows the best techniques to get the most out of your media content.

Chapter 3, Making Your iAd, shows you how to install iAd Producer—the tool from Apple that allows us to make rich iAds. With drag-and-drop simplicity and step-by-step examples, we'll create our first demo iAd!

Chapter 4, Making Sure it Works, shows you how to test your ads on the device, or in the iOS Simulator, if you don't have access to the required hardware.

Chapter 5, Templates and Objects, presents the benefits and limitations of a large selection of templates and objects as we build another example iAd, using a range of the pre-built templates and objects in iAd Producer.

Chapter 6, iAd Destinations, shows you how to use the core of our ad to engage your user and induce them to perform an action, such as sharing your brand with a friend via email or downloading your digital content from the iTunes Store.

Chapter 7, Building for the Big Screen, shows you how to build more immersive iAds for the iPad. With its large multi-touch screen, we'll make an ad with even richer interactivity that'll work exclusively on the iPad.

Chapter 8, Creating Interactive Ads, teaches you how to modify the JavaScript code that powers your iAd by adding simple code snippets to enhance your ad with dynamic SMS/e-mail sharing and calendar events, to keep engaging the user with your brand after they've left your advertisement.

Chapter 9, Managing a Successful iAd Campaign, presents the best ways to manage a successful iAd campaign, adding tracking analytics into your ad, measuring user insights, and the targeting options available, to ensure you reach the ideal target audience.

Chapter 10, Adding iAds into Your App, teaches you how to add iAd into an existing application, to begin generating revenue, and intelligently animate banners in and out of view, depending on their availability.

Chapter 11, Tracking Revenue and Fallbacks, shows you how to integrate additional ad solutions when the iAd Network doesn't have an available banner in its inventory. Finally, you'll learn how to analyze the number of ads your app is displaying, and more importantly, how much you're earning!

What you need for this book

You'll need to be a member of the iOS Developer program and have a Mac running Snow Leopard, OS 10.6 or later. We'll look at getting or updating a Mac and joining the iOS Developer program in the first chapter. It'll be useful to have an iPhone or iPad to test on, but isn't vital as you'll learn how to preview your ads without a device.

Who this book is for

This book is for brands, advertisers, and developers who want to create compelling and emotive iAd advertisements that generate revenue and increase brand awareness. You don't need previous experience of creating adverts or apps for iPhone and iPad, as you'll be taken through the entire process of making motion-rich, beautiful ads.

Conventions

In this book, you will find several headings appearing frequently.

To give clear instructions of how to complete a procedure or task, we use:

Time for action – heading

1. Action 1

2. Action 2

3. Action 3

Instructions often need some extra explanation so that they make sense, so they are followed with:

What just happened?

This heading explains the working of tasks or instructions that you have just completed.

You will also find some other learning aids in the book, including:

Pop quiz – heading

These are short multiple choice questions intended to help you test your own understanding.

Have a go hero – heading

These set practical challenges and give you ideas for experimenting with what you have learned.

You will also find a number of styles of text that distinguish between different kinds of information. Here are some examples of these styles, and an explanation of their meaning.

Code words in text are shown as follows: "Duplicate, by copying and pasting, the line that contains `CGPoint bannerOrigin` and rename `bannerOrigin` to `fallbackBannerOrigin`."

A block of code is set as follows:

```
if (bannerView.bannerLoaded) {
        // bring banner into view
        bannerOrigin.y -= bannerView.bounds.size.height;
    }
    else {
        fallbackBannerOrigin.y -= imageView.bounds.size.height;
    }
```

When we wish to draw your attention to a particular part of a code block, the relevant lines or items are set in bold:

```
if (bannerView.bannerLoaded) {
        // bring banner into view
        bannerOrigin.y -= bannerView.bounds.size.height;
    }
    else {
        fallbackBannerOrigin.y -= imageView.bounds.size.height;
    }
```

New terms and **important words** are shown in bold. Words that you see on the screen, in menus or dialog boxes for example, appear in the text like this: "From the right-hand menu, select **Set Up iAd Network**."

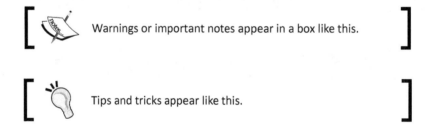

> Warnings or important notes appear in a box like this.

> Tips and tricks appear like this.

Reader feedback

Feedback from our readers is always welcome. Let us know what you think about this book—what you liked or may have disliked. Reader feedback is important for us to develop titles that you really get the most out of.

To send us general feedback, simply send an e-mail to feedback@packtpub.com, and mention the book title via the subject of your message.

If there is a book that you need and would like to see us publish, please send us a note in the **SUGGEST A TITLE** form on www.packtpub.com or e-mail suggest@packtpub.com.

If there is a topic that you have expertise in and you are interested in either writing or contributing to a book, see our author guide on www.packtpub.com/authors.

Customer support

Now that you are the proud owner of a Packt book, we have a number of things to help you to get the most from your purchase.

Downloading the example code

You can download the example code files for all Packt books you have purchased from your account at http://www.PacktPub.com. If you purchased this book elsewhere, you can visit http://www.PacktPub.com/support and register to have the files e-mailed directly to you.

Errata

Although we have taken every care to ensure the accuracy of our content, mistakes do happen. If you find a mistake in one of our books—maybe a mistake in the text or the code—we would be grateful if you would report this to us. By doing so, you can save other readers from frustration and help us improve subsequent versions of this book. If you find any errata, please report them by visiting http://www.packtpub.com/support, selecting your book, clicking on the **errata submission form** link, and entering the details of your errata. Once your errata are verified, your submission will be accepted and the errata will be uploaded on our website, or added to any list of existing errata, under the Errata section of that title. Any existing errata can be viewed by selecting your title from http://www.packtpub.com/support.

Piracy

Piracy of copyright material on the Internet is an ongoing problem across all media. At Packt, we take the protection of our copyright and licenses very seriously. If you come across any illegal copies of our works, in any form, on the Internet, please provide us with the location address or website name immediately so that we can pursue a remedy.

Please contact us at `copyright@packtpub.com` with a link to the suspected pirated material.

We appreciate your help in protecting our authors, and our ability to bring you valuable content.

Questions

You can contact us at `questions@packtpub.com` if you are having a problem with any aspect of the book, and we will do our best to address it.

1
Getting Started with iAd

iAd is an exciting mobile advertising opportunity from Apple.

In this chapter, we will look at:

- What an iAd is
- What makes an iAd awesome
- The anatomy of an iAd
- The technology that powers iAd
- The tools available to build your own iAds
- How to access to the tools

Learning what an iAd is

Announced by Apple in the summer of 2010, an iAd allows you to directly target customers with amazingly interactive ads integrated into applications purchased on the App Store. Each iAd begins as a small exciting banner on a user's personal device that once activated bursts to fill the screen, giving you, the advertiser, a chance to craft a deeply immersive experience.

Application developers on the Apple App Store designate space within their app for your iAd to be shown, with the banner sitting at the bottom of the screen throughout the use of the app. Often, iAds can be more interesting than the app they're in!

iAds are built into iOS 4.0 and, later, the operating system used by the Apple iPhone, iPod touch, and iPad.

Think of an iAd as a mini-app contained within another third-party application that a user has downloaded from the Apple App Store.

With an iAd, your advertisement is viewed by an audience that:

◆ Has installed more than 15 billion applications since the App Store opened in 2008

◆ Has activated over 225 million iTunes accounts, with each account being tied to a credit card for one-click billing (even within your iAd)

◆ Downloads 200 new apps every second worldwide

◆ Spends, on average, 73 minutes per day using apps

◆ Engages with iAd ads for an average of 60 seconds per visit

Apple sets a degree of quality in their products, which is often mirrored in the extensive range of applications available on their App Store. However, mobile advertising is often a jarring and unpleasant experience for the user. Unhappy with this, Apple decided to build a unique advertising platform right into the handsets of millions of users.

In early 2011, Apple announced iAd support for iPad, which gives us full access to a rich interactive multi-touch canvas to promote our brands or products in a way that was previously only imaginable to advertisers.

 Many companies using iAds create a promotional video just to show off their ad! You'll sometimes find that you get additional PR opportunities with iAd, as each experience is so dynamic and different people love talking about them.

Each iAd impression can be targeted towards:

◆ **Demographics**: A target gender or age

◆ **Application preferences**: A user's app purchasing and downloading trends can give an insight into their preferences

◆ **Music passions**: Although a user's taste in music isn't an obvious useful targeting technique, listening habits monitored by iTunes can identify a certain demographic. This is how radio advertising is targeted.

◆ **Movie, TV, and audiobook genre interests**: As each device is linked to an iTunes account, Apple has access to a user's store purchases and media interest

◆ **Location**: Every iOS device has location capabilities built in; so, if you have brick-and-mortar stores you can target nearby potential customers, possibly with local time-sensitive offers

- **Device (iPhone, iPod touch, or iPad)**: The iAd Network lets you design and target advertisements unique to the different iOS devices, tailoring each experience to take full advantage of the hardware available

- **Network (Wi-Fi, 3G)**: If a user is on Wi-Fi, they're more likely to be in a situation where they'll engage with your iAd, as Wi-Fi is mostly available in static positions with users having more time to focus on your ad

Apple manages the entire process of delivering your ads, including hosting them on the iAd Network and wirelessly delivering them to your audience on iOS devices.

Apple allows users to opt out of *interest-based ads* by visiting `http://oo.apple.com/` on their iOS 4.0+ device. This still delivers iAd's to the user, but without any user-specific targeting. Obviously, Apple doesn't publicize this and only a handful of power users ever opt-out.

Understanding problems with existing mobile advertising

Mobile advertising isn't a new idea but, until iAd, it was never quite right. It was filled with ringtones, wallpapers, and premium SMS that would unwittingly sign the user up to a subscription service. It was more about publicizing paid mobile media direct to the customer than promoting great brands and products.

In-application advertising is beginning to target more specific brands, but nearly all mobile adverts take you out of the application you're currently in and make it impossible to easily get back to where you just were. Typically, the user is pushed out of the app into the mobile browser, to a webpage that often isn't meant for mobile and lacks interaction and responsiveness for the user. Before iAd, a typical mobile banner would be a plain static strip hidden within a user's app, not an interactive ad built into the core operating system.

On the desktop, most advertising revenue comes from search, but mobile users are using more specific apps for finding the information they want. If you want to find a great place to eat, you're more likely to open up a restaurant directory app than go into the mobile browser and use a search engine. Context-aware applications are becoming the way users find things on mobile. Your iAd intelligently positions itself in these applications, providing relevant, contextual, and exciting marketing opportunities.

Discovering what makes an iAd awesome

Unlike traditional mobile advertising, each iAd provides an in-app interactive advertisement, which doesn't push the user out of the app. Never before have you been able to promote your brand or product with such an immersive experience, interacting with the fingertips of the users.

A study by Nielsen compared Campbell's Soup TV advertising campaign with their iAd mobile advertisement and found that users interacting with the iAd were:

- More than twice as likely to recall the ad
- Three times more likely to remember the messaging
- Four times more likely to purchase

People remember better when there's interactivity with the information that we want them to absorb. Each iAd is given access to deeply immersive device features, from the full multi-touch screen (allowing users to pinch and flick around images of your really cool product close up) to physical movements of the device (allowing them to use a shake to show a random message or fact about your brand), iAds offer an unparalleled opportunity for a compelling, interactive, and memorable experience.

The unique features integrated in an iAd make it possible to let users interact with your brand in several engaging ways, such as the following:

- **Download an app or buy iTunes media from within an iAd**: If you have content available on the iTunes Store or App Store, such as a movie or app that you want to promote, users can purchase this within your iAd with a single tap, without ever leaving the app they're in
- **Save screen images to photo albums**: Images like coupons, barcodes, recipes, or branded wallpaper can be saved straight to the user's device or instantly set as their background
- **View in-line audio and video**: Video can be played within a custom frame in your iAd, overlaid with interactive elements interactive elements
- **Find nearby stores**: With rich Google Maps built into every iOS device, it's easy to show a list of your nearby stores or retailers
- **Share content through Twitter without leaving the ad**: The iAd framework is completely extensible, so social sharing and almost any functionality can be achieved

At any time, the user can click on the close button, always in the top-left of an iAd, and get back to the app that they were in, which makes them more comfortable about tapping on an iAd and associates your brand with a positive experience. Here, you can see the close button in a demo ad:

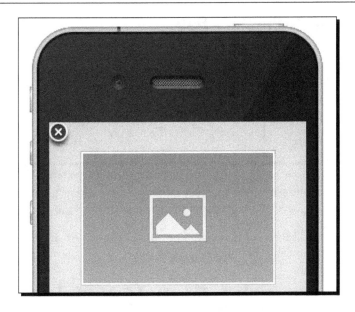

With iAd, Apple has built an experience that simultaneously combines the interactivity of traditional online advertising with the emotive aspects of television advertising.

 Check out the Nissan Leaf iAd promotional video (search for *Nissan Leaf iAd* on a video site such as YouTube); it's an amazing example of inciting emotion within an iAd and demonstrates the vast flexibility of the iAd platform.

Describing the anatomy of an iAd

An iAd consists of four key parts, which are as follows:

1. A banner ad.
2. Transition from the banner to the main advert.
3. A splash page.
4. The core ad unit.

Understanding the banner's role

The **banner** is the first impression of your advert; it's vital that it inspires the user to tap on it and explore all the other great content you've got waiting in your iAd. Banners are identifiable by their small logo in the bottom-right of the banner, as shown in the following screenshot:

The iAd logo increases the chance of the user tapping on your advert, as they know they'll be delivered a rich immersive ad without losing the place of the app they're in.

The banner is typically displayed either at the bottom of the screen or above the tab bar of a user's application, as shown in the following screenshot:

Using different banner types

There are two types of banners you can use for your iAd - a **static image banner** or a **dynamic HTML5 banner**.

Static image banner

A static image banner is a much more traditional banner and is often chosen because it's quick and simple to create.

Your static banner can either be the size of the banner frame or can be a screen-size static banner with only a slice of the image visible in the banner, revealing the full image when the user taps to view your ad.

Dynamic HTML5 banner

An HTML5 dynamic banner opens up much more opportunity for user engagement, as it allows for animated text and graphics. Adding motion and animation to your banner makes it stand out on the user's device, drawing their attention to your ad and increasing the chance they'll tap to find out more about your brand.

With an HTML5 banner you're able to update data in the banner remotely with real-time information, like latest sports scores or stock quotes.

Transitioning into the ad

The transition occurs when the user taps the banner to enter your iAd; it softens the entry to the splash page and creates a visual connection between the two. The transition can either be a **slide** or a **reveal**.

Slide transition

The slide transition is the most common way of presenting your splash page. It pushes a full color block up from your banner covering the app the user is currently in. A progress bar shows the status of the loading of your splash screen.

Reveal transition

You should only use reveal transition if you're using a screen-size static banner. It pushes apart the user interface elements in the users app to reveal your iAd splash screen. The following screenshot shows the reveal transition in an ad that we'll create later in the book:

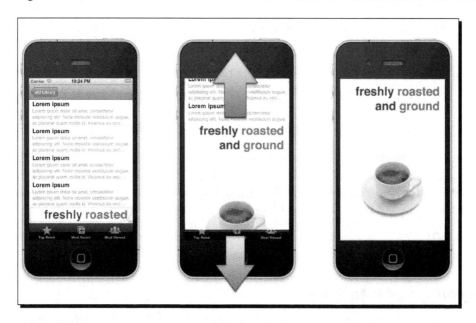

Making loading interesting with the splash page

The splash page is an optional screen; it is shown while the main iAd resources load, in between the user's tapping of your banner and their being able to interact with the core ad unit.

Although the splash page is optional, it's an ideal opportunity to convey your brand message while the resources for your ad load.

Apple estimates you've got 15 seconds to win the user's attention once they've entered your iAd, so an engaging splash page ensures that we keep them happy while they wait.

The splash page can be used to show interesting stats or features about your brand or product before transitioning into the main ad.

 Even if you think your iAd is lightweight and won't need time to download, users are often on slow mobile data connections where small ads won't load immediately.

A pre-roll video can also be used in the splash page although, with the lightweight CSS3 animations and styles available, we can apply dynamic effects to images and text that can often mimic video, without the large (and slow) download associated with streaming video.

Exploring the core ad unit

This is the main part of your iAd where there is a real opportunity to deliver your content in a range of exciting ways. The core ad unit is built up of multiple views; think of these as different pages of a website, each with a range of media and content to excite the user about your brand or product.

The ad unit starts with the **root view**, which is generally used for navigation, to toggle between the different views within your iAd.

The subpages of the root view offer the chance to provide: dynamic maps showing the location of the user to your nearest store or retailer, amazing 3D interactive video carousels and image galleries, or a blank canvas only limited by your own imagination! Here is a selection of the templates that can be used in your iAd to give you an understanding of the types of the content you can include:

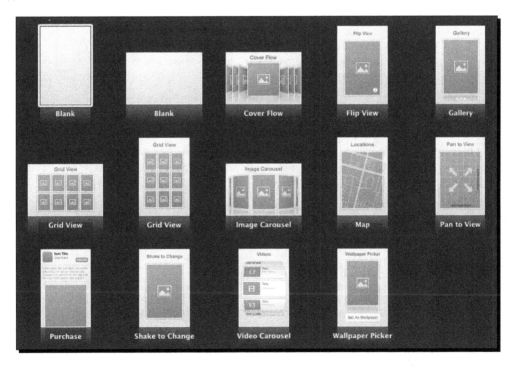

Understanding your iAd

An iAd is essentially a rich dynamic webpage contained within an application a user has installed. For the most part, we don't need to be concerned with what's going on, as the tools Apple provides manage this for us. That having been said, it is good to have an understanding of the magic that powers your iAd.

HTML5 is the underlying technology of the iAd framework. It is based on the future of the web with the next generation of HTML (and mistakenly marketed as including enhancements to JavaScript and CSS). Our iAds can use HTML5 in conjunction with many of the latest features in JavaScript and CSS.

Structuring with HTML

HTML5, the fifth generation of **HTML (Hypertext Markup Language)**, is the content and semantic structure of your page.

Video, audio, and other things that traditionally would require a plug-in, such as Flash (which iOS famously doesn't support), can now be done with HTML5.

 For those curious, if you right-click on a webpage and choose **View Source**, you can look at the underlying HTML that creates the structure and contains the content of that page.

Styling with CSS3

The third revision of **CSS (Cascading Style Sheets)** allows visual styling in your iAd. With CSS3, styling of rounded corners and background gradients can be done without images, which means that your iAd is lightweight and delivers your brand message much faster to the user. CSS3 has rich animation capacity, which can bring life to your iAd and banner.

CSS3 has smooth, hardware-accelerated 3D effects that you can apply to your iAd assets, combined with animations. Rich 3D motion adds to the interactivity of your ad.

Interacting with JavaScript

JavaScript is a programming language used to control the interactivity inside your iAd. Whenever tapping or pinching somewhere causes interaction with your iAd, behind the scenes, JavaScript will be controlling this. JavaScript is able to access user location to find local stores and provide location-sensitive promotions. JavaScript can be used to remotely fetch the latest offers and information from your website, using a technology called AJAX to create a dynamic, up-to-date experience.

Arranging the files

Each iAd is a folder full of the HTML, CSS, JavaScript, and media used for your banner and ad unit. In the following screenshot, we can see the file structure of a typical iAd:

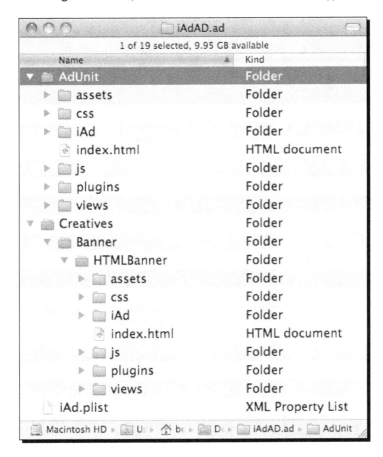

If you wanted to, you could create an entire iAd using just a text editor to manipulate these files. Luckily, **iAd Producer** creates and updates these files for us, when we're using it to create our iAd.

Using tools to create and test iAds

The main tool we'll be using to create our iAds is iAd Producer, a simple drag-and-drop tool for building, testing, and distributing amazing interactive iAds.

Introducing iAd Producer

iAd Producer manages all the HTML5, CSS3, and JavaScript in your iAd without your having to write a single line of code. In the following screenshot, we can see the rich visual interface of iAd Producer:

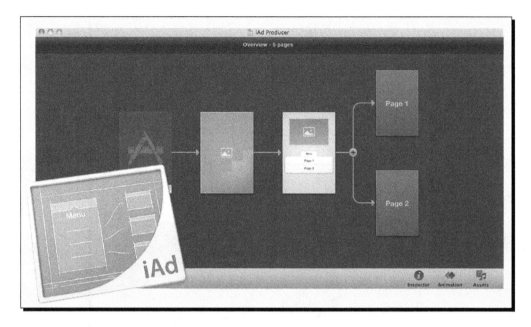

iAd Producer gives a visual overview of the structure and flow of your iAd. With it, you can add additional subpages and restructure your entire iAd in just a few clicks.

All your media assets are stored in the central asset library, which automatically manages support for high- and low-resolution displays by optimizing assets for the **Retina display** used in newer Apple iOS devices.

> The Retina display is Apple's high-resolution screen found in the iPhone 4 and iPod Touch onwards. It has double the resolution of older devices, giving it such a high pixel density that your eyes are unable to see the individual pixels. Such a vibrant, crisp, sharp screen can be taken full advantage of by your brand in your iAd. To find out more about Retina display, visit http://www.apple.com/iphone/features/retina-display.html.

We can build entire ads just by dropping images and videos onto motion-rich 3D carousels with iAd Producer's pre-built templates. Menus are auto generated for the user to explore and navigate around your iAd.

iAd Producer makes it easy to apply visual animations and effects to your content, a great way of adding character and excitement to your iAd, without the heavy overhead of video. These animations includes wipes, fades, spinning effects, and cube transitions that can be applied to media items, text, or even entire pages.

To create a visually impacting experience that users are familiar with, iAd Producer includes a rich library of carousels, buttons, audio or video players, and galleries; all these can be added into your iAd with a simple drag-and-drop.

Throughout making your ad, iAd Producer validates and checks your project, identifying common problems, such as images being the incorrect size or format, or you're having forgotten to configure a certain page. This means you can catch issues early and focus on creating your ad.

To extend your iAd's functionality beyond the inbuilt features of iAd Producer, we're able to view, edit, and extend the code it creates to create even cooler stuff like social sharing of your content, quizzes, or competitions.

Once you've finished your iAd, `iAd Producer` packages and optimizes your assets to reduce the size and time spent, delivering your complete ad experience to the user.

Testing with the iOS Simulator and the iAd Tester app

The **iOS Simulator** is a virtual iPhone or iPad that runs on your Mac's desktop and a quick way of testing on devices that you can't buy or that aren't publicly available yet. It supports most of the features a real device would have, such as **orientation** and **shakes**. Orientation allows the device to know when it has been rotated and update the screen content accordingly. Similarly, with shakes, we can update on-screen content when the users shake their device. In the iOS Simulator, we can emulate these rotations and shakes from the menu; unfortunately, shaking or rotating your Mac won't have similar results.

Even though you can test your iAd without a device, it's vital to test on a real iPhone, as an iAd will typically load and work faster in the simulator. This is because the simulator is able to use your entire system resources.

The **iAd Tester app** is a mobile application you can install on your iPhone, iPod, or iPad, through iTunes. The iAd Tester app is able to remotely connect to iAd Producer on your Mac and lets you test how your iAd will appear in other developers' apps.

To access iAd Producer, the iPhone/iPad simulator, or to test your iAd on a device, you'll need to join the **Apple Developer Program**.

Speeding development with iAd for Developers

If you have your own iOS application, Apple has a pre-built iAd package to drive downloads to your app, called **iAd for Developers**. To use this, you'll need to have an app live on the App Store, then contact Apple through the form available at `http://advertising.apple.com/contact/`, and choose **iAd for Developers, to promote an app**. The single page iAd is almost identical to your App Store listing and looks similar to the example, shown as follows:

Joining the developer program

To access full Apple documentation and iAd tools, you need to be a member of the paid Apple iOS Developer Program. This costs $99 per year and gives you access to iAd Producer, the tool we'll use throughout this book to build some great iAds for your brand.

Don't worry, despite it being called the developer program, you don't need to be a developer or have development skills for the techniques explored in this book.

Using the right hardware

The Apple software we'll be using in this book requires you to be on a recent version of their Mac OS X operating system and hardware.

You've got a Mac

If you've already got a Mac it needs to be an Intel Mac, running Mac OS X Snow Leopard, or later.

Time for action – checking your Mac

To check if your Mac is running Snow Leopard, follow the ensuing steps:

1. Click on the Apple icon in the top-left of your screen and select **About This Mac**. If the version has **10.6** or higher in it, you're running Snow Leopard or later and can install the tools that we'll be using.

2. If your version is less than **10.6**, we can see whether you're able to upgrade by checking that your processor has **Intel** in it, from **About This Mac**. Here we can see the OS version is **10.7.1**, that is, higher than 10.6, and so, compatible with iAd Producer:

If you've got an Intel processor, you can upgrade to Snow Leopard (v. 10.6) by buying a Mac OS X Snow Leopard upgrade disk from the Apple Store or a retailer. Once upgraded to Snow Leopard, you can optionally update to Mac OS Lion using the Mac App Store.

What just happened?

The **About This Mac** screen tells you the technical specification of your Mac and the operating system it is using.

If you don't have an Intel processor, and the **About This Mac** screen shows your processor as **PowerPC**, unfortunately, you can't upgrade to Snow Leopard; it's time for a well-earned new machine!

Time to get a Mac

Any Mac in the current lineup should be able to run iAd Producer; so, if you've had your eye on one for a while, treat yourself!

If you've already got a screen, keyboard, and mouse, the Mac Mini is the cheapest way to get started. If you're wanting to start afresh, a MacBook or an iMac will handle iAd production and development just fine.

If you're planning to buy a used machine, any mid-2009 or later model should be pre-installed with Mac OS X Snow Leopard and will be capable of running iAd Producer. Use the steps outlined earlier to see if a potential machine is suitable.

Becoming a registered developer

To access the iAd Producer tool and the extensive Apple iAd documentation, you'll need a paid developer account. Let's sign up to the iOS Developer program.

Time for action – signing up for the developer program

Follow these simple steps and you'll have access to the developer program in no time:

1. Visit `http://developer.apple.com/programs/start/standard/` and click on **Continue** in the bottom-left. You'll be setting up a new Apple Developer account and will be asked if you have an Apple ID you'd like to use. If you've got an iTunes or MobileMe account, you can use this. However, when creating iAds for your company or clients, you should create a new Apple ID. This keeps billing and invoicing separate from your personal account.

2. You can either set up an individual or company account; choose whichever is relevant to you.

 Setting up a company account can take around two weeks to verify your company information, so get it set up soon to avoid delays in your progress with building your iAds!

If you're setting up a new Apple ID, you'll now need to enter in your personal information, a password, and general security information, and press **Continue**. You'll be asked to complete a professional profile; this is just a survey for Apple and the values you select won't affect the account you set up. Apple will send you a confirmation e-mail within a few minutes; either click on the link in this e-mail to activate your account, or copy it into the text box in the signup process. Congratulations, you're a registered Apple Developer! Now, you'll need to enroll in the iOS Program.

3. Enter your billing address details and press **Continue**. You'll be asked to select which program you'd like to enroll into; check **iOs Developer Program** and click on **Continue**.

4. You've now got a chance to review your information, make sure iOS Developer Program is under Developer Program and your personal / billing information is correct. Confirm these details by clicking **Continue**.

5. Read the Apple Developer Agreement and check the box to accept it. Click on **I Agree**.

 The Apple Developer Agreement is mainly targeted at building and distributing applications on the App Store, but make sure you review it in full before accepting.

6. You can now buy the iOS Developer Program by clicking on **Add to Cart**.

7. Select **Checkout**, and, once your application has been processed, you'll be on the program.

What just happened?

Creating an iOS Developer account with Apple provides access to their development tools that we'll need to build great iAds. This developer account is the same that is used by developers who have apps available in the App Store. If you ever have an app that you want to make available in the App Store you can use this account to submit it.

 The $99 developer fee is only valid for one year, to continue using iAd Producer and creating iAds you'll have to renew your subscription to the program. Apple will notify you by e-mail with renewal instructions, when necessary.

Summary

We've learned a lot in this chapter. You now know that an iAd is an exciting marketing opportunity on Apple iOS devices, the iPhone, iPod touch, and iPad. iAds stand out because they offer an unparalleled interactive experience. Each iAd is a tiny interactive webpage, using HTML5, CSS3, and JavaScript. An iAd has four key parts:

1. **A Banner**: The engaging opportunity for users to tap on your iAd.

2. **A Transition**: A non-jarring animation between your banner and splash page.

3. **A Splash page**: Makes waiting fun for the user and keeps their attention.

4. **The Core Ad Unit**: The navigation and subpages that make up the key opportunities to impress the user.

iAd Producer is the tool that we'll be using to build your iAd. We can test our iAds in the iAd Simulator and on our devices using the iAd Tester App.

In this chapter, we have also:

1. Got the required hardware to run the tools we'll be using.

2. Signed up to the developer program to get the tools to build and test some great iAds!

Now that you have an understanding of what an iAd is and have access to the tools, we can move on to *Chapter 2*, *Preparing Your iAd Content*, where we'll look at preparing your media and content for an iAd and the constraints of delivering media to mobile devices.

 If you want to find out more about iAds before we get started building them, check out Apple's Sales Pitch at `http://advertising.apple.com/` and iAd Documentation at `https://developer.apple.com/library/iad/`[requires developer sign in].

2
Preparing Your Content for Mobile

You need great content to make a great iAd, and this content needs to be in the right format.

In this chapter, we'll look at the following topics:

◆ What media an iAd can contain

◆ Dealing with mobile constraints

◆ Editing and optimizing images for your iAd

◆ Getting audio in the right format for your iAd

◆ Changing your videos so that they'll work on iOS

Including media in iAds

iAds can contain images, audio, and video. Each of these needs to be in very specific formats and meet certain criteria before they can be included in your iAd.

Typical assets that you'll need to build an iAd include:

◆ Your product and/or company logo

◆ Emotive product imagery

◆ Compelling audio clips

◆ Immersive videos

◆ Map pins for marking store locations

◆ Background and themed artwork

When designing and producing the assets for your iAd, it's important to be mindful of the context in which your content appears

Overcoming mobile constraints

As with all mobile devices, the iPhone's smaller screen and portability means that there are limitations in the physical size, processing power, and connectivity available. These limitations shouldn't be feared, instead they're great opportunities to refine your message and deliver the most relevant experience to your future customers.

Designing for the small screen

Smaller screens means you need to make better use of the limited screen space available to you; for example, tappable areas need to consider the inconsistent accuracy of users' fingers. We need to make sure all tappable areas are at least 88px tall and wide, with sufficient space between each actionable element to prevent unintentional taps that are detrimental to the user experience.

 When designing your iAd banner, keep in mind that the bottom-right of the banner will be obscured by the iAd logo, so don't put any important information there.

It's important to remember that you shouldn't try to fit your entire product line or company ethos into your iAd. The captivating experience and unique opportunity to engage directly with the user should focus on just a few key products or points, encouraging them to act on and meet your ad goals.

When dealing with ads in a mobile context, users are often in an environment filled with distractions, so creating clear, responsive screens that are intuitive to the user is the key to achieving a successful iAd.

Delivering content when download speeds are limited

If you want your iAd to reach the widest audience, you need to assume that the majority of your users may be connecting over the generally slow cellular network. A slow connection means longer waits before users can see your awesome iAd! Because of this, certain restrictions and recommendations are in place.

Complying with file size restrictions

Apple restricts the file size of the initial parts of your iAd, the banner, and splash screen, so that they load quickly and engage the user within the key first 15 seconds.

Your HTML5 Banner can be up to the following size:

- 60KB on iPhone/iPod touch devices with high-resolution displays
- 40KB on iPhone/iPod touch devices with standard resolution displays
- 65KB on iPads
- 150KB for iPad fullscreen HTML5 banners

 The banner size limit includes both the portrait and the landscape versions of your banner, so it's important to design it in such a way that many of the same resources can be used in either orientation.

Your splash screen can be up to the following size:

- 256KB on iPhone/iPod touch devices with high-resolution displays
- 128KB on iPhone/iPod touch devices with standard resolution displays
- 300KB on iPads

Notice how you get twice the storage space for high-resolution displays; that's because there's twice the number of horizontal and vertical pixels in Apple's high-resolution displays (branded Retina display), so images end up being approximately twice the size as a result.

Always work with the high-resolution display size, as iAd Producer will scale down assets automatically, when you build your iAd.

 Try to keep the total number of resources that are loading in your iAd, at any one time, to 20 or fewer. Every request for a file includes some extra overhead that slows down the loading each time the network is accessed.

Your core ad unit can load larger resources, but it's a good practice to keep these resources small. Fortunately there are plenty of ways to optimize your assets for mobile delivery.

Working with images

Images are used throughout your iAd, for backgrounds, themed graphics, your logo, image galleries, and user-configurable wallpapers. They're probably the most common media type in your iAd and are available in a variety of formats, which can be manipulated and edited to enhance your ad's performance and experience.

Understanding the different image formats

In our iAds, images can be either **JPEG** or **PNG**, depending on what kind of image they contain or what they're going to be used for. JPEGs are typically smaller in file size, as they can be extensively compressed. PNGs often are better quality and more versatile, but this comes at the cost of their larger file size.

You should use JPEGs whenever you can. However, consider using PNGs when:

- **Your image contains text**: The crisp edges of text can get lost when the JPEG is compressed.

- **Your image contains sharp edges or shapes**: Just like with text, the JPEG compression process often blurs sharp line edges.

- **Your image has large sections of solid color**: JPEG compression can cause a blocking effect on large sections of color.

- **Your image has transparency**: Elements behind your image are still partially visible, if it has parts which are transparent. Therefore, you have to use PNG as JPEG doesn't suppot transparency.

Resizing an image

Chances are that most of your assets won't be of the correct size or in the right format to go straight into your iAd.

We can use **Preview**, a tool built into all Macs that is used for the manipulation of images and documents. Despite being called Preview, its little-known, built-in editing functionality is extensive, giving us a free, quick, and professional way to get our content into the right format for our iAd.

Time for action – cropping images using Preview

Let's take one of the provided sample files and get it ready for use in our iAd.

1. First of all, we're going to need one of the demo assets included in this book—if you've not already downloaded the complete collection of supporting files. Double-click the file `iAd_Book_Resources.zip` to extract the contents.

 You can download the assets by visiting `http://www.packtpub.com/support` and selecting **iAd Production Beginners Guide**.

2. Open the **Preview** app; you can find it in the `Application`'s folder on your Mac.

3. Select **File** | **Open**.

4. Navigate to the `book asset` folder, which is unzipped in step 1. Find the **dino stores** project folder and select **banner-background.png**. Click **Open**. You should now see the banner images that we'll be using later for our iAd:

This is an iPhone portrait banner, so it needs to be 640 x 100px on devices with high-resolution displays, and half that (that is, 320 x 50px) for standard display devices. Let's check if the size is correct:

5. To view the size of our image, go to **Tools** | **Show Inspector** in the **Preview** menu bar. This will bring up the information about our image. Look at the **Image size** value. Here, we can see the general info of our image, including its size and type:

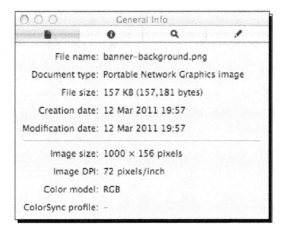

As you can see, this isn't the correct size; it's 1000px wide and 156px high. Let's resize it to the high-resolution banner size.

6. As iAd Producer will automatically make the lower-resolution images from the high-resolution assets, we only need to make assets for the higher-resolution displays.

7. The iPad currently doesn't have a high-resolution display, so there is only one set of assets we need to make for it.

To resize your image, in the **Preview** menu bar, select **Tools | Adjust Size**. We want this image to be **640**px wide and **100**px high. Type 640 into the **Width** box. This will automatically update the **Height** to be **100**, as the image is already in the correct aspect ratio. Check that the sizes are correct and then press **OK**:

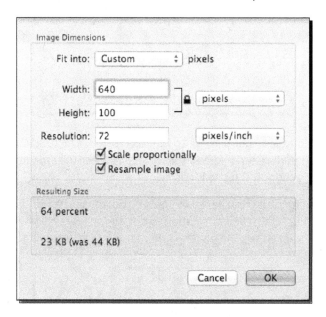

8. You should see the image snap to smaller size. Now, we need to save it. In the menubar, select **File | Save As...**. We'll want to convert the image from PNG to JPEG, as we don't need the benefits of PNG for this image. Change the **Quality** to about two-thirds. Now pick a place to save the file; we'll be coming back to it later.

What just happened?

We just resized ou first image using **Preview**. Use this example as a guide whenever you need to scale your images down.

Cropping a section from an image

If you only want a subsection of a larger image, we can select it and remove the part we don't want. This is called **cropping** and we're able to do it in **Preview**.

Time for action – cropping a selection

Taking a larger image we'll be using later in our ad, let's trim away the parts that we don't want appearing in our iAd:

1. If you haven't already, open **Preview** from your `Application`'s folder.

2. From the Preview menu bar, select **File | Open**. In the `book assets` folder we downloaded in the last exercise, find the **Dino Stores** folder and open **store-footprints.png**.

3. You should see three dinosaur footprints. We'll be using these later on the store finder for our iAd; however, we don't want all three footprints, just the red one.

 We're selecting the red image as users relate red markers on maps to destinations. A green marker shows a starting point, a purple for the user-selected destination, and a blue beacon for the user's current location.

4. In the **Select** option, make sure that the **Rectangular Selection** tool is active by clicking on the small arrow next to the **Select** icon and then choosing **Rectangular Selection**.

5. We're going to select a small area around the red footprint, so zoom in to the footprint using the **Zoom +** button, above the image. You may need to scroll to bring the right footprint into view. Here, you can see the select tool and zoom buttons on the toolbar:

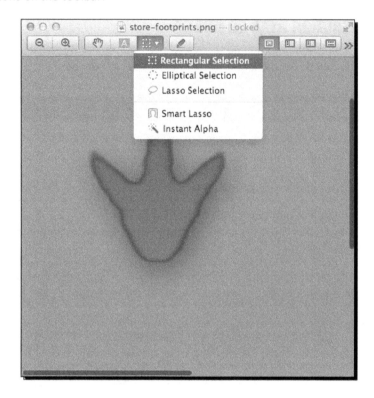

6. Now, hold down *Shift* and drag your mouse over the footprint so that a square box appears around it. There is a small box next to your mouse pointer, showing the size of your selection as you drag; once this has reached **160x160**, stop dragging.

 Holding down *Shift* while dragging forces a square selection instead of a rectangle to appear. Use this when you need precise and equal selections.

7. You should now have a square around the red footprint. If it's not centered, you can click-and-drag the square to center the footprint within it. You can also use the arrow keys to fine tune the positioning of your selection.

8. Once you're happy with the positioning of the square, choose **Tools | Crop** from the menu bar. The rest of the image should disappear, with just the red footprint remaining.

Now we can save the image; choose **Save As...**, so we don't overwrite the full image, and make sure that you save it with a different name, such as map-pin.png. Save it in a safe place; we'll be putting it on the map of our iAd later.

What just happened?

You now know how to extract just a subsection of an image using the **Preview** tool on your Mac. Cropping images can be useful to select just the interesting parts of an image, or to change their aspect ratio, say to make images square to fit better in a gallery.

Removing solid background colors

You'll often find your images have a solid background, but you want to overlay them on top of each other. Or you may have a background image on your iAd that you want to always be visible, and not obscured by this solid color. Transparent, layered images add depth to the content in your iAd, which, when combined with animation, can look incredible.

Time for action – removing solid colors

We're able to remove solid blocks of color using the **Instant Alpha** tool in Preview.

 The Instant Alpha tool can be used to remove solid blocks of color from images. It works by detecting similar shades of a color you select and replacing those pixels with a transparent color.

1. If you haven't already, open **Preview**.

2. Now open the grass-blades.png file, included in the Dino Store folder of the demo assets you download. You should see some green blades of grass on a cream background.

3. This cream background will interfere with the background image of our iAd, so we're going to remove it. Before we continue, make sure that **Show Image Background** in the **View** menu is checked. This will allow us to see where our image ends and which parts are transparent.

4. Click on the small arrow to the right of the **Select** button, above the image, and select **Instant Alpha**, as shown in the following screenshot:

 If you can't see the **Select** option, try resizing the **Preview** window a little wider, as it gets hidden if it's too small.

5. **Instant Alpha** lets you drag over an area of color you'd like to remove. The further you drag, the wider the range of color it selects. The area that will be selected is highlighted in red. Drag the cursor over the background until it turns red.

6. There should be dancing lines around the outside of the grass blades; click **Delete** to remove this area.

7. You should now see a checkerboard effect behind the blades of grass. This is used by image editing software to show an area of an image as being transparent.

8. Now, we need to save the image; click on **File** | **Save As** in the menu bar. Choose a place to save the image (we'll be using it later). Make sure the format is PNG and the transparency checkbox is ticked.

9. Click on **Save**.

What just happened?

We've now removed the background color on this image, so later, when we put this image over our background, only the solid parts of the image will cover it. The following screenshot shows how it would have looked before we added the transparency (on the left) and how it looks after we've added the transparency (on the right):

As you can see, this lets the background be visible through the transparent part of the image. Now that you know how to manipulate your images, we'll look at optimizing our images for mobile delivery by reducing their file size.

Speeding up our image downloads

When images are created, they contain extra information that can be removed, optimized, or compressed. We can process our images before including them in our iAd to keep within Apple's file-size limits and reduce the time our users have to wait before engaging with our brand.

Time for action – optimizing an image

There are many applications available to optimize images; we'll be using **ImageOptim** as it's free and open source.

 ImageOptim analyzes each image and determines the most efficient algorithm, or best way, to compress the content, then removes any unnecessary comments or color profiles. ImageOptim is lossless, so our images won't lose any quality.

1. Download ImageOptim from `http://imageoptim.pornel.net`.

2. Extract the downloaded file by double-clicking on it. Drag the application to your application folder.

3. Open ImageOptim.

4. Drag your images onto the table in the app; it'll automatically optimize and save each one. You can drag multiple images at a time or an entire folder, and ImageOptim will process them all and display the saving.

 ImageOptim can optimize all the file formats supported by iAd, so our JPEGs, PNGs, and GIFs all can benefit from sophisticated file size reduction.

5. Your images are now optimized! You can see the savings you make next to the image filenames. Close the app, but remember to optimize any images that you'll use in the future. Here's an example of the typical savings you can expect to make when using ImageOptim:

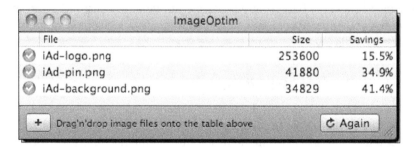

What just happened?

We've now reduced the size of our images, meaning they'll load quicker and can help keep us within the iAd file-size limits. Typically, you'll get between a 15- to 50-percent reduction in the size of your images, with no loss of quality!

Pop quiz – understanding images

We've covered a lot on editing images and their different formats. Try answering these questions based on what we've just learned:

1. Why do we optimize our images with software like ImageOptim?

    a. Because they'll look crisper and clearer

    b. To increase their file size and download time

    c. To decrease download time and keep within Apple's file-size restrictions

    d. Optimized images can have more colors so they look brighter

2. What tool should you use in Preview to remove a solid block of color in order to make part of an image transparent?

    a. Quick Selector

    b. Instant Alpha

    c. Fast Grab

    d. Mega Select

3. Which image format should you use whenever you can?

    a. JPEG

    b. PNG

    c. GIF

    d. TIFF

4. When would you need to use a PNG image?

    a. To keep file size down

    b. To have a transparent section of the image

    c. To have animated content

    d. When your image is black and white

Have a go hero – editing your own images

Why not take your own image, such as your company logo, and prepare it for your iAd by using what you've just learned? You could:

- Crop out just the content you need
- Make any solid background transparent
- Resize the image
- Save it as a JPEG or PNG, depending on which one is more suitable
- Optimize and reduce the file size of the assets that we've bee working with so far using ImageOptim

Including audio

Audio, music previews, character catch phrases, or background ambient sounds can be used to engage the user with the theme of your iAd.

Converting your audio

Just like images, your audio has to be in the Apple-recommended format to get the best performance from your iAd and the device it's running on.

 Apple recommends AAC audio files with the .m4a extension at a bit rate of 128 kbps. iOS devices have dedicated hardware chips inside them to effortlessly decode this format for crisp-and-clear, uninterrupted playback.

Time for action – converting an mp3 to work on iOS

iTunes includes a powerful audio engine that we can harness to convert our audio to the right format. To do this, follow the ensuing steps:

1. Make sure that the **iTunes** window is open. You should be able to find it in your `Application`'s folder.

2. In the `assets` folder, provided in the code bundle for this chapter, find the `Dino Store` resource folder, in which there is an audio file `roar-noise.mp3`. Drag this to the **iTunes** window.

3. We now need to set up iTunes to convert audio into the correct format. From the **iTunes** section of the menu bar, open **Preferences**.

4. On the **General** tab, click on **Import Settings**, near the bottom right. We want to import using **AAC Encoder**, picking the **High Quality** setting, so that your **Import Settings** match the following screenshot:

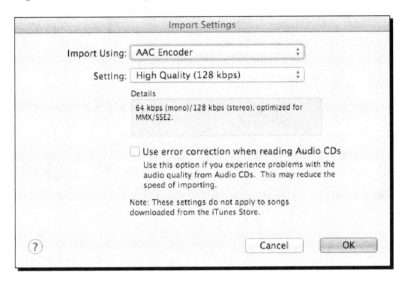

5. Click on **OK** and close the **Preferences** window. Now find the roar-noise audio file in your library. Right-click on it and select **Create AAC Version**. Once done, you should see two copies of the file in your library.

6. Right-click the second of the two files and choose **Show in Finder**. This will reveal the two files, roar-noise.m4a and roar-noise.mp3. We're only interested in the new .m4a file, so move this out of this folder to a place you can later easily access it at.

7. Once you've moved or made a copy of the file, you can delete them from **iTunes** to prevent filling your library with unwanted audio.

What just happened?

We just converted a .mp3 audio file into a .m4a AAC audio file, the format supported in iAds.

As users can adjust or mute the volume on their device, ensure that any audio essential to your iAd experience is also available with visual cues. If you choose to autoplay any audio in your iAd, such as in the background, you should include a clear visual way of pausing it.

Audio works great for engaging the user within your iAd, but for even richer content we can embed video into our iAd.

Incorporating video

Video can add compelling narrative and stories to your iAd; you can use it for movie trailers, product demos, or showing off your latest TV commercial. Great video pulls users into your iAd experience, and, if done correctly, can blend with the rest of your iAd to create a seamless memorable exposure to your brand.

Converting your video

Apple devices have built-in dedicated hardware to playback your video smoothly, but for this to work, it has to be in the correct format.

Time for action – encoding a video

Using **QuickTime**, included with your Mac, we're able to create iAd-compatible video in just a few minutes.

 QuickTime X (or 10) is the current version of QuickTime, provided by Apple with their Mac operating system. QuickTime provides audio and video playback and streaming, along with a simple interface for converting video to different formats. If you're able to run iAd Producer, you'll have the correct version of QuickTime installed.

1. Open QuickTime; it should be called **QuickTime Player** and you can find it in your `Application`'s folder.

2. Choose **File | Open File**. Open the `dino-stores-intro.mp4` file in the `Dino Store` folder, provided with the downloaded `book assets` folder.

3. The video should load in the QuickTime window. Hit the **play** button and check whether the video plays and looks as you'd expect it to.

4. Once you've watched the video, choose **File | Export for Web** from the menu bar.

5. Choose a filename and where to save it. Under **Export versions for:**, make sure **iPhone** and **iPhone (Cellular)** are checked and **Computer** is unchecked. Your export settings should be similar to those in the following screenshot:

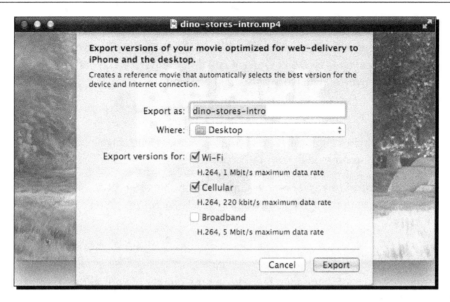

6. Hit **Save**; this will now process your video. It might take a few minutes, depending on the length of the video and the speed of your Mac.

What just happened?

QuickTime just created a few different files that allow iAd to display two different versions of your video. A high-resolution one for when your iAd is viewed over Wi-Fi, and a lower-resolution one for streaming over the cellular network.

It does this by creating what is known as a reference movie, in this case, the file `dino-stores-intro.mov`. The reference movie is loaded by the iPhone or iPad then decides if it wants the high quality (the larger file, in this case `dino-stores-intro - iPhone.m4v`), or the lower quality (the smaller file, `dino-stores-intro - iPhone (Cellular).3gp`). This means that no matter what connection your iAd user is on, they can watch your video with minimal buffering.

QuickTime also made a poster file, `dino-stores-intro.jpg`, which is used as the thumbnail for our video.

As this method is meant for embedding on the web, it made a webpage for us, `dino-stores-intro.html`; you can safely delete this if you want as we won't need it for our iAd.

Fine tuning your video

For advanced users, or if an experienced third party is creating your video assets, consider the following technical tweaks. Don't worry if you don't understand what's going on here. The video we just converted will work perfectly fine in our iAds.

Video content

Shoot your video in high definition 720p or 1080p. Working with high-quality video is vital to keep your viewers immersed in your iAd content.

Limit the use of zooms, fast camera moves, and transitional effects. Whenever a large percentage of the screen changes, your video's file size increases, due to the way in which videos are created.

Your video's audio

You can reduce the size of your video by reducing the quality of your audio. Typical audio is of CD quality; however, you can reduce the quality by half, while keeping the audio in your iAd sounding great.

 If you're considering the use of lots of audio and video to enhance your iAd, check out the **Video Delivery Settings** of Apple's iAd Asset Guidelines at `http://bit.ly/iAd-asset-guidelines`.

If you're including multiple videos in your iAd, make sure that they're all of a similar volume to avoid causing discomfort to the viewer!

Video dimensions

You don't have to include full-resolution video in your iAd to get beautiful video quality. iOS devices have a powerful rendering engine that's able to display fullscreen video at very high quality.

Consider these maximum sizes for optimal videos:

◆   iPhone & iPod touch—480 x 320px (landscape) or 320 x 480px (portrait)

◆   iPad—512 x 384px (landscape) or 384 x 512px (portrait)

Video durations

When including video within your iAd, Apple recommends the following duration limits:

- Any video that plays before your main ad unit, such as a pre-roll after your splash screen, should be around or below 15 seconds

- Any video within your main ad unit should not exceed 60 seconds

- You should keep the total amount of video in your iAd to under 2 minutes

- Not only will Apple's recommendations reduce the loading durations in your iAd, short videos generally keep the user more engaged. Longer videos are likely to cause the user to close the iAd and leave your experience. Video should be used to compel your users; however, to ensure they're engaged throughout your ad, you should focus on keeping them interacting with the ad's content.

Have a go hero – keeping in the guidelines

Apple occasionally updates its recommendations and guidelines based on feedback or when new technologies and best practices become available. It's important to stay up-to-date by exploring the Apple documentation.

Ensure you're following the correct and latest asset guide at `https://developer.apple.com/library/iad/documentation/UserExperience/Conceptual/iAd_Design_Guide/AssetGuidelines/AssetGuidelines.html`.

Read the design guide overview, which gives insight into the iAd experience and workflow at `http://developer.apple.com/library/iad/documentation/UserExperience/Conceptual/iAd_Design_Guide`.

 To access these documents, you'll need to log in with the Apple ID that we created/used when we signed up to the Developer Program in *Chapter 1, Getting Started with iAd*.

Pop quiz – audio and video

1. What audio format should you convert your sound files to?

    a. mp3

    b. m4a/AAC

    c. wma

    d. jpg

2. What does the reference movie created by QuickTime do?

    a. Show who made the video

    b. Allow you to edit the video remotely

    c. Automatically selects the high quality or low quality stream

    d. Contains footage of your next secret product

Summary

You can now manipulate, optimize, and convert your media into the best possible formats for your iAd. In this chapter, we've learned about:

- The constraints of mobile devices, such as screen size and download speeds
- Editing and resizing images to use in our iAds
- Converting audio files so they play on iOS devices
- Encoding and fine tuning video for our ads

Keep in mind that just because you can include audio, video, and imagery in your iAd, it doesn't mean you have to try to find a way of fitting them all in. In the next chapter, things are about to get exciting as we'll look at installing iAd Producer and using the assets we just created to make our first iAd.

3
Making Your iAd

We can now start using the content we optimized to work well with iAd, to build our first ad.

In this chapter we'll be covering the following topics:

- ◆ Installing iAd Producer on your Mac
- ◆ Familiarizing ourselves with the iAd Producer interface
- ◆ Setting up a blank iAd to work with
- ◆ Using templates to build each section of your iAd
- ◆ Tweaking the templates to make your ad even more awesome
- ◆ Using Safari to preview the animations in an iAd

Getting iAd Producer

iAd Producer is the tool that allows us to assemble great interactive ads with a simple drag-and-drop visual interface. Download and install iAd Producer on your Mac, so that you can start creating an ad.

Time for action – installing iAd Producer

To install iAd Producer, follow these steps:

1. To download and use iAd Producer, you need to be a paid member of the iOS Developer Program. In *Chapter 1, Getting Started with iAd*, we signed up to the developer program, so you'll need those login details before continuing.

2. Go to `http://developer.apple.com/devcenter/ios/` and click on the **Log in** button.

3. Enter your Apple ID and password, and click on **Sign In**.
   After you've signed in, find the **Downloads** section at the bottom of the page. Click on **iAd Producer** to start downloading it. You can see the download highlighted here:

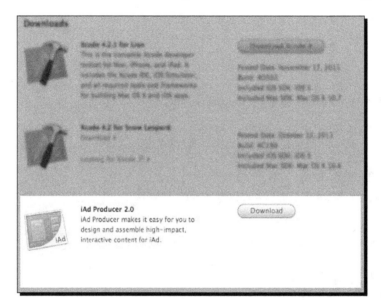

 If you cannot see **iAd Producer** in the **Downloads**, make sure you're logged in and your developer account has been activated.

4. After the download is complete, open the file and run `iAd Producer.mpkg` to start the installation wizard. Follow the steps in the installation and enter your Mac password, if asked for it.

When installing certain software, you need to enter your Mac password to allow it to have privileged access to your system. Don't confuse this with your Apple ID that we set up for the iOS Developer Program. If you don't have a password on your Mac, just leave the password area blank and click on **OK**.

5. When you've gone through the installation steps it'll take a couple of moments to install. After you get a **The installation was successful** message you can close the installer.

What just happened?

We now have iAd Producer installed; whenever you need to open it, you can find it in the `Applications` folder on your Mac.

Working with iAd Producer

Let's take a look at some of the main parts of iAd Producer that you'll be using regularly, to familiarize yourself with the interface.

Launch screen

When you first open iAd Producer, you'll be able to start a new iPhone or iPad project from the project selector, as shown in the following screenshot. As the screen size and experience is so different between the two devices, we have to design and build ads specifically for each one:

From the launch screen, you can also open existing projects you've been working on.

Default ad

Once you have chosen to create either an iPad or iPhone iAd, a placeholder ad is created for you, showing the visual flow. This is the overview of your ad, which you'll be using to piece the sections of your ad together. The following screenshot shows the default overview:

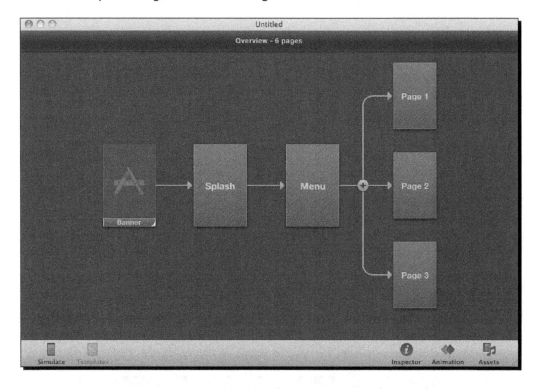

Double-clicking on any of the screens in your ad flow will ask you to pick a template for that page; once assigned, you're then able to design the iAd using the canvas editor.

Template selector

Before we edit any page of an ad, we have to apply a template to it, even if it's just a blank canvas to build upon. iAd Producer automatically shows the relevant templates to the current page you're editing. This means your ad follows a structure that the users expect. Templates provide some great starting points for your iAd, whether it's for a simple banner with an image and text or a 3D image carousel that the user can flick and manipulate, all created with easy point and click. The following screenshot is an example of the template chooser:

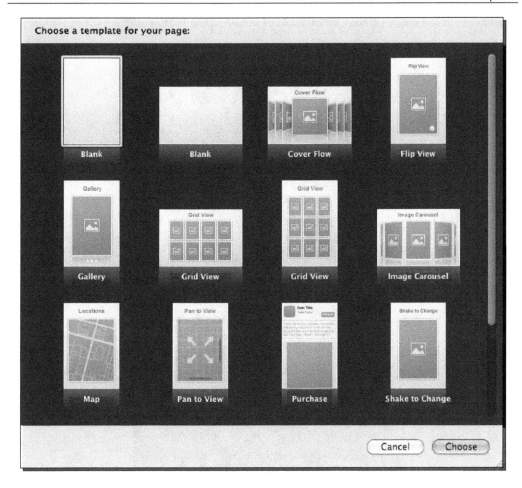

Asset Library

The Asset Library holds all the media and content for your iAd, such as the images, videos, and audio. When adding media to your **Asset Library**, make sure you're using high-resolution images for the high-resolution Retina display. iAd Producer automatically generates the lower-resolution images for your ad, whenever you import resources.

 If you wanted an image to be 200px wide and 300px high, you should double the horizontal and vertical pixels to 400px wide and 600px high. This will mean your graphics look crisp and awesome on the high-resolution screens.

The following screenshot shows an example of media in the **Asset Library**:

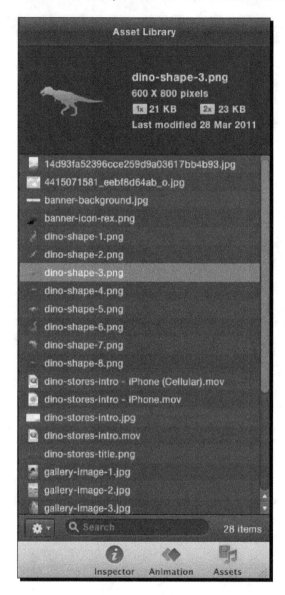

Ad canvas

Once you've selected a template, you can double-click on the item in the **Overview** to open up the canvas for that page. The ad canvas is where you customize your iAd with a powerful visual editor to manipulate each page of your ad. Here's an example of the ad canvas with a video carousel added to it:

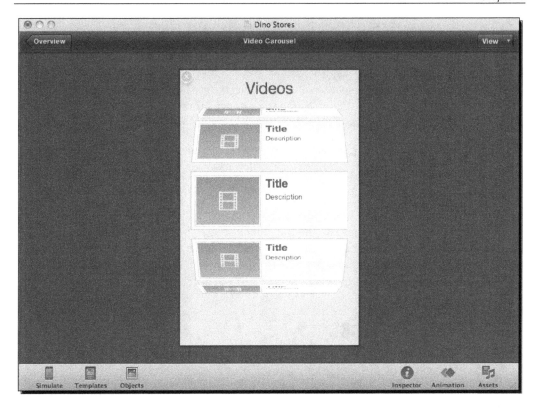

Setting up your ad

Let's create and save an empty project to use as we create our iAd; you'll only need to do this once for each ad.

Whenever you're working with something digital, it's important to save your iAd whenever you make a significant change, in case iAd Producer closes unexpectedly. Try to get into the habit of saving regularly, to avoid losing your ad.

Time for action – creating a new project

In order to create a new project, follow the ensuing steps:

1. If you haven't created a new project already, open **iAd Producer** from your `Applications` folder.

2. Select the iPhone from the launch screen and choose **Select**. You'll now see the default ad overview. iAd Producer has automatically made us a project called `Untitled` and populated it with the default set of pages.

3. From the **File** menu, select **Save** to save your empty iAd, ready to have the components added to it later. Name the project something like `Dino Stores`, as that is the ad we'll be working on.

4. You can now save the progress of your project at any time by choosing **File** then **Save** from the menu bar or pressing *Command + S* on your keyboard.

What just happened?

You've now seen the project selector and the launch screen in action, and have the base project that we'll be building upon as we make our first iAd. If you quit this project you can now open the project from within iAd Producer by clicking on **File | Open**, from the menu bar; or, simply double-click the `project` file in Finder to automatically open it.

Getting the resources

In this chapter, we'll be using the `Dino Stores` example resources that are available to download with this book. If you want to use your own assets, you'll need the following media:

◆ An image for your banner, approximately 120px wide and 100px high

◆ An image of your company logo or name, around 420px wide and 45px high

◆ An 80px square image, with transparency, to be used as a map pin

◆ A loading image, approximately 600px wide and 400px high

◆ Between six and 10 images for a gallery, each around 304px wide and 440px high

◆ Two or more images that will change when the iPhone is shaken, each around 600px wide and 800px high

◆ An image related to your product or service, at least 300px wide, to use on the main menu page

 These pixel sizes are at double-size to account for the high-resolution Retina display found on the iPhone 4 and later. iAd Producer will automatically create the lower-resolution versions for older devices.

Building your banner

The banner is the hook to encourage the viewer to click and explore your iAd. We'll be using an image and an advertising slogan to create a simple but effective banner.

Time for action – making the banner

In order to make the banner, follow the ensuing steps:

1. Open up the Dino Stores project and double-click on the **Banner** in the ad overview. It should be the first item on screen.

2. Before you're able to edit any page of your ad, you need to assign a template to it. From the template chooser, you should see the available templates for banners. In this banner, we'll be using **Image and Text**; select this template and click on **Choose**.

3. After choosing the banner type, select the banner again, from the iAd overview. You should now have the banner canvas open, ready to customize the banner, as shown in the following screenshot:

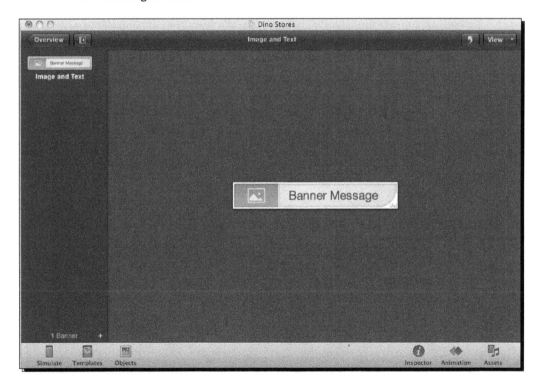

4. The first item that we'll change is the **Banner Message**. Double-clicking on the text will change it to editing mode. Now, enter your own text, such as Rawr-some Pets. Click outside of the label to leave the editing mode.

 In iAd Producer, each area of text is referred to as a *label*. They're called this because the user of the iAd cannot edit them. For editable areas of text, we can use a text box.

5. Now let's make the text slightly bigger and center it, so it sits correctly in the banner. Click on the text again, so a selection box appears around it, and then click on the **Inspector** option in the lower-right corner of iAd Producer. This opens the **inspector pane**, which is used to adjust the appearance and styling of elements in your iAd.

 The inspector pane can be toggled to open and closed by clicking on the icon again. You can use this to enlarge the maximum area available to the canvas so that you can edit your ad with more precision.

6. In the inspector pane, click on the **Text** section to expand the text formatting options. We can center the text with the middle button in the alignment setting, then increase the font size to around **25**. You can see the font size and alignment highlighted in the following screenshot:

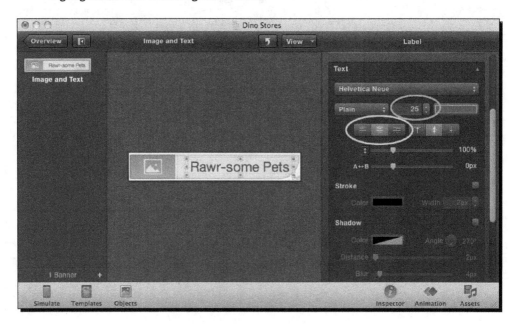

What just happened?

We selected the **Image and Text** template to create the base layout of our banner. Then, we used the ad canvas for the first time, to edit the default. Now you know how to select a template, then edit and adjust its text and appearance.

Have a go hero – writing good banner text

When writing the text for your banner, you can use certain language and words to entice and grab your user's attention so they'll tap your banner. Consider updating your banner to use a call to action, where you combine the following:

- ◆ An actioning verb to encourage the user to tap the banner, such as, "try", "join", "take", "find out", "create", or "play"

- ◆ A word to add value or importance in order to motivate the tap action, such as free, now, or fast

- ◆ Keep content to a minimum, so as to not deter the user from reading it

The following screenshot shows an example of a complete call to action:

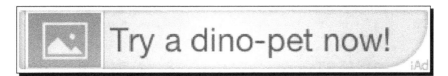

Time for action – changing the background

We have edited the text on our banner; let's now change the background to make it more prominent in the applications that it will appear in. We'll use a gradient to fill the background, fading between two colors.

1. Click away from the label on the grey background to select the background properties in the inspector pane. Now click **Background**, to open the background properties section.

2. A **radial gradient** had already been selected for us when we chose the banner template, so we only need to change the two colors that make the background.

> A radial gradient is a smooth transition between two colors; think of them as blending two colored circles into one, from the center of the area they are filling.

3. You should see a white-to-grey gradient strip with a small arrow and box at each end; click the box on the left to open the color selector. The color selector has a variety of ways to choose a color. We'll be using the simplest—the crayon selector. Select this by clicking the crayon box on the color selector. In the following screenshot, we can see the **Background** section along with the crayon color selector:

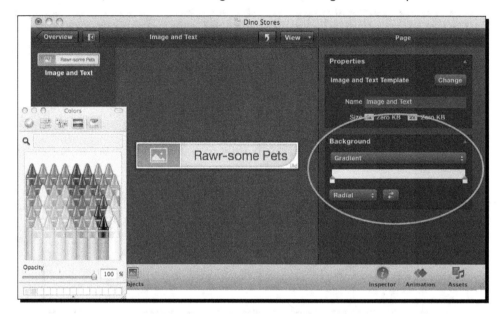

4. We now have a selection of crayons to pick our color from. The first color we select is the inside of your radial gradient; select the naturally prehistoric orange (named *Cantaloupe*) from the bottom-left of the colors. You should see the inside of your banner turn to that color. If it hasn't, make sure that the first box on the gradient strip is selected and try again.

5. Next, select the small gray box on the right of the gradient strip to change the outside color of the radial gradient. We'll change the outer color to white (named *Snow*), the far-right crayon on the bottom. Once both the colors have been selected, you can close the color picker.

6. We can now fine tune the gradient by dragging the orange box on the left about one quarter of the way towards the right. This changes the start point of where the gradient fades, so more of the orange is visible in the center.

What just happened?

We just used the inbuilt gradients in iAd Producer to create a gradient with code instead of images, meaning they can scale to the high-or low-resolution screens with no loss of quality, while having a significantly smaller file size. iAd Producer automatically produces the CSS.

Have a go hero – learning about CSS3 gradients

CSS3 is a work-in-progress specification that is currently receiving support in the latest generation of browsers. If you're curious about CSS3 gradients and how they can be applied to websites, check out the following resources:

- The CSS3 Gradient Generator is a visual web tool which allows you to generate and view the CSS code for complex gradients; visit it at `http://gradients.glrzad.com/`.

- CSS Tricks has a comprehensive but understandable overview on browser support and quirks at `http://css-tricks.com/5700-css3-gradients`.

- The W3 writes and maintains the in-depth specification on CSS3 gradients; available at `http://dev.w3.org/csswg/css3-images/#gradients`.

Time for action – adding an image

With the background gradient in place, we now need to add the final component of our banner, a small graphic to complement the text:

1. To add an image into our iAd, we need to add our media into the **Asset Library** of iAd Producer. We can add multiple assets at a time, so we'll import the entire `Dino Stores` project files. In iAd Producer, select **Assets** from the far bottom right to open the **Asset Library**. You should now see the **Asset Library** appear in the right of iAd Producer, as shown in the following screenshot:

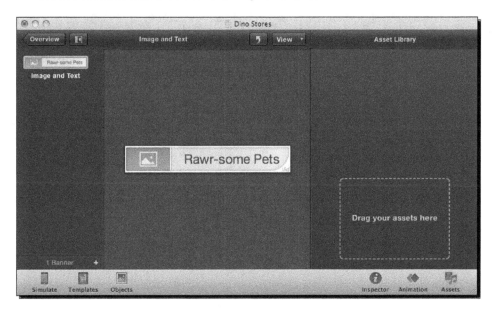

2. Select **File | Import Assets** and find the `Dino Stores` folder provided with this book's assets. Within this folder, there is a `final` folder with all the assets prepared for this iAd; select **final** and click on **choose**. You can also drag media straight from Finder to your **Asset Library**.

 The assets in the `final` folder for the `Dino Stores` example have already been resized and optimized for use in this project. If you want to use the assets that you prepared in *Chapter 2, Preparing Your iAd Content*, or if you've chosen to make your own resources, then import them now.

3. Wait while iAd Producer imports your media and assets. It should then display a list of all the assets available for use in your iAd. Click-and-drag `banner-icon-rex.png` to the placeholder image (a landscape silhouette with a moon) on the left of the banner canvas. It should update with our new picture.

4. Note that this is a PNG image; we picked PNG as we want the transparent areas to show the background gradient, something we cannot do with JPG. Now the new image is in our iAd, and the text seems to be too far to the right, so click on the text label and drag it slightly nearer to the left.

What just happened?

We imported the set of resources that we'll be using in our iAd to the **Asset Library** and updated our template to have our own image in it.

Time for action – supporting all orientations

Apple suggests that our banners should work in both portrait and landscape, and doing so ensures your iAd looks great and can appear in any app that supports iAd. We'll now look at modifying the banner to support both orientations:

1. To see how the current banner looks in landscape, select **View** then **Landscape** from the menu bar. You'll see the iAd resize itself to match the new dimensions; we now have a thinner and longer canvas to customize our ad on.

2. As you can see, our text is now too big and the image has been cut off. Select the text and change it to a more suitable size, such as **22**. You might need to move the text to be centered in this new view.

3. We'll now fix up the image; click to select the image. If the inspector pane isn't visible, open it from the bottom-right menu in iAd Producer.

4. Under the image properties section in the inspector pane, change **Actual size** to **Stretch to fit**. This allows us to shrink the image down to fit in the banner.

 By scaling the same image we used in portrait, we keep the total size of our banner down as we don't need to load in any extra resources for the landscape version of our banner.

5. Still in the inspector pane, expand the **Layout** section and check the **Constrain proportions** option. Constraining the proportion means the image will always remain the right ratio when we resize it. Here, we can see the **Layout** section and the **Constrain Proportions** option selected for our image on the banner:

6. Now, drag the image from one of the small boxes around the edge of the image, called **drag handles**, to resize it to fit correctly within the thinner landscape banner. If the image needs to be repositioned, drag it into a place where it looks good.

 When dragging or moving elements on the ad canvas, iAd Producer will suggest certain points you could use; these are indicated by yellow lines appearing and the element snapping to them.

7. Unfortunately, some of the changes we've made also affect the view in portrait because they share the same assets and some settings. Choose **View** then **Portrait** from the menu bar, to return to the portrait view.

8. You may have noticed that the image has now shrunk and doesn't fit the banner correctly. This is because the **Stretch to fit** setting we chose is conflicting with this view. We can fix this by dragging the image from the drag handle to resize it to fit how it should.

9. Reposition the image so that it's back in the correct position.

 The arrow icon above the canvas next to the **View** drop-down menu can be used to quickly jump back and forth between the landscape and portrait versions of your banner.

10. Check the banner again, in each orientation. Everything should be looking great now; if it isn't, fix up the issues until you're happy with the banner.

11. Save your iAd project using the **Save** option in the **File** section of the menu bar.

What just happened?

We completed our banner by supporting both the landscape and portrait orientations to ensure that our ad is compatible and will, therefore, appear within as many apps as possible.

If you were using the supplied assets, your banner should look something like the following screenshot:

Pop quiz – making banners

1. Why should we tweak our iAd banner to look good in both portrait and landscape modes?

   a. So our banner works upside down

   b. To make our iAd look great in any orientation

   c. In case the user is seeing our banner on a train

   d. Apple requires us to support both orientations

2. What is a radial gradient?

    a. A circle with a color in it

    b. Two colors that look good together

    c. Two colored circles that fade into each other

    d. A button with an image

Now that we have a completed banner, let's look at transitioning our users into our core ad unit smoothly, with a splash page.

Making a splash

The splash is your chance to keep the user interested while they wait for your core ad unit to load.

Time for action – making the splash screen

Let's make a splash screen that shows a bouncing image and three messages fading between each other:

1. If you're continuing on from the last exercise, click on the **Overview** back button in the top-left of iAd Producer. If you aren't, then open iAd Producer and choose **Open Project**; find the `Dino Stores` project we've been using so far.

2. You should now see the overview of your iAd and the flow between each component. Double-click the **Splash** page to open the template selector. For this splash page, we'll be using the **Bouncing Logo** template. Double-click the page again to open it on the canvas.

3. Open the **Asset Library** pane from the **Assets** option, on the right of the bottom bar. This should show all the assets we imported earlier. Drag **Pterodactyl.png** to the large image placeholder box on our splash's canvas.

4. You may have noticed our pterodactyl's wings and head have got cut off. We can fix this by resizing the image box using the drag handles. Once you've changed the size of the image box to show the entire image, make sure it is still centered by dragging the entire image, so that a yellow line appears down the middle of the canvas and the image snaps to it. This is iAd Producer suggesting the ideal position for it. The following screenshot is an example of the yellow–lined, suggested positioning in iAd Producer:

5. We've added the image into our splash; now, we'll customize the text. The **Bouncing Logo** template comes with a `Multi-Label` object, similar to a standard label, but it let's us change between different messages with a transition.

6. Double-click on the **multi-label**; at the moment, it should say **Loading Message 1**. This opens the multi-label editor and fades out the rest of the canvas while we edit it.

7. Click on the text again to highlight it and replace it with your own message, say **It's taken 180 million years.**

8. To move the message to the next cell, the sub-label of the multi-label, click the down arrow to the right of **1 of 3 cells**. In the following screenshot, this cell navigation arrow is highlighted:

9. Now, enter the text for the second cell, say but finally... Move on to the third cell and add the final message, for example, they're here.

10. iAd Producer will now automatically transition between these cells, while our ad is loading. To ensure our message gets a chance to complete a full cycle, we need to adjust the timing of the multi-label. We'll change the time each cell is visible for and the length of the transition, and make sure the splash is visible for a certain time.

11. To change the multi-label duration, click anywhere outside of the cell to exit the editing mode. Now single-click back on the multi-label to select it, but don't enter back into the editing mode. If the inspector pane isn't visible, open it up and find the **Effects** section. We'll want to change the **By Letter** to **Line**. This means the effect is applied to an entire line at a time, instead of each individual letter. Check that the **Show For** is **2s** and the **Hide For** is **0.5s**; change these if they're not. Your final effects should look like the following screenshot:

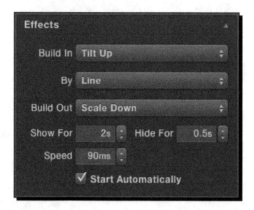

12. Now let's change the minimum duration of the splash to **7.5s**. Click the background of the iAd to modify the main splash properties. In the inspector pane, change the **Show Page for at Least** value to **7.5s**, by dragging the slider to the right.

> We chose a minimum duration of **7.5s** , as this allows the entire effect animation on the multi-label cell to complete. Each cell is visible for 2 seconds and hidden for 0.5 seconds, making a total of 2.5 seconds. Then we have three cells in total, making a total duration of 3 x 2.5 seconds, or 7.5 seconds. It's important to keep the splash screen visible for as little time as possible, to prevent the user from closing your ad before they even reach the content!

13. Finally, we'll add a background gradient to our splash. Under the **Show Page for at Least**, find the **Background** section. Just as we did with the background of our banner, we'll use a radial gradient. We're going to click on the first color on the gradient strip and select *Snow*, the white crayon on the bottom right. Now click the second color box on the gradient strip and choose *Cantaloupe* from the bottom left.

14. Save your project from the **File** menu. That's our final splash, and it'll look similar to the following screenshot:

What just happened?

We've now made our first splash screen, transitioning the user into the core ad unit. You modified the animation effect timings to ensure the full splash animation gets viewed by the user.

As our splash page includes animations that can't be previewed in iAd Producer, let's take a quick look at how to simulate them using Safari.

Previewing the ad

Whilst iAd Producer gives a great overview of the positions, styling, and flow of your iAd, it doesn't show us animations or let us interact with our ad. Fortunately, as each iAd is built using the latest web technologies, we're able to use **Safari**, the built-in web browser on your Mac. Safari uses the same engine to display web pages as the iPhone, so the representation should be accurate; however, remember your Mac is a lot faster than your iPhone, so performance may be worse on that device.

Time for action – testing your iAd

Let's take a moment from building our iAd to check over the Dino Stores ad that we've been creating so far to check that the animations provided by the templates and multi-labels are working:

1. If it isn't open already, open the Dino Stores project that we've been working on and open up the banner on the canvas editor. You might need to return to the overview to find the banner.

2. From the menu bar, select **Export** then **Preview in Safari**. This will open Safari, with your banner in it. You should see the text slide in from the right and the image fade up. Don't worry if you can see the text before it enters the main banner area, which would be out of the visible frame on the iPhone.

     You might have noticed that the iAd logo and frame is missing from the preview in Safari, this is added by the iAd system on the iOS devices and is not available in Safari.

3. Let's view the animation again by refreshing the page. From the menu bar in Safari, choose **View** and then **Reload page**. If you make changes to your iAd in iAd Producer, reloading the page won't show the updated iAd, so you'll have to go back into iAd Producer and choose **Preview in Safari**, again, to update it.

4. If you're happy with the banner, open the splash in iAd Producer and select **Export** and then **Preview in Safari**, from the menu bar.

     Whenever you're working on an iAd with animations or effects in it, you can preview the iAd at any time to see how it will look when using this technique.

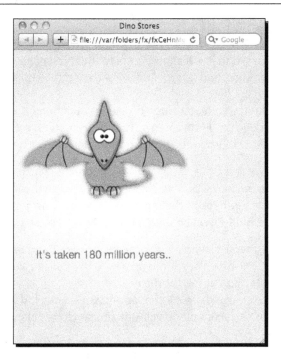

What just happened?

You just previewed what your ad looks like running in Safari—just like in the previous screenshot. In the next chapter, we'll look at device testing being able to touch our ads and immerse ourselves, which makes it much easier to get a feel of what our iAd experience will be like.

Now that we've seen how our banner and splash page are going to look, let's continue building the rest of our ad.

Adding a menu

The menu is the root view of our core ad unit and is used as the primary navigation between the subviews of our iAd. The flow of the ad typically means users will go from the menu to a page, then back to the menu and on to another page.

Time for action – making a menu

Let's make a menu for our iAd that will allow access to the three pages in our ad—an image gallery, a shakeable image view, and a store finder. To make the menu, follow the ensuing steps:

1. If you haven't done so already, open up iAd Producer and the `Dino Stores` project we've been working on. From the overview screen, double-click the **Menu** page in the app. Then, flow to open the template chooser.

2. For this menu, we'll use the `Hide-Reveal` template, which gives us a menu that slides out to the bottom when we change pages and that can slide back in when the user wants to get back to the main menu. Select this template and click **choose**. Double-click the **Hide-Reveal** menu in the ad flow to open up the menu canvas.

3. Double-click the menu area to open its editing mode. Then, double-click on **Page 1** to change the text. The first page of our ad will be the image gallery, so enter some text, say **View our pets**. Repeat this for the next two items, the shakable image view and the store finder. You could use **All shapes and sizes**, and **Find us!** for these items. With the new text, your selected menu will look similar to the following screenshot:

4. The default style of the menu isn't very compelling, so let's restyle it. Exit the editing mode of the menu by clicking the background of the ad, and then single-click the menu again to select it. However, don't enter edit mode. Expand the background section of the inspector pane to reveal the gradient strip and click on the first color box to open the color picker.

5. This time, we're not going to use the crayons to select our color because they offer a very limited choice. On the color picker, click the rainbow-filled circle to open the **color wheel**. The color wheel gives us a large circle with the color spectrum in it, allowing selection of any color that we want. The following screenshot shows what each part of the color wheel selector is for:

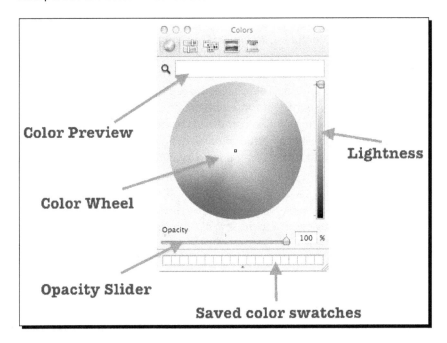

6. For our first color, select a light, orangey yellow by clicking the color you want on the color wheel. The preview area and iAd canvas should update to show your selection. You can click-and-drag on the color wheel to get a live update of the color you're selecting.

7. Once you've found a color you like, select the second color by clicking the second color box on the gradient strip in iAd Producer to open that color in the color picker. This time choose a darker, deeper orange that complements the first. You can use the lightness slider to change between lighter or darker colors to select from.

8. Now that you've selected the colors for the menu, let's make sure it's a linear gradient. A linear gradient has a start and finish color, and fades from the first to the second color. In the **Background** section of the inspector pane, check whether the type under the gradient strip is **Linear** and not **Radial**.

 When creating linear gradients for tappable items, you should keep the top color lighter than the bottom, to create the illusion of depth. A light-to-dark gradient gives a pushed-out effect, which gives the button that realistic, tappable feel. If you need to swap around your colors, there is a button in the **Background** section with two arrows on it. Clicking that will reverse the direction of the gradient.

9. We've styled the inside of our menu; let's now change the border. Under the **Background** section, you should see a border section; if it's not expanded, click it to reveal the border settings. Click the color box to open the color picker. Change the default white to another color, such as deep brown. We can increase the width of the border to **3px** to make it more pronounced. If you want, change the radius to **20px**, to increase the rounded corners of the menu. The border style can be changed from a solid line to dotted or dashed; however, if you try changing it you'll quickly see these don't suit the menu we're making.

 If you've made a custom color that you'd like to save in order to access easily later, you can drag the big block of the color in the preview area to the strip of empty boxes along the bottom color picker. This is useful when you use the same custom colors throughout your ad and want to keep them consistent.

10. You may have noticed the main **Menu** tab at the top hasn't had any styling applied to it, so let's change it to match the rest of the menu. Double-click inside the main area of the **Menu**, then single-click on the top part of the menu, where it says **Menu**. Selecting the **Menu** tab can be quite difficult, so don't worry if you have to try this a few times before you can select it.

11. Firstly, let's get the background color of the menu tab to match the border, so it looks like one complete unit. In the inspector pane, find the **Background** section, change it to a solid fill and replicate the same red we used for the border.

 iAd Producer unfortunately hides the area on the canvas we're editing behind a dark grey mask, so you might need to deselect the **Menu** tab occasionally to see the changes you're making.

12. The darker background of the **Menu** tab has meant the text is no longer readable, so let's change the text color. From the inspector pane, find the **Text** section and expand it if you need to. Click on the block of grey color and change it to white. Here, we can see the selection of the **Menu** tab with its colors adjusted:

13. Click back on the main ad canvas to see how the menu looks and edit any part you think needs tweaking, The menu is done!

14. We've added the menu, let's now change the background of our page. Click the background on the ad canvas and open the **Background** section in the inspector pane.

15. We'll want the background to match the splash screen to ease the transition into our core ad unit. If you used the suggested colors for the splash screen, you'll want to change the first color to white (*Snow*) from the crayon section of the color picker, and the second to orange (*Cantaloupe*). The default template should have a radial gradient already applied. Check whether it does and change it if you need to.

If you're using iAd Producer 2.0 or later, (released Q4 2011) then you can set the **Shared Background project** property from the inspector pane on the ad overview. This will cause all future page backgrounds to share the same default.

16. That was easy; let's add a couple of images to our advert's menu. Open up the **Asset Library** by clicking the **Assets** icon in the bottom-right corner of the iAd Producer window. Drag the **t-rex.png** image from the **Asset Library** onto the placeholder image area on the canvas. Reposition the image on the right of the canvas, so it slightly overlaps the edge of the screen.

17. Now drag the **dino-stores-title.png** image onto the canvas and reposition it so it is sitting next to the dinosaur. You might want to position the logo image in between the teeth of the dinosaur, as shown in the following screenshot:

 When dragging an image onto the canvas, if you put it over the top of an existing image, the existing image will be replaced. If you want to have overlapping images you need to drag the new image to a place on the canvas that doesn't already have one, then reposition it.

18. Let's add a reflection to the dino-stores-title.png image. Select the **Dino Stores** image on the canvas, and then click on the inspector pane. Find the **Reflection** section and expand it, if you need to. Tick the checkbox to enable the reflection. Now, we can tweak the reflection settings to improve its appearance. Changing the **offset** to **0px** means the reflection will start precisely where the image ends, it's generally a good idea to do this. We'll leave the size at **100%**, but you can use it to crop the reflection if you don't want the whole image mirrored underneath it. The **strength** is how transparent the reflection is; try a value around **15%** for a subtle and stylish reflection, similar to the following screenshot:

19. If you haven't done so already, make sure to save your iAd.

What just happened?

Congratulations, you just made your first-ever menu page for an iAd. Having a great menu page is essential to encourage the user to drill down into your iAd and find out more about the compelling message you have.

Have a go hero – menu pages

Why not try selecting a different template for the menu page and styling it like we just did with the `Hide-Reveal` template? You could do the following:

◆ Change the template of a page by opening it in the canvas editing view and pressing the **Template** button on the left of iAd Producer's bottom bar

◆ Try changing the template from the `Hide-Reveal` template to the `Buttons` template

◆ Restyle your template to match the ad

Be warned—changing the template resets the entire page, so you'll have to restyle all the components and add your custom images back.

Building the core ad pages

We've built the navigation to get between the pages, now it's time to put some great content in them! We'll be adding a **3D interactive image gallery**—a page that changes between images when it's shaken, and a store finder that uses the inbuilt GPS to pin point a users nearest store or outlet.

Inserting an image gallery

Let's get started with the image gallery; we'll be using a 3D carousel that can be flicked back and forth by the user to browse the images.

Time for action – making the image gallery

In order to make the image gallery, follow the ensuing steps:

1. We'll be adding the gallery to our existing Dino Stores project. If you haven't already, open the Dino Stores project that we've been working on in iAd Producer.

2. Double-click **Page 1** to open the template chooser. Select the **Image Carousel** template and press **Choose**. Now, double-click the page again to enter the canvas.

3. We're now on the page's canvas, ready to edit our gallery. To add images to the gallery, you must drag them all at once to the gallery object on the canvas.

4. Let's select the group of items that we want to add. Open the **Asset Library** from the bottom bar and find the group of images labeled **gallery-image-1.jpg**, **gallery-image-2.jpg**, and so on. Single-click the first image, **gallery-image-1.jpg**; it should become highlighted. Now hold down the *Shift* key on your keyboard while clicking the last image, **gallery-image-6.jpg**. This will select all the images in between the two selections. With the selected group of images, drag them onto the image gallery object on the canvas.

> Note that we're using JPG images in the gallery. Our images don't have areas of transparency, so we can use JPG and benefit from the smaller file size. If you're using your own images, the image carousel requires high-resolution images that are 304px wide and 440px high. iAd Producer automatically generates the lower-resolution resources for you.

The gallery should now fill up with our images and add a 3D perspective to them. Your project should be shaping up and look similar to the following screenshot:

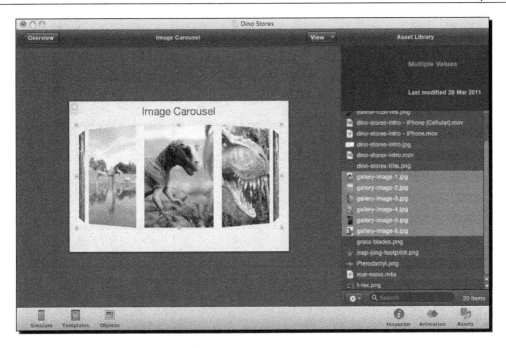

5. To give the images a polaroid effect, let's add a 4px white border around the outside of the pictures. Select the image carousel by clicking on it. In the inspector pane, expand the border section. Tick the checkbox to turn on the border, and then change the color to white using the color picker; increase the width to **4px**.

 Don't be tempted to add a shadow or reflection to your 3D image carousel. Shadows and reflections can perform poorly when they're in a 3D view. Save them for static or 2D elements.

6. All we need to do now is add the background gradient to match the rest of our iAd and change the title. Click the background of the ad canvas; then, open the inspector to change the background of the page. We'll want to use the same radial gradient that we got in the splash and menu, so set the first color as *Snow* and the second as *Cantaloupe*.

7. Once you're happy with the background gradient, double-click the **Image Carousel** label to change the text in it. Type a heading for the page, say `Our Pets`. You might also want to make the font bigger and change the color from the text section in the inspector pane.

What just happened?

We just assigned the `Image Carousel` template to the first page of our ad and added some images to it. We learnt how to select multiple images at once and apply them to a gallery object.

When adding your own images, try to keep them between six and 10 images per gallery, for the best experience.

Have a go hero – cover flow gallery

Now that you know how to select multiple images and add them to an image gallery, why not try using one of the other gallery templates? The `Cover Flow` template can be used to make a 3D gallery of images similar to the animated album view in iTunes. You'll also have to resize your images in this view to each be 440 pixel-wide squares.

Shaking a view

So far we've only been using the touch screen of the iPhone, so let's begin to take advantage of the other capabilities of this device. The **accelerometer** built into the iPhone is used to detect rotation and motion events, so that we can make a page that responds to a user shaking their iPhone by changing an onscreen image.

Time for action – shake shake shake

Using the built-in `Shake to Change` template, we'll create the second page of our iAd. We'll then add multiple images that change each time the user shakes the device.

1. Continuing with the `Dino Stores` project in iAd Producer, double-click the **Page 2** page in the project overview. From the template picker, select **Shake to Change** and press **choose**.

2. Now open up the page in the canvas by double-clicking on it. Expand the **Asset Library** and find the images **dino-shape-1.png** to **dino-shape-8.png**. Now click on the first image to highlight it, and then click on the last image in the list while holding the *Shift* key to select all of these images. Now drag the selection to the placeholder area in the middle of the canvas. In the following screenshot, we can see the multiple images selected and ready to be dragged:

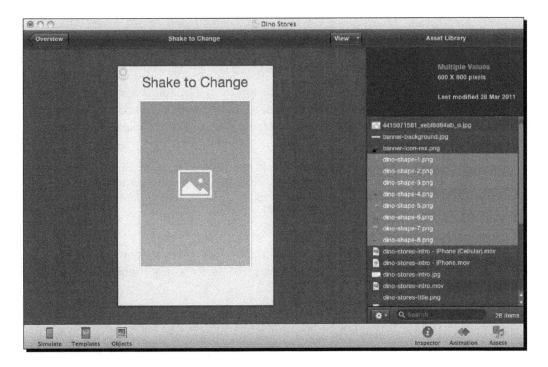

3. Some of the images are larger than the placeholder area, so we need to expand it using the drag handles. Try making it the whole width of the canvas and increasing the height so the first image isn't cut off. You might want to reposition the image to ensure that it's still centered correctly. The yellow helper lines should appear to help you while you're dragging it.

4. We'll now flick through each image to check whether it fits correctly. To do this, we need to double-click the first image to enter the cell editing mode. Just like with the multi-label, this shakeable image view is set up with multiple cells that it transitions between. You should see the **1 of 8 cells** navigation box appear beneath the image; click the left and right arrows to cycle through each image.

 When you change between cells, you should see the images wobble and fade between each other; this is the animation that will happen when the user of your ad shakes their device.

5. Navigate to each image and check that they're not cut off around the edges; if one is, click outside the image to exit the cell editing mode and make the image area larger to fit the full picture in.

6. Once you're happy with how each of the images is displayed, click the background of the ad canvas and open the inspector pane. Let's change the background to match the rest of our iAd. Use a radial gradient with *Snow* and *Cantaloupe* as the colors.

 If you find the gradient looks more washed out than you expected, try reselecting the radial gradient option for the gradient. Sometimes iAd Producer doesn't update the view properly and doing this forces it to refresh the preview.

7. If you want, change the text at the top of the page; however, keep in mind you'll want a way of telling the user that shaking the device will let them interact with your iAd.

What just happened?

We just used the page template Shake and Change to add a page to our iAd that changes each time the user shakes it. You can use the device hardware features to add extra interactivity to your ads, delivering a memorable and immersive experience to users.

Letting users find our stores

Now that we've got the user interested in our product, let's give them a way to buy it! Using the built-in GPS functionality of the iPhone, you can show your users their local stores and provide them with contact information to get in touch.

 Although the iPod touch doesn't have built-in GPS, it can use its wireless Internet connection to approximate the user's position. It's generally incredibly accurate!

Time for action – store finder

This will be the final page of our Dino Stores iAd; we'll be using nearby Apple Stores as an example location set.

1. If you're not continuing on from the last exercise, open iAd Producer and select the project that we've been working on. Go to the ad overview There should still be one page without a template; this is the final page in our iAd. Double-click **Page 3** and select the **Map** template.

2. Once you've selected the template, double-click the page to open it in the canvas editor. Let's start by customizing the map; click the placeholder map area in the center of the canvas and open it in the inspector pane.

3. In the **Properties** section, find the **Site ID**. By default, this is set to **demo**; it is the example ID used by Apple and shows the location of their Apple retail stores. You'd typically update this to your own **Site ID**, which needs to be set up by Apple. When you partner with Apple for the iAd Program, you can contact them to request one.

4. The **Radius** value defines how far from the user's location the ad should look for stores. Depending on how many stores you have, you might want to change this; the higher number or density of your stores, the lower the search radius should be. For the demo **Site ID**, set this to **50mi**.

5. Still in the properties section, click the drop-down file selector in the **Custom Pin** to select a custom image to show each store location. Choose the image you want to use, for example **map-pin-footprint.png**; this is a red icon, as red is used to signify destinations on iOS maps. Depending on the image, you may need to adjust the offset to center the pin over the location; for example, try pin values of **-9px** for **Offset X** and **5px** for **Offset Y**. Your pin should appear centered in the map on canvas, such as the one shown in the following screenshot:

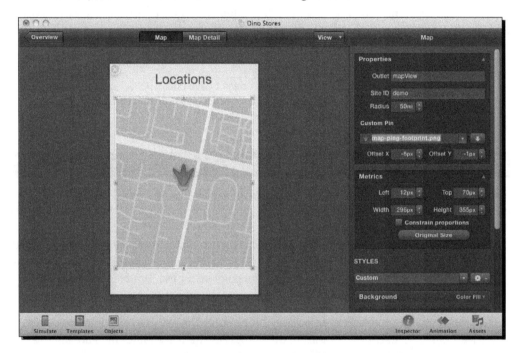

6. That's the **Map** view finished, but let's add a couple of visual tweaks to it so that it looks even better. With the **Map** view selected, scroll down to the border section of the inspector pane and add a **4px**, solid-white border to frame the map.

7. Let's also add some shadow to pop the map out from the background. Below the border section, enable **Drop Shadow** by ticking the checkbox and click the color to open the color picker. Change the opacity slider to a lower setting, around **40%** or so, to reduce the transparency of the shadow and make it less harsh on the screen.

8. With the map view styling finished, let's now add radial gradient to the page background. Click the canvas and expand the **Background** section in the inspector pane. Add the gradient you've been using throughout the ad. If you've been using the suggested gradient, choose *Snow* and *Cantaloupe* as the colors from the crayon color picker.

9. Let's change the **Locations** text to something like Find a store . . . by double-clicking on the label to enter editing mode.

10. Let's also add the number for our head office. The template doesn't provide any other labels with this template, so we need to add our own. On the left of the bottom bar, click on the **Objects** icon to open the object library, and scroll down till you find the **Label** object, as shown in the following screenshot. Select it to add an empty label onto the canvas;

11. Double-click the new label on the canvas to enter editing mode. Enter some text, say `Call us: 555-1051`. You might need to resize the width of the text area to fit the whole message. Now, move the text area to the bottom of the screen.

You might have to make the map smaller and move the label away from the bottom of the screen. The slide-reveal menu template we're using adds the top part of the menu to each page of the ad, so that the user can get back to the main page. Preview the ad in Safari to see if you need to reposition it—navigate to the ad overview and choose **Export | Preview in Safari** from the menu bar. The menu will only show up if you start the preview from the overview and then click the **menu** to navigate to that page.

12. Once you're happy with the positioning of the label, save your completed iAd!

What just happened?

We just added the last page to our iAd so customers can find our nearest stores. You've now finished creating your first iAd. Well done! Your overview screen should be similar to the following screenshot:

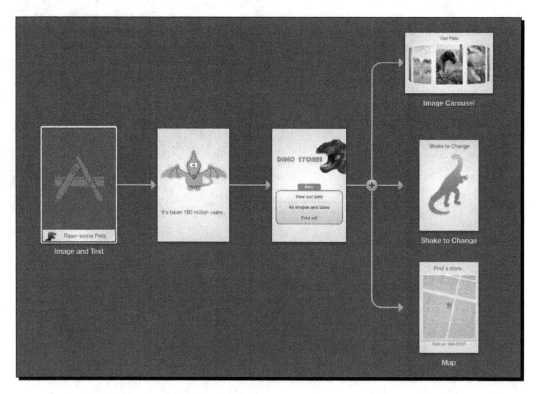

Pop quiz – iAd Producer

Now that you're familiar with iAd Producer, see if you can answer these simple questions:

1. Where would you go to find media you've imported into your iAd?

   a. The inspector pane

   b. The canvas

   c. The file menu

   d. The asset library

2. What is the name for a text box that changes between multiple values?

   a. Multi-label

   b. Lots-a-Labels

   c. Text transitioner 5000

   d. Fading text box

Summary

You've learned a lot in this chapter, and made your very first ad in iAd Producer. You should now know how to:

◆ Create a project in iAd Producer

◆ Build banners, splash pages, menus, and subpages

◆ Choose a template for each view

◆ Add radial and linear gradients to elements' page backgrounds

◆ Extend the templates by adding your own custom objects

◆ Preview your iAd using Safari

Now that you've made a great iAd, we'll look at testing it on physical devices and in the simulator, how to fix issues that arise, and common problems with your iAd.

4
Making Sure It Works

Now that we've built our first iAd, we need to test its functionality and performance, to ensure we deliver the best possible experience to our users. Thorough testing will help establish the value of your brand with an ad that shows quality and class.

In this chapter, we'll take a look at:

- Learning the limitations of testing in Safari
- Testing in the iOS simulator
- Interacting with the simulator
- Emulating hardware events
- Deploying and "touching" our ads on the device
- Debugging common problems
- Sharing our iAd using a demo

Testing in Safari

In the last chapter, we took a brief look at previewing an animation in our iAd, using Safari. Now, let's dig deeper and use it for testing, where we'll quickly discover the limitations.

Time for action – going on Safari

Lets open a project to preview and test in Safari.

1. Open a project in **iAd Producer**, such as the `Dino Stores` project we have been working on.

2. From the ad overview, select a page of the iAd by single-clicking it; a yellow border should appear around it. Now, choose **Export**, then **Preview in Safari**, from the menu bar, or use the keyboard shortcut *Cmd + Shift + Enter*.

     If you don't select a specific page when previewing from the overview, iAd Producer opens the splash page by default.

3. That page of your iAd will open in Safari; you can now click around to test your ad. Click the menu item to navigate to other pages of your ad.

     To test an ad directly from the canvas, select **Export**, then **Preview in Safari**, and iAd Producer will automatically open the current page you've been working on.

4. Try interacting with the ad; you'll quickly see there are some limitations. The preview in Safari lacks the iAd frame around the banner, and elements that would not usually be visible can be seen before they animate into view. While images, audio, and video elements will work, items such as maps and shakeable views aren't available in the Safari preview.

    If certain objects aren't available, Safari will show a warning prompt informing you which components can't be loaded.

What just happened?

We just opened our iAd in Safari both direct from the overview and when editing a specific page on the canvas. This is useful for quick testing, but has limitations in the objects it can display and the hardware interactions we can use; for example, shaking the device and multitouch are unavailable.

Safari on your Mac is likely to be using a newer version of **WebKit** than is available in iOS, which means you're less likely to see issues that may appear when using iOS.
WebKit is the open source rendering engine that decides how web pages should be displayed. It's used by web browsers like Safari (on desktop and mobile devices) and Chrome.

We're unable to test the flow and interactions between certain sections and pages of our iAd within Safari, so let's open an iAd using the iOS Simulator.

Testing in the simulator

The iOS Simulator allows us to test on devices that we may not have, and is useful for quickly deploying tests in an accurate environment for compatibility checking.

The iPad apps available at launch were built entirely using the simulator, as developers were unable to get access to the physical devices before they went on sale.

Installing Xcode and the iOS Simulator

To use the iOS Simulator to test on iPhone and iPad, you need to install the iOS SDK from Apple, which is included with Xcode. An **SDK** is a **Software Development Kit**; it contains the tools needed to build and test software for a specific platform.

Xcode is available for download either from the Mac App Store or manually from the developer portal. The Mac App Store is preferable but is only available in later versions of Mac OS X. Let's take a look at installing with the Mac App Store and how to get Xcode manually if it's unavailable.

You'll need approximately 10GB of free disk space available on your Mac to install Xcode and the developer tools. You have to install Xcode on your main hard drive, as it needs to update core system tools that can't run from an external disk.

Time for action – installing Xcode with the Mac App Store (easy)

We'll now discover if the Mac App Store is available on your Mac and install Xcode if it is.

1. From the Apple icon on the far-left of the menu bar, select **App Store** to open the store.

If you can't find the menu button, it means your Mac OS version doesn't support the Mac App Store. To update your OS, select the Apple icon and choose **Software Update**. Complete any required updates and start this exercise again.

If you still don't see the Mac App Store, skip ahead to the next exercise—*installing Xcode manually.*

2. With the App Store open, search for Xcode or visit `http://itunes.apple.com/gb/app/xcode/id448457090` to automatically open Xcode.

Older versions of Mac OS X, before Lion, may try and charge you to download Xcode from the Mac App Store. If Xcode doesn't appear as a free download, follow the manual steps in the next exercise instead, to install it for free.

3. Once the app Install Xcode has been downloaded, double click it to open the installer. Follow the installation steps and Xcode will be installed!

What just happened?

By using the Mac App Store to download our app, we avoid a lot of the manual and laborious task of downloading it from the developer portal. You'll automatically be informed of the updates when opening the store; or, if the App Store icon is in your dock, a badge will appear when updates are available.

You can safely delete the Install Xcode app, if you require disk space after installing. However, keeping it will mean future Xcode updates can download quicker, because only the changed parts of the installation need to be downloaded.

If you weren't able to download Xcode from the Mac App Store, then follow the next exercise to download it manually.

Time for action – installing Xcode manually (harder)

If you don't want to or can't use the Mac App Store, we can manually download and install Xcode from the developer portal. If you've successfully downloaded the app from the App Store, skip this exercise.

1. To access the iOS SDK, we need to log in to the iOS developer portal. Go to `http://developer.apple.com/ios/` and log in with your Apple ID and password.

2. We need to download the iOS SDK, the application used to develop iOS applications for iPhone and iPad. Once logged in, find the **Downloads** section near the bottom of the page and click on **Download Xcode 4** to start the download. In the following screenshot, we can see the option to download Xcode in the developer portal:

Downloads

Xcode 4.1 for Lion
This is the complete Xcode developer toolset for Mac, iPhone, and iPad. It includes the Xcode IDE, iOS Simulator, and all required tools and frameworks for building Mac OS X and iOS apps.

Download Xcode 4

Posted Date: Jul 20, 2011
Build: 4B110
Included iOS SDK: iOS 4.3
Included Mac SDK: Mac OS X 10.7

The Xcode and iOS SDK download is several gigabytes in size and can take a while to download; if you have a slow connection, it might be worth leaving it overnight to complete.

Once downloaded, open the Xcode and iOS SDK.mkpg installation package by double clicking on it. When prompted **This package will run a program to determine if the software can be installed**, click **Continue**.

3. Read and accept the **Software License Agreement** and continue to the **Installation Type** screen. Make sure all the options are checked, as we need to install all the components for the iOS Simulator. Your installation window should look similar to the following:

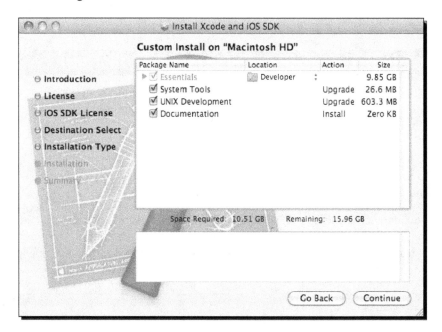

4. Click **Continue** and then **Install**, to complete the installation.

 By default, Xcode and the related tools are stored in the `Developer` directory on your hard drive; you shouldn't need to change this.

What just happened?

You just installed Xcode manually from the developer portal (those of you who had been unable to install Xcode through the Mac App Store, or to whom it hadn't been freely available).

You now have the tools installed to build iOS and Mac apps, which includes the iOS simulators for the iPhone and iPad. Although we won't be using Xcode to develop our ads, we still had to install it for the simulator to work.

Time for action – opening an ad

Now that we have the iOS Simulator installed, we can test an iAd running in the full iAd framework.

1. Open up iAd Producer and load an existing iAd project, for example, the `Dino Stores` project we made earlier.

2. From the ad overview, click the **Simulate** button in the bottom-left bar to open the simulator. You can use *Cmd + Enter* to open the simulator from the keyboard.

> iAd Producer will automatically open the iOS Simulator as an iPhone or iPad, based on the type of project you're working on.

3. The iOS Simulator will appear in your dock, and then, shortly after, the simulator will appear. iAd Producer automatically installs and opens your iAd in the iAd Tester app. You should see your banner appear at the bottom, after it has loaded, similar to the following screenshot:

The iAd Tester app is a *fake* placeholder app that emulates an app where your ad could appear. Typically, your iAd will appear at the bottom, above the tab bar, which is used for navigating between the screens in an app.

4. Click the banner to open your iAd. You can now play around and test your iAd, as you would if it was on a device.

What just happened?

You now have tested your iAd in the exact software environment it will run in. Whenever you want to update the preview in the simulator, just press the **Simulate** button in iAd Producer and it will be redeployed.

Interacting with the simulator

For quick checks, the simulator is better to use than Safari, as your ad is framed correctly and has access to the full iAd features and components. Unlike Safari, we're able to simulate hardware events whilst we're interacting with an iAd.

Time for action – simulating hardware in the simulator

With a real device, we can shake, pinch, and rotate the iPhone or iPad to interact with an iAd. These events can be emulated within the simulator.

1. We'll be using an example project with a selection of objects we can interact with. Open the `Interaction Demo` project included with the book assets.

2. From the ad overview, click the **Simulate** button to open the simulator. First up, let's look at rotating the device.

3. You should see the banner appear in iAd Tester. We'll now rotate the simulator to check how our banner looks in landscape. From the menu bar, select **Hardware** then **Rotate Left** or **Rotate Right** to rotate the device. The simulator will then rotate and the banner should update to show in landscape. Now rotate the iAd back to portrait, either by rotating once in the opposite direction or by rotating the simulator in the same direction three more times, to get back where we started.

You can also use keyboard shortcuts to rotate the simulator; try pressing the *Cmd* key with the left or right arrows.

4. Now click the banner to enter the iAd. From the menu, select **Shakey Time**. We'll now learn how to simulate the user shaking their device. From the hardware menu, select **Shake**; the ad should update to show you've shaken it. Try shaking it a few more times. You can see the **Shake Gesture** in the **Hardware** menu item in the following screenshot:

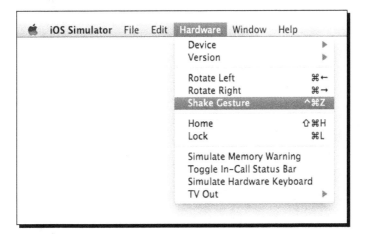

 Unfortunately, shaking your Mac won't update the ad in the simulator. However, *cmd* + *ctrl* + *Z* on the keyboard, gives you a quick way to shake the iOS Simulator.

5. Click the menu button to get back to the start of the demo iAd. Now select the second item **GPS/Multitouch**. This will open a prompt, requesting access to your location, simulating the GPS hardware found in real devices. As your Mac (probably) doesn't have a GPS in it, the simulator defaults to Apple's headquarters in Cupertino, California.

6. Now that the map has found your *location*, let's simulate a pinch to zoom in and out of the map. Move the mouse pointer near the middle of the map and hold the *Ctrl* key on the keyboard; two circles should appear, representing the touch points of two fingers. Keep holding *Ctrl* and click-and-drag outwards from the map to zoom in. To zoom back out, repeat the process but start from the outside of the map and drag inwards. The following screenshot shows the simulated touch points of a multi-touch drag:

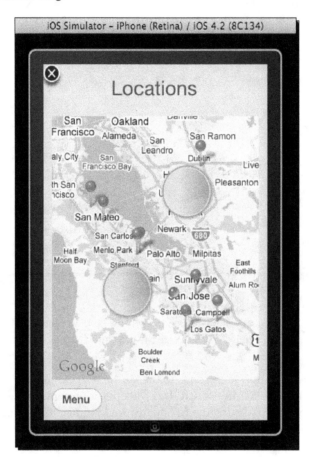

7. Try pinching and de-pinching the map to zoom in and out; it can take a while to get used to, so don't worry if you don't get it the first time. When you're confident with these gestures, click **Menu** to go back to the main ad screen.

8. Finally, we'll try flicking a panorama view. Open the **Flick** page from the menu. You should now see an image; this image is in a scrollable view, so it can be moved around within its frame to reveal a different section. Click-and-drag the image around to see this. To flick the image, click-and-drag quickly and sharply; you should see that the image continues to move after you have let go.

 Flicking is used to navigate large scrollable areas quickly. iOS calculates the speed and distance of dragging gestures and adds momentum to the scroll, so it keeps moving after you've removed your finger from the screen. The scroll then gradually decelerates to a natural end.

9. Once you're satisfied you're able to interact with the iOS Simulator, quit it by choosing **iOS Simulator** from the menu bar and clicking **Quit**, or use the keyboard shortcut, *Cmd + Q*.

What just happened?

We just tested out simulating hardware events, such as rotations, shakes, and multitouch. Keep in mind that certain hardware features in the simulator don't perform identically compared to the device; for example, GPS spoofing a location and the mouse pointer giving you increased tapping accuracy compared to a finger.

Pop quiz – the iOS Simulator

See if you're able to answer these questions about the iOS Simulator:

1. What did we have to install to use the iOS Simulator?

    a. Xcode and the iOS SDK.

    b. Just Xcode.

    c. Just the iOS SDK.

    d. The developer preview of iOS.

2. How do you do a pinch gesture using the iOS Simulator?

    a. Squeeze the screen.

    b. Press *Cmd + Z* on the keyboard.

    c. Pinch two fingers on the trackpad.

    d. Hold *Ctrl* to show two touch points, then click and drag.

Time for action – simulating different devices

By default, iAd Producer opens the simulator as an *iPhone 4 with Retina Display* for iPhone ads, or a *generic iPad* for iPad projects. The iPhone 4 simulator is scaled to 50 percent to counter the higher pixel count so it can still fit on your screen. We can also open a standard resolution display iPhone to see how our lower-resolution assets appear. Let's try simulating in the iPad, standard resolution iPhones, and different software versions of iOS.

1. Let's open an iPad project to see how the simulator looks when testing iPad ads. As we've not created an iPad ad yet, open the **Interactions Demo - iPad** file from the book assets. Once loaded, click **Simulate** to open the simulator.

2. The simulator should automatically open with the iPad. Try interacting with the iAd—the same hardware controls apply for shaking and rotating.

 It can be hard to distinguish between the iPad and iPhone 4 retina simulators; if you're unsure which simulator is open, check the title bar, which should say whether it's running as an iPad or iPhone.

3. By default, the iOS simulator scales the iPad to 50 percent of its resolution, if your screen isn't large enough to show the iPad at its native size. To show the iPad simulator at the correct scale, choose **Window** from the menu bar. Now click **Scale** and select **100%**. You can also change to 100 percent scale using *Cmd + 1* and back to 50 percent using *Cmd + 2* on the keyboard. When zoomed to 100 percent, you may have to scroll around the simulator to access off-screen parts of the iPad, as shown in the following screenshot:

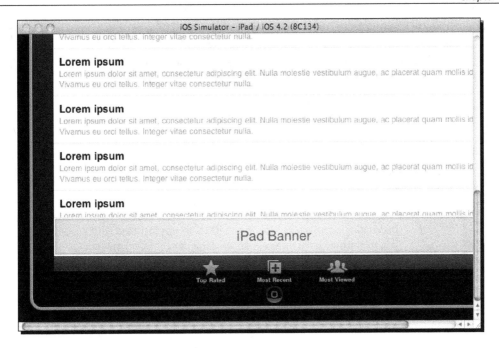

4. Close the iPad simulator and open an iPhone project, such as the `Interactions Demo`. We'll now test the standard resolution, non-retina version of our iAd. Open up the banner of the ad from the overview; it should now appear on the editing canvas. From the **View** drop-down menu in the top right, change it from **iPhone (Retina) - 50%** to **iPhone**, as shown in the following screenshot:

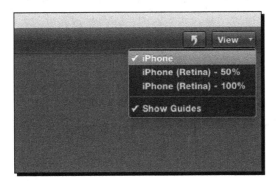

5. Now, click **Simulate** to open the standard resolution iPhone simulator. The simulator should now have a proper iPhone frame surrounding it, without a title bar. You should use the standard-resolution simulator to check that iAd Producer has correctly downscaled your images to display on these devices.

6. We can also specify different versions of iOS to test our iAd in. Older versions of iOS may have different rendering quirks and may display content differently, so it's important to test in as many as you can before deployment. To change the iOS version the simulator launches in, select **Export** from the menu bar in iAd Producer, then **Simulator iOS Version**; try changing the version and click **Simulate** to launch the ad again.

 Depending on which version of the iOS SDK was installed with Xcode, you might only have one version available for the iOS Simulator. Apple regularly updates the SDK whenever a new version of iOS is released, so keep an eye out for e-mails from Apple announcing updates to the SDK. You can then re-download the latest Xcode and install the update to have access to the latest simulators.

What just happened?

Using the simulator, we were able to emulate different types of hardware and software conditions to test a range of situations our iAd could appear in.

Have a go hero

Why not try testing the iAd we made in *Chapter 3, Making Your iAd*, or an iAd of your own in different simulator conditions to check if it works as intended. You could try:

◆ Testing it in the simulator

◆ Previewing how your assets look in high resolution retina and standard resolution displays

◆ Testing interaction with hardware, such as shakes and using GPS location

◆ Using your iAd in different versions of iOS

Testing on the device

Testing on your computer is great for checking whether graphics look like you expect them to, previewing animations, and trying out the flow of your ad; but they don't compare to the experience of touching and interacting with your immersive iAd.

Installing iAd Tester

iAd Tester is the *fake* placeholder app we used in the iOS Simulator to test our iAd. Apple has made the app available so we can install it and test ads directly on our iOS devices. With iAd Tester, we can access iAds on our device, remotely on our Mac, and wirelessly from the iAd Test Server.

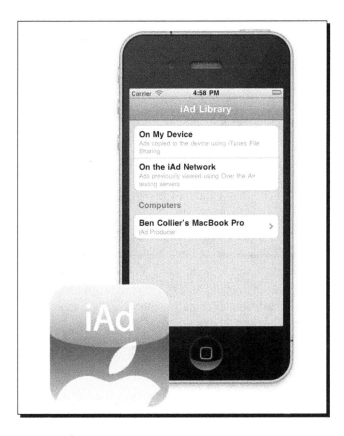

In the previous screenshot, you can see the iAd Tester running on an iPhone 4.

Time for action – putting iAd Tester on your devices

When you installed iAd Producer, it placed a version of iAd Tester on your Mac. We can use iTunes to install this on our iOS devices.

1. iAd Producer copied a version of iAd Tester to the `Developer` folder of your Mac. Open Finder and navigate to `Developer`, then `iAdJSDeveloper`; now open the folder `iAdTester-Device`. You should see a file called `iAdTester`.

2. Open iTunes and drag the file to your library, as you can see demonstrated in the following screenshot:

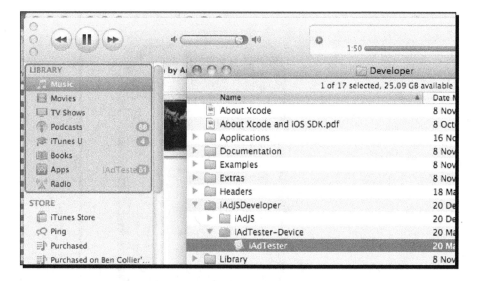

3. This adds iAd Producer to your iTunes library, so it can be synced to your iOS devices. Now connect an iOS device, such as an iPhone or iPad, to your Mac using a dock connector cable. iTunes should now recognize the device and it will show in the side bar. Click the device icon to open the overview, and change the tab to **Apps**. Make sure **Sync Apps** is checked and find `iAdTester` in the app list on the right; check the box to select it for syncing. Your iTunes apps page should look similar to the following screenshot:

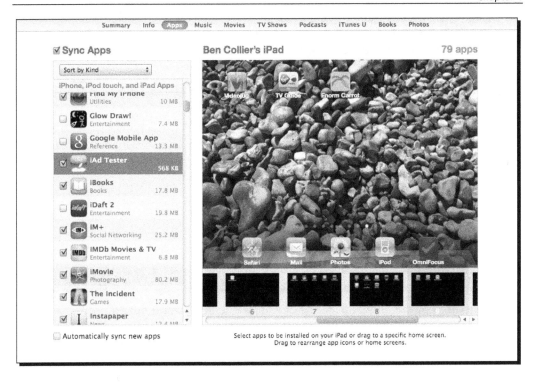

4. Click **Apply** and wait for the device to synchronize. iAd Tester should now be installed.

Your iOS device can only sync with one machine at any time; if you want to synchronize it with a different machine, you might end up losing your media and applications on it.

5. Repeat for all the iOS devices you have to test on.

What just happened?

Using iTunes, we copied iAd Tester to our iOS devices that we want to use to test our iAds. You should try to test on many devices, so install iAd Tester on every device you can.

Leave your iOS device connected and iTunes open, as we'll now look at exporting and accessing our iAd with iAd Tester.

Accessing your development iAd

iAd Producer allows you to export and copy your iAd to the device or broadcast your project wirelessly over the network. Let's export our iAd and copy it to a device with iOS Tester installed.

Copying to a device

We can copy our ads to the device using iTunes. This is useful if you want to test your ads when you don't have a wireless connection or want to demonstrate your iAd away from your Mac.

 If you're having an exciting meeting to discuss the progress on your awesome iAd, copying it to the device means you can show off without the need for your Mac to be powered on and connected to the same network.

Time for action – exporting our iAd

Before we can copy our iAd to an iPhone or iPad, we need to export our ad.

1. Open the project you want to export in iAd Producer, for example, the iPhone iAd `Dino Stores` we made in the last chapter.

2. From the **Export item** in the menu bar, select **Export to Disk (Optimized)**. Now choose a location to export your iAd and save it.

 When you export an optimized ad, iAd Producer automatically generates two extra files, `WebArchive.manifest` and `WebArchive@2x.manifest`. These manifest files are a part of HTML5 and tell the web browser or iAd framework that all the file names contained within them should be downloaded for offline use. This means the content in your iAd begins to load before it is needed so your ad content appears instantly as your user browses your iAd. Optimized ads are also compressed, with whitespace and comments removed from the code.

What just happened?

We've just exported an optimized version of our iAd project to a folder on our Mac. Now that we've got the ad in the correct format, we can copy it to a device and begin testing.

Time for action – copying our ad to the device

The *File Sharing* feature of iTunes can be used to copy our iAd to the device so that it can be opened with iAd Tester. Make sure you're using a recent version of iTunes that has *File Sharing* enabled—select the Apple logo from the menu bar then **Software Update...** to download any updates that may be required.

1. In Finder, locate your exported iAd; it should be a folder called `Your-Project-Name.ad`. If you're curious, have a look at the structure of your exported iAd. iAd Tester requires a zipped or compressed version of our exported project, so right click on the folder containing the export and choose **Compress** "`Your-Project-Name.ad`". You can see our `Dino Store` project being compressed, in the following screenshot:

2. After the ZIP file has been made, check that iTunes is open and connect an iOS device with iAd Tester installed. Click on the device in the sidebar to open the overview. Now, open the **Apps** tab and find the **File Sharing** section near the bottom.

  Don't make any changes, such as modifying the assets, to the files in your exported iAd, as exported projects cannot be imported back into iAd Producer.

3. In the **File Sharing** section, select **iAd Tester**, so it is highlighted. You can now either drag your compressed ZIP file to the documents area, or click **Add...** and find the file you want to copy across. The file will now sync to the device. In the following screenshot, we're syncing our previously compressed `Dino Stores` ad:

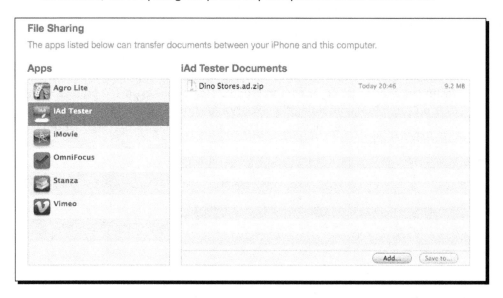

 If iAd Tester doesn't show up in the list of apps, make sure it's installed by checking the home screen of your iOS device for the icon. If it isn't, try installing it again.

What just happened?

We've now transferred our iAd to our device so we can test it. If you want to delete an ad (or any document) from your iPhone or iPad, highlight the item in the document list and press the *Delete* or *Backspace* key.

Testing on the device

Once we've successfully used iTunes to transfer our ad to an iPhone or iPad, we'll want to run and experience it for the first time.

Time for action – testing the ad

With iAd Tester installed on your iOS device, and the ad transferred to it, we can now open and test our ad:

1. Open iAd Tester from your device by tapping its icon on your home screen.

2. Now tap **On My Device** to show a list of the files you have copied to the Documents folder of iAd Tester, using iTunes file sharing.

3. Select the iAd you want to preview; if you're using the Dino Stores project, select **Dino Stores** from the list.

4. iAd Tester now shows you a mockup app where your iAd might appear; tap the banner to begin interacting with your iAd. Here, you can see the three screens you need to navigate to demo an ad:

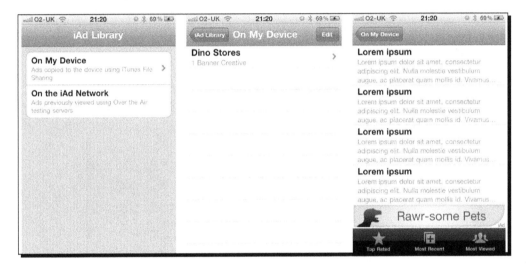

5. If you want to close your iAd, just tap the **X** in the top left to return to the mock app. If you want to change which ad you're using, tap **On My Device** from the navigation bar and select a different one (if there are any available).

What just happened?

We can now test our iAd on an actual device; this is the key to understanding exactly how our ad performs on the constrained mobile device hardware.

That was quite a few steps to go through just to view our ad, so let's try wirelessly testing our iAd using a Wi-Fi network.

Wireless testing

Fortunately, for quick testing, we don't have to sync a new version of our iAd to the device each time we want to preview an update. If our iOS device and Mac running iAd Producer are on the same network, we can wirelessly access our projects.

Time for action – wireless deployment

iAd Producer is able to share open projects wirelessly to iAd Tester. Make sure your iOS devices and Mac are connected to the same network before continuing.

1. Open iAd Producer and the project you want to test with. Make sure the project matches the device you're testing on; for example, iPhone projects will only be available on iPhones or iPod touches. Open the Interactions Demo project to test it on an iPhone.

2. Once the project is open, we'll need to enable wireless sharing. Open the preferences menu by selecting **iAd Producer** from the menu bar, then **Preferences**, or use the keyboard shortcut *Cmd + ,* (a comma).

3. From the **Preferences** menu, open the **Testing** tab and confirm that the **Enable iAd Testing on Devices** slider is set to **ON**. If it isn't, slide it across to start it. The following screenshot shows the iAd Testing settings you should use:

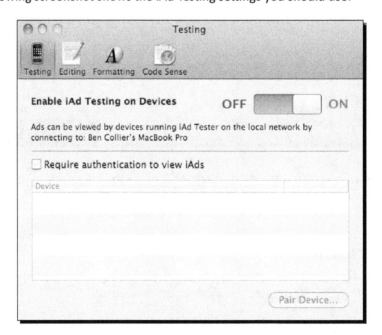

You can also toggle the wireless sharing on and off using the **Share Ads Locally** option from the **iAd Producer** item in the menu bar.

4. You can now close the preference window and open iAd Tester on your iOS device. All your open projects in iAd Producer will be broadcast and available to view in iAd Tester.

5. From iAd Tester, you should now see a **Computers** section, where your computer name should be listed. Tap your computer name to view a list of open iAd Producer projects.

 If you can't find your computer, ensure both devices are connected to the same network. If you can't find your project, keep in mind that new projects in iAd Producer that are yet to be saved will appear as **Untitled**.

6. Select the ad you want to preview. You'll now see the same mock placeholder app used if your ads are saved on the device using iTunes file sharing.

7. Now try modifying your ad in iAd Producer and previewing it again in iAd Tester. You may need to close and open the ad to preview the update, as the device needs to download the changes.

8. When you close iAd Producer, or a project, it will no longer be available remotely until you open the project again in iAd Producer.

What just happened?

iAd Producer now broadcasts your iAd locally over your Wi-Fi network so they can be accessed on devices running iAd Tester. This is a great way of testing your ads easily and, often, on an actual device; use it whenever you can!

Have a go hero – securing iAd Producer

Currently, anyone connected to the same Wi-Fi network as you can see the ads being broadcast. This should be safe if you're on a trusted network, such as your home or office, but, if you're using public Wi-Fi, you can secure which devices are able to access your iAds.

Try following these steps:

1. If you've not already, open iAd Producer and enable sharing ads locally.

2. From the iAd Producer preferences, check the **Require authentication to view iAds** box. Now press **Pair Device...**

3. iAd Producer will show you a pin number. Open iAd Tester on your device and tap your computer name; it should say **Open for pairing** underneath. Enter the pin. The following screenshot shows an example pin:

4. Repeat this for any other devices you want to pair.

Your iAds can now only be accessed wirelessly from authorized devices. Alternatively, you can just toggle the **Share Ads Locally** option when you don't want your ads being broadcast.

Remember, iAd Producer only broadcasts iAd projects that are currently open; when you close iAd Producer, no ads are available to you or other people on your network.

Submitting your ad

Once you've completed your iAd, you can submit it to the Apple iAd Network to test it from the live servers. This is useful as it mimics the exact delivery procedures your iAd will undergo when it is live, and allows you to test download performance on cellular networks.

Time for action – publishing on the network

To enable your account for use with the iAd Test Server, you need to contact Apple, who can enable your Apple ID for testing. You'll only be able to do this when you're in the final stages of iAd production and have an iAd Account Manager at Apple.

1. Choose **Export**, then **Upload to iAd Test Server**. You'll need to sign in using your Apple ID. The **Upload Options** dialog will then appear.

2. Enter in the details of your iAd, such as the ad name and description.

 If you upload an ad with the name of an existing ad, it will be overwritten; to avoid this, make sure you use a unique name.

3. Click **Upload** and your iAd will begin uploading to the test server. You won't be able to edit the ad while it uploads, but you can continue working on other iAd projects.

4. Once the upload has completed, you're able to e-mail an announcement to your team that the iAd is available on the testing server. The e-mail will have instructions which can be used to view the ad on your device.

What just happened?

You just uploaded your ad to the iAd Test Server; this enables exact replication of the conditions your iAd will load in, such as network speeds and latency issues. You should now test your iAd on all the different connection methods you can, such as Wi-Fi, cellular, and under poor network signal.

Pop quiz – when to test on what

Although it's best to test on the device whenever you can, it's often easier to preview our ad in other ways when we're making quick iterations to our iAd. See if you can suggest the most appropriate way in these situations:

1. If you wanted to test the buttons in your iAd, which is the best to use?

    a. Safari.

    b. Always test on device.

    c. iAd Producer's canvas preview.

    d. iOS Simulator.

2. You've changed the animation of one of your elements and want to see how it looks which method would you use?

    a. Device.

    b. Simulator.

    c. Safari.

    d. Canvas.

    e. Upload to the iAd Testing Server.

3. You've imported some extra assets and want to check they've been scaled correctly; which of these would you use?

    a. iAd Producer's canvas preview.

    b. A device.

    c. Safari.

    d. iOS Simulator.

Tackling common problems

You need to ensure your iAd conforms to Apple's regulations and guidelines, and know how to fix common problems that may arise throughout the development of your iAd. Let's look at finding potential issues, and overcoming some problems you'll likely come across.

Validating your ads

You may have omitted certain elements or settings in your iAd that are required, or your assets sizes might be outside the Apple guidelines. Fortunately, iAd Producer is able to uncover potential problems with your ad that may prevent it from working correctly and suggest improvements to increase the performance of your ad.

Time for action – validating your iAd

Whenever you're working on a project in iAd Producer, you can check the status of your ad at any time.

1. Open in iAd Producer the project you want to validate, for example, Validation Example in this book's assets.

2. Once the project has opened, select **Export** from the menu bar and then **Show Project Warnings**. This will open the **Project Report** window. An example of the **Project Report** is shown as follows:

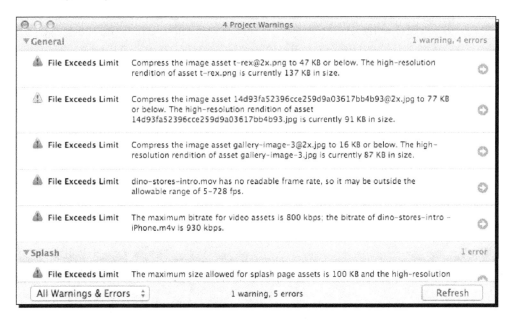

The report is split by general and page-specific issues, and falls into two sections:

◆ Errors—highlighted with a red circular icon

◆ Warnings—highlighted with an orange triangle icon

Errors mean the project is invalid and would not be accepted by Apple into the iAd program until they're rectified. Warnings are suggestions and hints at things you may have missed, or ways to improve your iAd. Warnings don't prevent your iAd from being accepted by Apple, but it's important to check and fix them if you can.

Let's fix the errors with our project first.

1. If you're using the example ad, you'll have noticed the errors are due to the file size of one of our images. We can fix this by resizing the image to the correct size, using **Preview**, and optimizing the image with **ImageOptim**. Whenever we update an asset outside of iAd Producer, we need to tell it to update its local copy.

    iAd Producer makes a copy of each asset and saves them within your project when you add them to the asset library.

2. To refresh our asset library with the latest version of an asset, open the asset library by clicking the **Assets** button in the bottom left of iAd Producer. Assets that have been updated have a circular arrow next to them; right-click on the asset and select **Update**. Confirm that you want to update the file, and the revised asset will now be in your library. In the following screenshot, we can see an example of asset update confirmation:

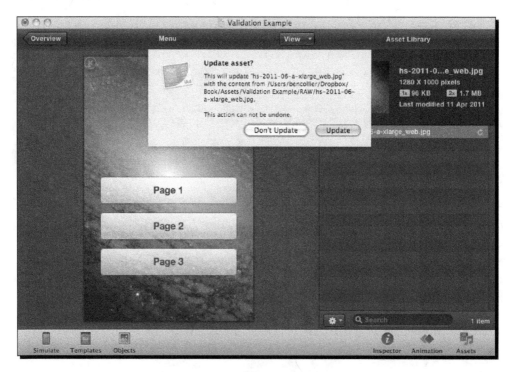

3. If you're using the example project, reopen the **Project Report**; it should now no longer have the file size errors.

 If the **Project Report** still shows errors or warnings you have fixed, try clicking the **Refresh** button in the bottom right. The report usually automatically updates, but sometimes you need to force it to check your project.

Once all the errors in your project are fixed, take a look at the remaining warnings. The example project has several warnings, mostly like "The page named 'Page 1' has not been changed". This warning is generated as we haven't applied a template or changed this page. Go through each of the 'has not been changed' errors and add a template and some custom content.

Other common warnings include:

◆ "The object with outlet 'video' on page 'Preroll Video' is missing one or more required attributes": This warning can be safely ignored if you don't have any pre-roll in your ad; if you do, make sure you have added the video to the preroll tab on the splash page.

◆ "Image asset 'image-name' height/width is greater than containing component ImageView1's height/width": This means the dimensions of an image are larger than the dimensions of the view that contains it, and you can resize the image (and reduce the file size), as it's bigger than it needs to be.

Don't worry if you can't fix all the warnings, as long as you know them and are conscious of the implications.

What just happened?

We just used the Project Report tool in iAd Producer to highlight errors in our project that prevent it from being accepted by Apple, and fix some warnings that are issues in our ad that can affect its performance. You can also find the **Project Report** tool from the inspector pane of the ad overview. Now, we can look at problems you might come across that are not detected by the project report.

Troubleshooting common issues

It's likely you'll come across some common issues when you're building your iAd; the following are some potential solutions.

Warnings about the file size of images

I've reduced the size of my images, but iAd Producer is still showing warnings or errors.

Large image sizes can be reduced by ensuring you're using the right type of image; for example, if you don't need transparency then make sure you're using JPG for your image. When saving a JPG image in Preview, we can increase the compression level to reduce the file size. Select **File**, then **Save as**, from the menu bar in Preview, and change the quality slider until the image size reduces to an acceptable level. Keep in mind, though, that reducing the quality of your images too much can cause blocky and pixelated images. Experiment with different quality levels until you find an acceptable trade-off. In the following screenshot, you can see an example of the quality and file size dialogue when saving an image:

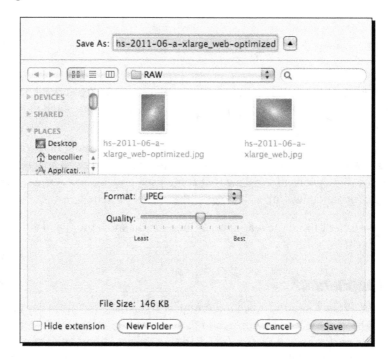

Slow performance

My ad performs great in the simulator, but it's really slow on the device.

Your Mac has considerably more resources and power than your iOS device (although they're quickly catching up), so you're likely to see some performance degradation when testing on the device.

This is why you should test on the device often throughout the development cycle. You'll be able to catch issues early and track down the cause. Make sure you test on different device models, as well, since certain devices have more power than others.

Typically, the performance of your iAd can be optimized by isolating the component that is slowing the ad down; check for elements with the following:

1. **Large shadows**: Each shadow has to be dynamically drawn onto your iAd, and larger shadows take longer to generate. Try reducing the distance and blur of your shadows if you're seeing poor performance.

2. **Slow or jumpy animations**: Objects won't animate smoothly if there isn't enough power in the device to redraw each frame of the motion. Typically, this will occur if you have too many animations occurring at once, or the animated elements have too many styles applied to them. Try reducing the amount of items that are concurrently animated, and remove or reduce intensive styles, such as shadows, reflections, or opacity.

3. **Images briefly only showing a section of them**: This is often caused by your iAd not prefetching the assets used by your ad. iAd Producer only enables the prefetching on exported optimized ads, so when you test your ad on the iAd Test Server, you shouldn't see this occur as often.

 Even when your exported iAd is optimized, you still might see images partially appear whilst they download. An optimized ad starts downloaded assets before they're needed; but, if you're on a slow connection, or have many assets, they may not be downloaded before you need them.

Imported images appear small

When I open images in iAd Producer, they're smaller than I expected.

iAd Producer assumes you're importing high resolution images for the retina displays, so it reduces the visible size of your image by half to accommodate this. You should always export your images at double the horizontal and vertical resolution that you want them to appear as.

For example, if you have a full-screen image, export it at 960px by 640px, double the standard screen size of 480px by 320px.

You should try to keep your source images as large as possible, as it's easy to scale images down, but impossible to make them larger without any loss of quality.

iAd tester doesn't show any ads

My ads aren't appearing in iAd Tester when sharing them wirelessly.

If you're unable to see your ads in iAd Tester, make sure that the project you want to share is open in iAd Producer. Only open projects are broadcast on your wireless network. If you have the project open in iAd Producer, make sure that it is sharing your ad project—you can turn on local sharing from the iAd Producer item in the menu bar.

If iAd Producer is definitely broadcasting your open project, but you're still unable to see your computer listed in iAd Tester, make sure your iOS device and Mac are connected to the same network.

Time for action – checking the network you're connected to

Let's assume your Mac wireless connects to your network; if it has a cabled connection, you'll need to ensure your iOS device connects to the same access point.

1. On your Mac, click the Wi-Fi icon in your menu bar to show the available networks. Take note of the network name with a tick next to it; this is the currently-connected wireless network.

2. On your iOS device, open the **Settings**; then, choose the **Wi-Fi** item from the menu. This will now show you a similar list of available networks. Check that a tick is next to the same network name as your Mac is connected to; if it isn't, tap that network name to connect the device. You might have to enter the network password to access the network. In the following screenshot, you can see both the settings for the iPhone and on the Mac:

What just happened?

We just checked that our Mac and iOS device are connected to the same network, so that iAd Producer and iAd Tester can successfully connect to each other.

If you're still unable to access your iAds, you might have turned on the authentication setting in iAd Producer; either pair the devices or turn off the authentication from the iAd Producer preferences.

Sharing a demo

When you're developing your iAd, you might want to share your progress with colleagues, for comments and suggestions. We can share snapshots of our iAd, record quick screen demos, or even share a work in progress ad with other members of our team.

Taking screenshots

To give a quick visual snapshot of our iAd, we can take a screenshot of one of the screens.

Time for action – taking a screenshot

We can take screenshots on an iOS device or by using the simulator of your Mac.

1. To take a screenshot on our iOS device, open up a screen you want to capture, such as a page of your ad in iAd Tester.

2. Find the home button (the circular button at the bottom center of your screen) and the lock button (the button at the top of your device used to turn it off) and press these at the same time. You should hear a camera snap and the screen flash white briefly. If this doesn't happen, try again and make sure that you press them at precisely the same time.

3. This saves a copy of the entire screen image to your camera roll, which you can find in the Photos app on your iOS device. Open up the image you just took, and you can send the picture via email.

4. If you want to take a screenshot on your Mac, open your iAd in the iOS Simulator. Once you've got the page of your ad that you want to share, press *Cmd + Shift + 4*, on your keyboard. You can now click-and-drag over the area of your screen you want to capture, or press the *Spacebar* and click on the highlighted simulator, which will just capture that window.

You can also take a screenshot of your entire screen by pressing *Cmd + Shift + 3* on your keyboard.

5. Your screenshot is saved as a PNG file on your desktop. You can share it with your colleagues by dragging it to your e-mail client.

What just happened?

You can now take screenshots on your Mac and iOS device. These shortcuts aren't limited to just iAd Tester; you're able to capture any screen or app you want.

If you need to demonstrate the animations and interactions in your iAd, we can record a screen cast to share with your team.

Recording a screen cast

A screen cast is a short movie recording the actions on the screen of your Mac. Screen casts are useful if you want to send a work-in-progress demo to other members of your team who don't have access to iAd Tester or an iOS device.

Time for action – lights, camera, action

There currently isn't an easy way to record the output of our iOS device, so we'll use the iOS Simulator and QuickTime to record our iAd.

1. Open your ad in the iOS Simulator, making sure your ad isn't fully open, so that just the banner is visible.

2. Now open **QuickTime Player** from the `Applications` folder. Choose **File**, then **New Screen Recording**, from the menu bar.

3. QuickTime will now show you a window with a red recording button in it. When you want to start recording, click this button. The **Start Recording** window with its instructional dialogue is shown in the following screenshot:

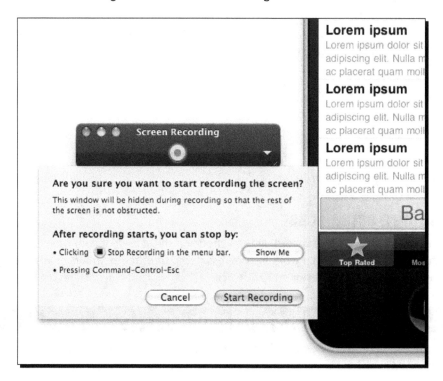

4. Before recording, QuickTime will show you instructions on how to stop the video; you can either use the **Stop Recording** item in the menu bar or the keyboard shortcut *Cmd + Ctrl + Esc*.

5. Click **Start Recording** and start interacting with your iAd. Once you've got the footage you wanted, stop the recording.

> Using the keyboard shortcut means your video won't end with you trying to find the stop button!

6. QuickTime will now show your screen recording ready to be played back. Check over the video; if you're happy with it, choose **File**, then **Save as..**, from the menu bar. If you want to try recording the video again, close this movie and start a new screen recording.

What just happened?

Using QuickTime, we were able to record the contents of our screen to produce a demonstration video to share with our team. QuickTime-created screen captures are saved as `.mov` files in the H.264 format, which should be playable in most modern video players, and on many mobile devices, such as those based on Android and iOS.

Have a go hero – creating a demo

Why not try sharing a recording of your iAd with a colleague or friend? You could:

- Record each screen of your iAd and interact with the elements
- Use the simulator hardware controls to show different orientations and shake events
- Change the iOS simulator to the standard, non-retina device when recording demos, as it puts a better device frame around the outside of the simulator
- Set the background of your Mac to a plain white for a more professional look
- Download PhoneFinger, a tool to replace your mouse cursor with a hand for a more authentic demo. It's a free download from `http://wonderwarp.com`
- Share your ad with your team by exporting it from QuickTime

You're now able to create a great demo of your iAd; you can also use these techniques to create promotional material for your finished iAd.

Sharing an ad

You can share your iAd with anyone who has iAd Tester installed on their device. Use iAd Producer to export an optimized iAd; compress the folder, just as you would if you were using iTunes file sharing to test your iAd, but instead of copying it to your device, send the `.zip` file to your team.

Summary

We're now able to test and share our ads in a variety of different ways and know the most useful techniques to use at the right times. You can now:

- Simulate devices and iOS versions you don't have access to using the iOS Simulator
- Test on your devices quickly and wirelessly, transferring them for offline use
- Fix some common problems you may come across
- Share snapshots and video demos of your iAd

In the next chapter, we'll explore advanced use of templates to provide rich functionality, such as videos and wallpaper pickers, along with animations and transitions to increase the emotivity and responsiveness of our ads.

5
Templates and Objects

We've used some of the available templates in iAd Producer to build our ads so far, but what can we do to go beyond the basic template design and functionality.

In this chapter, we'll look at when to use which templates, and how we're able to use objects to enhance the functionality of our ads, including:

- What each template does
- Setting the user's wallpaper
- Adding preroll video
- Animating our objects
- Transitioning our pages

The templates

With a wide range of templates, we're able to build interactive ads simply by dragging-and-dropping media onto the ad canvas. Templates are useful, as they offer familiarity to the user; because they follow Apple's standards and are used by other ads available on the network. We'll take a look at the different templates available for each part of our iAd, and then make a basic ad, using templates that we'll later extend with objects.

If you plan on using your own assets, you'll need:

- A preroll video, under 10 seconds, and relevant media used to create it. This video needs to be encoded for Wi-Fi and cellular, to be used in an iAd.

In *Chapter 2*, *Preparing Your iAd Content*, we looked at using the **save for web** feature of **QuickTime X** to export our videos for Wi-Fi and cellular, so our iAd can load the appropriate movie for the user's connection.

◆ An icon for your banner, approximately 100px high and wide.

◆ Three or more full-screen images the user can set as their background, 640px wide and 960px high.

◆ A large image, filling around half the screen, to be used on a voucher page, approximately 640px high and wide.

◆ A full-screen, 640px-wide, and 960px-high image that will be rubbed off the screen by the user.

◆ One larger image made up of three or more smaller, icon-like images, similar to the ones shown in the following screenshot:

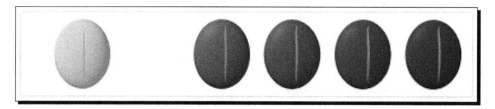

Creating a banner from a template

Let's set up a new project and add a basic image banner to it, using the **Image and Text** template.

Time for action – creating a banner

In order to create a banner, follow the ensuing steps:

1. Open iAd Producer from your `Applications` folder, and select an iPhone project.

2. Choose **File | Save as** from the menu bar, and enter a name for you project, such as `Coffee Beans`.

 If you're using the example files for this project, you can find them in the `Coffee Beans` folder included with the book assets.

3. Now, add your assets to the project, by dragging your assets to the asset library pane. The example assets can be found in the `final` folder. If you're using your own assets, make sure you optimize your images and convert your videos.

4. Double-click on the banner, on the ad overview, to open the template selector. Select the **Image and Text** banner type. Now, double-click the banner again to open it on the editor canvas.

5. Drag **coffee-cup-small.jpg**, or your banner icon, to the image placeholder on the canvas. You'll see a coffee cup with a white background appear.

6. As the image isn't transparent, let's update the banner to match the white background of our image. Click on the background of the banner to deselect the image, and then open the inspector pane. Expand the **Background** section if it isn't already and then change the **Background** type to **Color Fill** and the color to white.

7. Double-click on the text labeled **Banner Message** on the canvas to begin editing the banner text, enter something like `Coffee Beans`. Your banner should look similar to the following screenshot:

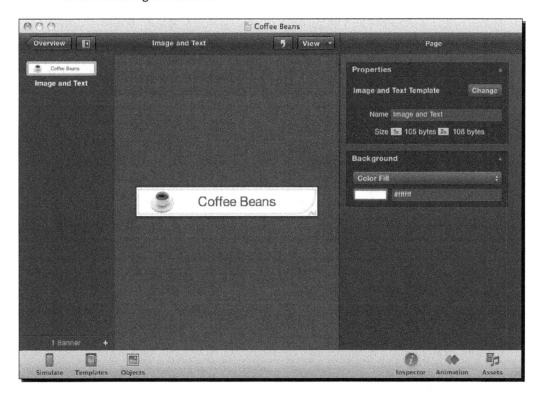

8. If you haven't been regularly saving your project, be sure to click on **Save**.

What just happened?

Using the skills that we learned in the previous chapter, we quickly made a banner using the **Text and Image** template and customized it with our own icon and message.

Exploring other banner templates

The **Image and Text** banner type gives a great impact, while still being lightweight and appearing on a user's device quickly. If you have a strong message or great copy that is self-standing, the plain **Text** template can help you deliver this quickly and easily. The **Image** template provides a good starting point, but by default, doesn't apply any animation or text and, so, shouldn't be used without any modification.

Every template chooser has a **Blank** template available that you can use with objects to build entirely custom pages.

Using splash screens and preroll videos

For this iAd, we're going to transition from our splash page to a preroll video. We'll make the **Splash** page look like the first frame of the video, so they smoothly transition between the two.

Time for action – prerollin'

We'll continue with our `Coffee Beans` project and add a short video of a steamy cup of coffee:

1. If you haven't already, open the `Coffee Beans` project, or if you're working on your own ad, open that now.

2. The preroll video is set up with the splash screen, so we'll need to add a placeholder **Splash** screen before we can add our preroll. Double-click **Splash** from the ad overview to open the template chooser. Select the **Mosaic** template. The **Mosaic** template cuts an image added to the canvas into multiple sections that are transitioned onto the screen. Double-click on the **Splash** page again, to open the ad overview.

3. Open the asset library pane and drag the **coffee-steam-video.jpg** to the canvas. This is the **poster frame** of our preroll video and can be used to transition smoothly into the ad while the main video loads. A poster frame is a snapshot image from the first second of our video and is created automatically when converting it in QuickTime.

4. While still in the splash editing canvas, change the toggle above the canvas from **Splash** to **Preroll Video**, as shown in the following screenshot:

5. You should now see a grey video placeholder where the preroll video will go. Single-click the placeholder to select it. Open the **Inspector** from the bottom bar to edit the settings of the video.

6. We need to select the video file and poster frame for our preroll. Make sure that the **Properties** section of the **Inspector** is expanded, and click on **Select a Video**, under the **Video** heading. From the list of files, select **coffee-steam-video - iPhone. m4v** (if you're using your own video, select your movie); the video object should now update to black.

If you're using your own video, such as the one we created in *Chapter 2, Preparing Your Content for Mobile*, you'll need to replace (Cellular) with -3G, for the video's cellular file. For example, the video file video-name - iPhone (Cellular).3gp would be renamed to video-name - iPhone-3G.3gp. This allows iAd to load the correct video for the connection.

7. Repeat this step for **Poster Frame**, and select coffee-steam-video.jpg. **iAd Producer** might assume your poster frame is meant for retina display and shrink its size by 50 percent, despite Apple's recommendation to only support standard resolution for video. If you're using the assets included with this book, this has already been done for you.

8. If your placeholder is only showing at half the size, we can use **Preview** to resize the image to twice the resolution. Switch to **Asset Library**, right-click on the poster frame for the **coffee-steam-video.jpg** image, and select **Open in External Editor** to open the file in **Preview**, as shown in the following screenshot:

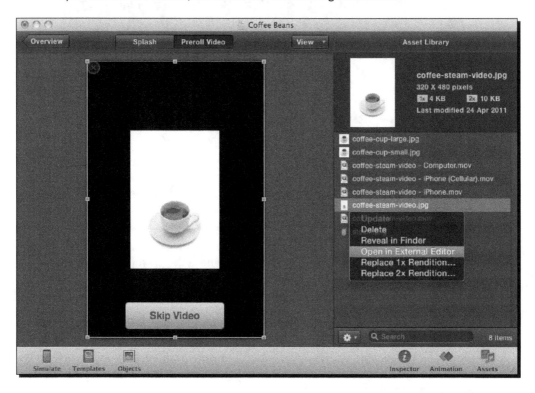

9. In **Preview**, select **Tools | Adjust Size** from the menu bar. We want to double each resolution, so enter 640 as the width; the height should automatically change to 960, to preserve the ratio of the image.

10. Save the image by choosing **File | Save**, from the menu bar, or *cmd + S*, on the keyboard. Close **Preview** and go back to **iAd Producer**.

11. We need to update the asset by right-clicking it in **Asset Library** and selecting **Update**. Confirm that you want to update the asset, and the image should now fill the entire video object. If it still is only half the size, try reselecting the placeholder frame in the inspector pane.

 While upscaling an image to a larger size isn't ideal, as some quality is lost, it won't be noticeable as we're transitioning to a standard quality video.

12. Now, switch back to the **Splash** page, using the toggle above the canvas. We'll change the image's effect from the default mosaic animation that was automatically selected when we chose the template.

 Don't forget, whenever you want to see how an effect looks, you'll need to preview it on the device, in the iOS Simulator, or by using **Safari**.

13. Click the image to select it, and open the inspector pane. If they're not already, expand the **Properties** and **Effects** sections. In the **Effects** section, change the **Build In** effect to **Fly In**, and the **Direction** to **Puzzle**. The **Build In** effect is how each cell of the mosaic appears on the screen, and the **Direction** is the order they appear in. We should also reduce the total duration of the effect by selecting **2s** in the **Duration** area.

14. As we've reduced the duration of the effect, let's also lower the number of cells the image is split into; this prevents the ad trying to animate too many items too quickly. From the **Properties** section, change **Rows** to **6** and **Columns** to **4**. Your **Mosaic View Properties** should look similar to the following screenshot:

15. Make sure no elements are selected, and open the inspector pane. Let's change **Minimum Display Duration** to **2s**, by dragging the slider to the left, so it matches the duration of our splash effect. This will prevent the placeholder frame that we added from being shown any longer than we need it to be.

16. Let's also change the background of our splash screen to a dark grey or black, using the color picker in the **Background** tab; this will really make our splash effect shine.

17. Make sure that you've been saving your iAd regularly.

18. Now is a great time to preview your ad, either using safari the simulator, or on your device, using **iAd Tester**. With the splash effect and video, it's going to look awesome!

What just happened?

We used the **Mosaic** splash template to show the poster image, the first frame of our video, which then transitioned into our preroll video. By combining a splash page and preroll video, we made entering our iAd a great experience for the user.

Alternative splash screen templates

As the **Splash** page is what the user sees while your main content loads, it's vital that you select the right template and customize it to grip the user and keep their attention:

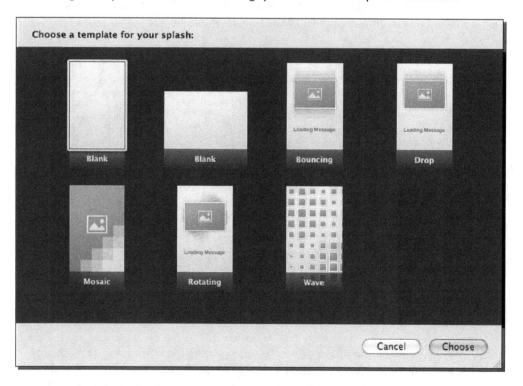

The preceding screenshot shows the selection of templates available in iAd Producer.

Bouncing, dropping, and rotating

Each of these templates gives us an area for an image, and a multilabel cell that fades between a number of messages while our core ad unit loads.

The image is also animated, depending on which template we selected. The bouncing template floats up and down; we used it in *Chapter 3, Making Your iAd*, to make our dinosaur look as if it was flying. The **Drop** template's image falls from the top of the screen into place, and the **Rotating** template twists the image like a corkscrew while loading your content.

 The best way to understand these animations is to view them. It's easy to create a new project and try out these different types for yourself. By default, iAd Producer creates placeholder images and text, so you don't even need to add any assets to a project to preview the animation.

The **Bouncing**, **Drop**, and **Rotating** templates allow you to create lightweight and quick splash pages just by dragging an image onto the screen and editing some text.

The Wave template

The **Wave** template takes one small icon image and duplicates it to fill the screen. Each instance of the icon is then scaled from small to large, to create a watery, wave-like effect. The **Wave** template works well, if you have a small identifiable product image or logo that can be replicated multiple times to create a bold splash screen.

Have a go hero

Let's look at the different effect combinations of the mosaic template and experiment with other splash templates and configurations. Why not try the following:

- Creating a new temporary project
- Using the splash **Mosaic** template with other effect settings, such as **Door Left** for the **Build In** effect, and **Random** for **Direction**
- Adding an icon to a **Wave** template and adjusting the mode and spacing
- See the different animations applied to the image, when using the **Bouncing**, **Drop**, and **Rotating** splash templates
- Previewing the effects and their performance, on your iOS device

Using the menu templates

The menu page provides the core navigation between our ad's pages; using the menu templates in iAd Producer creates menus that automatically update when we modify, add, or remove the pages from our ad.

Time for action – making the menu

Let's quickly set up a simple way of navigating our iAd, using a menu template:

1. We'll be continuing with our `coffee beans` example project; if it's not already open in iAd Producer, open it now.

2. From the ad overview, double-click on the **menu** page to open the template chooser. For this page, we'll use the simple **Button** template. Select it, and then double-click on the **menu** page again, to open it on the editing canvas.

3. Open **Asset Library** and drag **coffee-bean-ribbon.jpg**, or your company logo image, to the image placeholder on the canvas. You should see the image appear on the canvas; however, it has been cropped at the corners.

4. To fix this, with the image selected, open the inspector pane and expand the **Layout** section. Click on the **Original Size** button, as shown in the following screenshot, and the image's container will automatically resize to the correct dimensions, to show the entire image:

5. This image is a JPG, so it doesn't support transparency. This means we need to make sure that the background of the page matches the white of the image and that no other elements overlap behind it, or else they'll be hidden. Click on the canvas background, and change the background to white, using the **Color Fill** option, in the **Background** section of the inspector pane.

6. The buttons look a little boring against the plain white background. Let's restyle them by adjusting their background color, adding a shadow, and removing the border.

7. Click on the button object to select it, and then open the inspector pane. Find the **Background** section, and select a background **Gradient** for the buttons. Select two colors for the **Linear** gradient, for example, *Snow* and *Silver*.

 Remember that when using gradients on buttons, the gradient should go from light at the top to dark at the bottom. This will make the button look more like a physical, pressable object as it'll appear pushed out from the rest of the objects.

8. Expand the **Drop Shadow** section and tick the checkbox to enable the shadow. Try reducing **Distance** to **0px**, which means the shadow is visible on every edge of the button.

9. Now that we've added a shadow around the outside of the buttons, let's remove the border by disabling the checkbox in the **Border** section, on the object's inspector.

The following screenshot shows the **Border** properties disabled, and the overall look of our menu, so far:

10. Save your iAd.

What just happened?

We added a **Button** menu page to our iAd, so that our users can navigate between the pages of our ad. By using the template as a guide and modifying it to match the style of our brand, our menu page looks unique but feels familiar to our users.

Trying the available menu templates

Each non-blank menu template provides the same functionality, just with some additional objects and changes. For example, the **Hide-Reveal** menu type is similar to the **Buttons** template that we just added to our Coffee Beans ad, but groups the buttons into a container that animates in and out of the screen, as you move between pages. The **Wipe Clear** menu template hides your menu behind an image that the user has to wipe to reveal. Here, you can see the templates available in the template chooser:

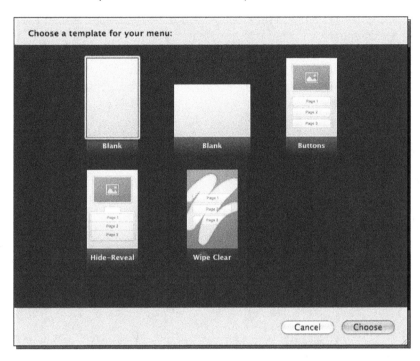

iAd Producer has a limited set of menu templates, but the most useful object provided by the non-blank templates is the set of buttons that are used to open our subpages. The buttons automatically update when you change the structure of your ad. Although iAd Producer has blank templates available, consider using one of the other templates and removing the items you don't want. This way, you'll still have a menu that updates when you modify your ad.

Pop quiz – menu

See if you can answer this question about menu templates:

1. If you want a blank menu template with navigation, what should you do?

   a. Use the blank template

   b. Make your own menu, using a button object

   c. We don't need to set a template; iAd Producer will automatically make a menu

   d. Use one of the non-blank templates, and delete the items we don't need

Now that we've got the user into our ad and have a way of navigating around it, let's add some content for them to interact with.

Creating more pages

Apple has a large selection of templates available for the pages of our iAd, that can be adapted to fit our needs and create amazingly interactive ads. With the page templates, you can quickly build the base of your iAd.

Time for action – pages

Let's create a wallpaper-selecting page and two blank template pages, which we'll use later to create our own view from the ground up, using objects:

1. Let's add some pages to our `coffee beans` iAd. If you haven't got it open in **iAd Producer**, open it now.

2. First up, let's set up our two blank templates. Double-click the first page on the **ad overview** to open the template chooser. There are two blank templates to choose from, either portrait or landscape; we want a portrait page, so select the taller, thinner of the two. Repeat this step for the next page as well.

3. Now, double-click the third page, and select **Wallpaper Picker** from the template chooser. Double-click the wallpaper page again, to open it on the canvas.

4. The **Wallpaper Picker** template requires one or more images that it'll display in a gallery. The user can flick through the images and set their favorite as the background on their device. Let's add three images to our wallpaper picker. Open the **Asset Library** pane, and highlight the three image files **wallpaper-1.jpg - wallpaper-3.jpg**. To select multiple items, single-click on the first file, and then hold the *shift* key down while clicking on the last file. Drag the highlighted group to the placeholder image on the canvas.

5. The first image should appear on the canvas. Now that we've added the images, we can update the style of the page to improve its appearance. Images look great against a black background, so we'll update the background color of our page to black.

6. Single-click the background of the ad, and open the inspector pane. In the **Background** section, set **Background Type** to **Color Fill** and the color to black.

7. With our new black background, the title of our page is hard to read; as we have the **Set as wallpaper** text in the button, we can safely delete the label without confusing the user as to the purpose of the page. Single-click the label with the text **Wallpaper Picker**, and press the *delete* or *backspace* keys to remove it from the canvas.

8. As we have extra screen space available now, let's enlarge the size of our images in the wallpaper picker gallery. Single-click the gallery to select it, and then click-and-drag the top-center drag handle towards the top of the page. You may notice that the left and right drag handles are already at the full width of the page, even though our image is quite thin. This is due to **iAd Producer** adding **padding** to our image. Padding bulks out the area an object takes up by adding empty space around it. We can adjust the padding; with the object still selected, open the **inspector** pane and expand the **Layout** section. In the **Layout** section, we can change **Padding X**, the horizontal (or left and right) padding, and **Padding Y**, the vertical (or top and bottom) padding. We only want to adjust the width, so try reducing **Padding X** to a smaller value, for example, *75*.

Keep in mind that there is always a button visible at the top-left of our iAd, to let users close the ad. This should be visible in iAd Producer, so avoid placing objects near it, and never have tappable, interactive buttons close to it, in case users close your ad instead of performing their intended action.

9. Once you're happy with the size of your images, let's continue tweaking our gallery. iPhone applications often use paging dots underneath flickable areas, to show which page you're on, and to indicate when more pages are visible. You may have noticed them on the home screen of your iPhone or iPad, where all your apps are shown. We can add these dots to our gallery by ticking the **Show Dots** checkbox in the **Properties** section of the inspector pane. You might need to adjust the height of the gallery to accommodate the dots. Our complete gallery should look like the following screenshot:

10. Now, preview the ad in the iOS Simulator or on a device. You may notice that you're unable to return to the menu, from the gallery, as the **Menu** button seems unresponsive. This is due to the iAd framework placing our gallery over the top of the button, even though it doesn't appear this way, in iAd Producer. We can make sure that the button is always on top of other objects by right-clicking on the button and selecting **Bring to Front**, as shown in the following screenshot:

11. Test your iAd again, and you should be able to return to the menu from the wallpaper picker page.

12. Now open the ad overview by clicking on the **Overview** navigation arrow in the top-left of **iAd Producer**. You can now see the structure of our ad forming, but what if we want to change the order in which our pages appear? In the ad overview, we can click-and-drag the pages of our iAd, to adjust how they appear in the ad. Try dragging the **Wallpaper Picker** page from the last page to the middle. The menu templates in your ad will automatically update to show the new order of your pages.

 Remember that you can only change the order of your pages, and not the banner, splash, or menu/core ad unit, in your iAd. Your ad has to follow that set flow defined by Apple.

13. Before we finish with our pages, we can rename the blank templates ready for us to build up with objects later. Continuing to remain in the ad overview, single-click the first page to select it. In the **Properties** section of **inspector**, change the name to Bean Blender. Repeat this for the final blank page, and call this Steamy Savings.

What just happened?

We used the **Wallpaper Picker** template, to leave a lasting message on the user's device by providing great backgrounds. Every time the user looks at their device, they'll be reminded of your ad experience and brand.

Highlighting the notable page templates

There's a great range of page templates available; here are some of the best and most useful templates taken from the template chooser, as shown in the following screenshot:

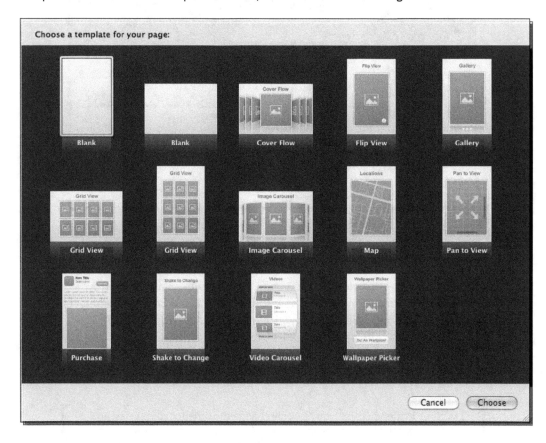

Interacting with images: Cover Flow

Just like the iTunes cover flow, where a user can flick through a 3D gallery of their album images, we can drag a group of images from **Asset Library** to the **Cover Flow** template. Here you can see the cover flow gallery focusing on the center item:

Using a 3D gallery: Grid View

The Grid View adds an amazing twist to a gallery. It automatically creates small thumbnails of your images that, when tapped, rotate around to reveal the full-sized image. This view looks great; if you're using it, be sure to adjust the rows and columns settings in the **Inspector**, to match how many images are in your gallery.

Revealing info with: Flip View

The Flip View gives you a large area for an image, which rotates in 3D to reveal its back side. You can add custom objects to the back of the image; this would typically be used to show more information, such as product and price details.

Have a go hero

Why not make another iAd project to try out each of the different page templates? You could:

◆ Use some images from the examples in this book, or your own images, to try each of the different galleries. Pay particular attention to the **Grid View** and **Cover Flow** templates, as these produce some pretty awesome galleries.

◆ Add a large image to the **Pan to View** template, which allows the user to flick around a close-up of your image and tweak its style on the page. This works great with picturesque, landscape images, or close-up views of products.

◆ Test some of the templates on different devices, to see how they affect performance.

We've seen most of the page templates available in iAd Producer. Now, let's take a look at styling the objects within our template.

Creating more advanced styles

iAd Producer has powerful editing tools to make your ad production simpler, more consistent, and deliver a better experience to the user. Let's look at creating style presets and creating advanced button states.

Using style presets

It's likely you'll be using the same styling throughout your iAd to keep a consistent and memorable experience. iAd Producer lets you save certain style combinations as presets to use in your ad.

Time for action – where's your style?

It's easy to use iAd Producer's style presets to keep track of, and apply commonly used styles in each of our ads:

1. In **iAd Producer**, open the `Styles Demo` **example** project included with this `book assets` folder.

2. From the ad overview, you should see this ad has two pages; the first page has some snazzy, styled text, while the second has some boring default text on it. We're going to copy the style of the first page and apply it to the second. Double-click the first page to open it on the canvas.

3. Single-click on the area of text to select it; then, open the inspector pane, if it isn't already open. Under the **STYLES** heading, there is a drop-down textbox with **Custom** written in it; click on the cog icon to the right of that, and select **Save as...**, to save a new style preset.

4. iAd Producer shows which properties will be included with the style. Let's not include opacity for this style preset, by removing the tick next to **Opacity**. Different styles are available, depending on what object you're editing, so make sure you take note of which properties are being included.

5. We'll also want to give the style a memorable name, so we'll know which one's which, when we have multiple presets. In the **Name** textbox, enter something descriptive, such as `Large Text in Box`. Click on **OK**, to save the style. The following screenshot shows the available properties:

6. The **Custom** drop-down textbox should now update to match the name of the style. Go back to **Overview**, and open up the second page with unstyled text; you should see some plain, default text, filling the page.

7. Select the plain-text label by single-clicking on it. From the inspector pane, click on the drop-down area under **STYLES**, and select the style you want to apply from the list, for example, **Large Text in Box**. The styles we saved should be applied so that the text matches the text in the first view.

 Remember that only the styles we selected to save with the preset will be applied.

8. Try adjusting one of the style properties, for example, expand the **Text** section in the **Inspector**, and change the background color to red. The **STYLES** drop-down will update to show that the style has been modified. Click on the cog icon next to it, and select **Save** to update the style, as shown in the following screenshot:

9. Every object with the style applied will now get updated to match the new style; check for yourself by going back to the first page of the ad. Your text should now be red. You can also duplicate a style by choosing the **Save as...** option instead of **Save**.

What just happened?

Using the built-in style preset function of iAd Producer, we were able to ensure that the styles within our ad are consistent. Using styles with our objects means we can update many objects at once, whenever we edit a style.

The styles are saved and unique to each iAd Producer project, so you're unable to transfer them between ads, but you can save as many styles as you need, per project.

Changing states

Tappable objects, such as buttons, can have different styles applied to them, depending on what state they're in. States change depending on the interactions of the object; a button can be **normal** (this is how it will usually appear), **highlighted** (when the user has pressed or tapped the button), and **disabled** (when the button is visible but won't respond to interactions).

We can modify the style of our buttons for each state using the style editor in iAd Producer. Changing button states increases how responsive our ad feels, as the user is instantly rewarded with feedback when they interact with your iAd.

Time for action – what a state!

Let's adjust the states of the menu buttons in our Coffee Beans example project:

1. If you haven't already, open the Coffee Beans project that we've been working on. Double-click on the **Menu** page to open it on the canvas.

2. Single-click on the menu object to select it, and then open the **Inspector** and find the **SETTINGS** heading. Beneath the heading, next to the **STYLES** drop-down, is the state selector, a selector that lets you change between editing the **Normal**, **Highlighted**, and **Disabled** states. When you select a different state, any styles you apply will only appear when the button is in that state. You can see the state selector in the following screenshot:

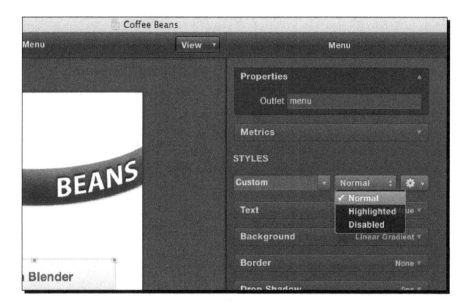

3. Change the selector to **Highlighted**; this button state should use an inverted or reversed version of the normal linear gradient. Expand the **Background** section, and select the same gradient as your normal state. If you're using the example colors, use a *Snow* to *Silver* gradient, using the crayon selector.

4. Now, we can invert the direction of the gradient by pressing the gradient reversal button, shown next to the gradient type drop-down, and highlighted in the following screenshot. This simply switches the order of the colors around. Inverting the gradient gives a depressed, or pushed-in, feel to your buttons:

 iAd Producer sometimes doesn't update the canvas to show your changes; if this happens, you should save, close, and then reopen your project. If you still can't see the changes, use either the iOS Simulator or a device to test your button states.

5. Now, change the state selector to **Disabled**. As disabled buttons won't do anything when clicked, they should feel flat and use lighter colors to appear washed out; the easiest way to achieve this is to reduce the opacity of our disabled button state.

6. Expand the **Opacity** style section and drag the opacity slider to around 40 percent. Lowering the opacity makes the button slightly transparent, washing out the color, and showing the background slightly behind it. The disabled style isn't generally ever seen by the user of our iAd, as the only way to disable a button is by using JavaScript code. So, you only need to set it when you know you'll be using it.

7. Finally, save your iAd and test it on a device. You should feel the effect that the states have, as you interact with your buttons.

What just happened?

We just used the state selector to change the appearance of our buttons when they're highlighted or disabled. We also learned what styles should be applied to each state, and why that style was appropriate.

If you're using the default styles provided by iAd Producer for a button, it automatically applies the correct states for normal, highlighted, and disabled buttons.

Pop quiz – styles and states

Try to answer these questions on using button states and style presets:

1. How do you know what styles are saved when creating a style preset?
    a. Only the styles you've modified are saved
    b. All the styles are saved
    c. The background and text color are the only styles saved
    d. A checklist is shown when you save the style

2. Whenever you save a style preset, you're shown an editable checklist of the styles that will be stored with the preset. What styling should you apply to a highlighted or tapped button?
    a. A linear gradient, the same as the normal state but inverted
    b. A radial gradient, using the same colors as the normal button state
    c. A solid, dark color
    d. We don't need to style the highlighted state as it's never used

3. You should invert the normal button gradient to create a depressed, pushed-in feel, mimicking a real button. What color should be applied to a button in the normal or default state?
    a. A solid light color
    b. A linear gradient, from light at the top, to dark at the bottom
    c. A radial gradient, from dark in the middle, to light at the edges
    d. A linear gradient, from dark at the top, to light at the bottom

Going beyond templates with objects

We can build our own pages by selecting the blank template, or use a template as a starting point and build upon it using objects. Let's take what we've created so far and enrich our iAd.

Time for action – adding objects

We'll add to the Coffee Beans example that we've been building so far, by creating two custom pages, using the blank templates that we had selected earlier when creating our project. To add objects, follow the ensuing steps:

1. Open the iAd project for the Coffee Beans ad that we have been working on. From **Overview** open the first blank page on the canvas: it should be titled Bean Blender. You should see a blank page, with a menu button, ready for us to add our custom objects to. Before we get started, set the background of the page to a solid **Color Fill** white, so that it matches the menu page.

2. We'll be making a page that changes between shakes, displaying different facts about coffee beans. Click on the **Objects** button in the bottom of iAd Producer, to open the object gallery.

> There's already a shakable view template that we can use for this! However, we'll build this page ourselves, to demonstrate how most of the templates are simply built using the objects available to you.

3. From the object gallery, click on **Shake View**, and a placeholder shake view will then be added to the canvas. By default, a **Shake View** assumes you want to shake between a gallery of images, however, we're going to delete the placeholder images from each cell and add our own objects to the view.

4. Double-click on the **Shake View** to open the cell editing mode; the rest of the page will be made darker to indicate the change, as you can see in the following screenshot:

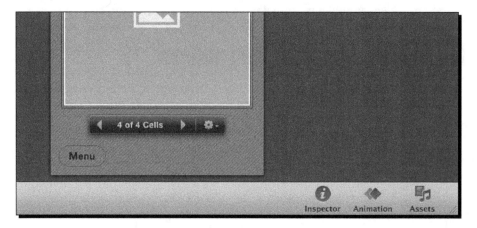

5. Now, single-click on the placeholder image and press the *delete* or *backspace* keys on your keyboard. We need to repeat this for each cell of the view, change between cells using the cell navigation arrows, and delete the placeholder until you've removed them all. You can use *Cmd* + left arrow or right arrow to navigate between cells using the keyboard.

6. With the placeholder images deleted, we should resize our **Shake View**, click outside the cell to exit the editing mode, and reselect the **Shake View** with a single-click. Now click-and-drag the top middle drag handle upwards, so it starts just below the close button.

7. We'll add our custom objects into the **Shake View**; make sure you're on the first cell by double-clicking on the **Shake View** to enter editing mode and using the cell navigation arrows to change cells, until the page indicator says **1 of 4 Cells**. Open the **Objects** page and click on **Label**; this will add a placeholder label to the **Shake View**. Change the label text to Unroasted Beans; you'll need to resize the text area so the whole text is visible and on one line. Now, reposition the label in the top-left of the shake view, and drag the label so it's the full width of the view; this will ensure it's aligned correctly. Let's update the text style to **bold** and the alignment to **left**, using the **Text** section of the inspector pane.

8. Let's add a second label; again, click on **Objects**, and then select **Label**. Update the text to Unroasted coffee beans are green & come from the seeds of the coffee plant, and reduce the font size to something like **17**. Reposition the label in the bottom of the **Shake View**, and resize it to fill the full width.

9. While still in the cell editing mode, click on **Objects | Image**, to add an image to the cell. From **Asset Library**, drag the image **beans-1-un-roasted.jpg** to the image object we just added to the canvas. Single-click on the image to select it, and then open the **Metrics** section on the **Inspector**. Press the **Original Size** button to resize the image object to fit the image inside it. Consider styling the image, possibly with a thick, light-grey border and drop shadow.

10. When you're happy with the style of the image, add one more image to the canvas from the object gallery. Resize the image on the canvas to be 65px wide and 50px high; you can use the **Layout** section on the **Inspector** to set the exact size values. Reposition the image object in the top-right of the cell; use the yellow rulers that appear to guide you.

11. From **Asset Library**, drag the image **coffee-grades-sprite.jpg** to the placeholder image object. You should see two coffee beans appear; however, if you take a look at the source image, you'll see it's really a strip of several coffee beans. We're going to use a technique called **CSS Sprites**; with sprites, we take several separate images we want to use and combine them into one large image.

Then we only show the section of the image we want at that time. Combining the images into one decreases the loading time, as each file included in your ad increases the requests to the iAd network. We can position the image sprite inside the image object to just show the part we want. Double-click on the image object, and the hidden areas of the sprite will become visible, although slightly lighter, to show what parts are visible and hidden:

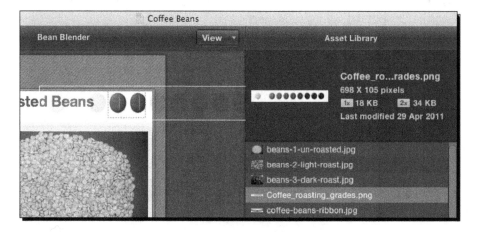

12. Click-and-drag the sprite, and move it, so just the green unroasted bean on the far-left is visible. Once you're happy, the sprite and the cell look similar to the following screenshot. We'll continue adding the remaining cells to our **Shake View**:

13. Each cell of our **Shake View** is going to have the same structure, just with different text and images. We can copy the objects from one cell and paste them into the next; this saves time and keeps each cell consistent with the last.

 It's important to have consistency in your iAd, especially when transitioning between two views or cells, as in a **Shake View**.

14. We want to select all the objects in our cell; to do this hold the *cmd* key down on the keyboard while clicking on each object that you want to select. Once you've selected all the objects, in this case, four objects, right-click on one of the objects and select **Copy** from the menu, or press *cmd + C*, on the keyboard. Now, use the cell navigation arrows to change to **cell 2 of 4**. Right-click anywhere within the cell and choose **Paste** from the menu, or use *cmd + V*, on the keyboard. The objects we selected in **cell 1** should now appear in **cell 2**. First, update the title label at the top of the cell to Lightly Roasted, and the bottom label text to After several minutes the beans "pop" or "crack" and visibly expand in size. From **Asset Library**, drag the image **beans-2-light-roast.jpg** to the main image in the cell. Finally, adjust the positioning of the image sprite, to show the two darker beans to the right of the current green bean.

15. Repeat this for the final cell, and copy and paste the objects that you'll need. Then, use Dark Roast for the title label and After a few more minutes the beans begin popping again, oils rise to the surface. This is called second crack for the bottom label text. Update the main image to beans-3-full-roast.jpg, and move the image sprite across to the next two beans.

16. We have one empty cell left; switch to it using the cell navigation arrow, and then click on the cog icon to the right of the arrows. Select **Delete Cell**, as we only need the first three.

 When making a page that requires an interaction and isn't immediately obvious, you should add an onscreen cue to help the user. Consider adding a Shake to change label to this page, so the user knows what to do.

17. Test your ad on a device; if you notice the transition between the cells can get stuck, consider removing the drop shadow on the images to increase the performance.

What just happened?

You just built an entire page from scratch by adding objects to a blank template. Using the Shake View object, we made the page interactive so the user can shake through different the cells that we copied and pasted (to save time and keep experience consistent between the users shakes).

We used an image sprite, combining several images into one larger image, and showing only the section that we wanted to display. Image sprites are a technique originating from early video games and reduce the requests to the iAd network, so our ad loads faster.

Have a go hero

Why not improve your **Bean Blender** page by doing the following:

- Adding an extra cell to the **Shake** view object about double-roasted coffee (see Roast Flavors, at http://en.wikipedia.org/wiki/Coffee_roasting).

- Creating a style preset for each item, so you can update one cell's style and the other cells will change to match it.

Time for action – more objects

We still have one blank page on our canvas; let's add a page full of steam a user has to wipe clean before revealing a promotional offer:

1. We're continuing with our Coffee Beans example project, so if you haven't already, open it in iAd Producer. From **Overview**, open the last blank page, titled Steamy Savings. Set the background to a solid white, using the **Color Fill** option.

2. Open the objects library and add a Wipe Clear object to the canvas. The Wipe Clear object shows an image, which disappears as a user wipes it with their finger. Drag the image **steam-mirror.jpg** from **Asset Library** to the Wipe Clear object. You'll see the object fill with the image; resize the Wipe Clear object by using the **Original Size** option, in the **Layout** section of the **Inspector**. The image should now fill the screen. Test the page on a device or in the iOS Simulator; you can wipe or rub the screen to remove parts of the image.

3. You may have noticed that your ad automatically faded the image out before you had a chance to wipe all of the image off. It does this so users who don't interact with your page can still get to the content. Let's tweak this setting though, to keep our content on screen a little longer.

4. Open the **Properties** section of the **Inspector**, and change **Fade Delay** to somewhere between **7.5s** and **10s**, and **Duration** to **3s**. The fade delay is how long it takes before your iAd starts to fade the ad, if the user hasn't cleared it all, and the duration is how long the fade out animation lasts for.

5. Your properties should look similar to the following screenshot:

6. We can also adjust the transparency of the Wipe Clear object, so that the page content can be seen slightly through the steam. In the **Inspector**, expand the **Opacity** section, and use the slider to reduce the amount to around **90%**.

7. Lets add the objects that'll be revealed once the wipe clear has faded. At the moment, the `Wipe Clear` object fills the whole page, so we can't get to the canvas. Drag the entire object off the canvas, either to the left or right side. iAd Producer will fade the object out to show that it's not included, as shown in the following screenshot. We'll reposition it on the canvas once we've added our elements:

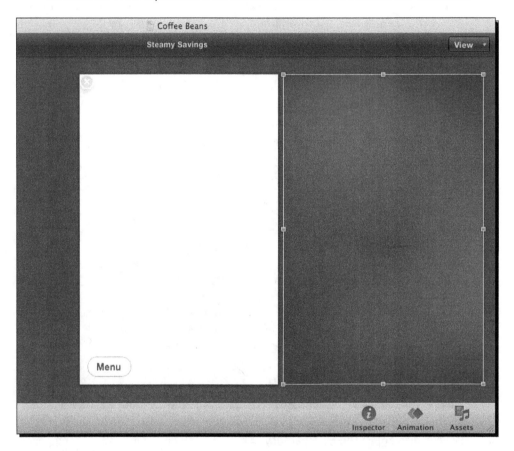

8. With the `Wipe Clear` object off canvas, add a label to the page from the object library. Position the label in the top-center of your ad, and update the text to `Steamy Savings`. Next, we'll add an image to the page, but instead of using the image object, drag the image **coffee-cup-large.jpg** from **Asset Library**, straight to an empty space on the canvas. The image should appear as iAd Producer automatically generates an image object for you. Position the coffee cup in the center of the screen.

9. Now, add a `Multi-Label` object to the canvas, and add a voucher code to each cell, with a quick description, for example, `#HALFOFF - 50% off` for **cell 1**, `#EXTRA - double serving` for **cell 2**, and `#SAMPLE - free expresso` for the final cell. Add a label with the text `Voucher codes:` above the multilabel, so the user knows what they are. Also, add some small text at the bottom of the screen identifying how to use the codes, for example `Present voucher codes in store`.

10. Style and position the elements, so your page looks similar to the following screenshot:

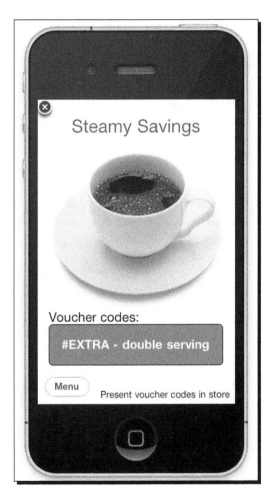

 When in cell editing mode on a supported object, you can use the **Apply Style to All Cells** button to quickly duplicate your cell style to the other cells.

11. When you're happy with the layout of the page, reposition the `Wipe Clear` object onto the canvas, by clicking-and-dragging it. You might find some objects overlay on top of the wipe clear; if that happens, right-click on the `Wipe Clear` object and select **Bring to Front**. This will make sure that the object is the foremost element on screen.

12. Save and test out your ad on a device or the simulator.

What just happened?

We've now finished the main structure of our `Coffee Beans` iAd; it focuses on being more informative and interesting about coffee, then offers a user a chance to action their new interest with an offer on the **Steamy Savings** page. Some of the best ads don't push their product and brand at every opportunity and subtly gain the user's interest.

Tweaking the transitions

Transitions are used to animate between pages of your ad; you can set an appear and disappear animation for each page, to add some motion and effects when your pages are opened and closed.

Time for action – transitions

Let's improve the feel of our `Coffee Beans` ad by changing the transitions so the user flows smoothly through our content and pages:

1. Open the project `Coffee Beans` in iAd Producer.

2. By default, iAd Producer adds fade in and out transitions to each page, fading out the first page and fading in the second. This causes a flicker between our splash page and preroll video, as we made these pages match the same content. Let's remove these two transitions for a seamless change between the splash and preroll. Double-click on the **Splash** page on the **Overview**, to open it on the editing canvas.

3. Make sure the top page toggle is set to **Splash** and expand the inspector pane from the right of the bottom bar. We still want our **Splash** page to fade in when it appears, but don't want any transition when the page disappears and the preroll starts.

4. Expand the **Transitions** section and make sure that the transition is set to **Fade In**. Now, change the toggle to the **Preroll Video** and set the transition to **None**:

5. Preview your ad, and you should notice the improvement; things will be much smoother!

6. Return to the ad overview and make sure the inspector pane is still open. We can quickly change the page transitions for the ad **Overview**. Single-click on the menu page to select, but not open, it. Then, in the **Transitions** section, select **Slide Left**. Repeat this for each page, with transitions of your choice.

7. Save your ad, and preview the different transitions on a device or in the iOS Simulator.

What just happened?

We changed the transitions between the splash and preroll video into the main ad unit to create a seamless flow between the sections of our ad.

Adding some animation

Each object on our page can also have an appear and disappear animation, similar to the full-page transitions. Adding motion to our ads, grabs people's attention and makes the experience more engaging.

Time for action – animations

We'll add some animations to our `Coffee Beans` project that'll move our objects around on their pages:

1. Open the `Coffee Beans` project in **iAd Producer.** Double-click the menu page to open it on the **canvas.** Click on the menu object, and expand the **Actions** pane.

2. We want our menu to slide in from the bottom of the screen when the page loads, and slide out when it's closed. Make sure the title of the pane says **Page Appear** and click the + icon to open a list of available actions.

3. From the list of actions, find and select **Slide In**. This will add the action; change the **Direction** to **In From** and **Bottom**. Double-check to make sure your action's properties match the following:

 If the list of available actions doesn't include anything listed under **ANIMATIONS**, make sure you have the menu selected.

4. We're able to tweak the animation by modifying the **Duration, Delay**, and **Timing**. A **Duration** of **0.75s** generally works well; try adjusting that and previewing the animation. The timing option changes how the animation behaves, for example, the default ease in and out option will start off slowly and decelerate at the end, and a **Linear** option travels at a constant speed from start to end.

 When setting animation durations for key objects, such as menus or text, try to keep them under 1 second. Longer animations make your ad feel slow and unresponsive.

5. Click on **Page Appear** in the title of the **Actions** pane and change it to **Page Disappear**. This will let us set the actions for when the page is about to disappear. Add a **Slide Out** action, and change the **Direction** to **Bottom**. You can use the play triangle icon to preview the animation.

 It's good to match your page's disappear actions with the appear actions. So, if an object slides in from the bottom when it appears, it should slide out to the bottom when it disappears.

6. As we have the menu appearing from the bottom of the screen, let's make our main image move in and out from the top of the screen. Repeat the preceding steps for the image, but change the **Direction** properties to **Top** for **Page Appear**, and **Top** for **Page Disappear**.

7. Save and preview your ad. You might want to add some actions to the objects on other pages of your ad.

What just happened?

We used actions and animations to build up the components of our page and enhance the page transitions as the user navigates around our ad.

Pop quiz – animations and transitions

Test what you've learned so far, by answering the following questions about animations and transitions:

1. Why might you want to prevent the transition between your splash page and preroll video?

   a. To make your content load faster

   b. To prevent a flicker between them

    c.   It will prevent our ad from using too much battery power

    d.   Transitions can be replicated in the video

2.   When does the **Page Disappear** action start?

    a.   Immediately, when the ad opens

    b.   Before the ad closes

    c.   Just before the page disappear transition

    d.   Just after the page disappear transition

Finishing touches

To make your iAd that bit more special, we can touch up a few rough edges to make the most polished, engaging ad possible. It's these last tweaks that are really noticeable while using your iAd.

Have a go hero – touched up

Let's try fixing the final few issues with our `Coffee Beans` project; consider trying some of these suggestions:

- Make all menu items match on each page (using style presets)
- Update the **Skip Video** button on the preroll, so it looks great; don't forget to modify its states
- Try different transitions between the core ad pages
- Place a message above the `Wipe Clear` object, telling the user to wipe the screen
- Make a new banner by adding objects to the blank banner template
- Add animations to elements on other pages
- Check whether the banner works in both orientations

If you need some inspiration on touching up your iAd, check out the completed project, `Coffee Beans`, in the `assets` folder.

Summary

In this chapter, we've focused on using templates and objects to create customized, unique iAds; with these basic skills, you're able to quickly build advanced ads. You now know the following:

- How to add preroll video to an ad
- What templates are available
- How to build upon templates with objects
- How to use the blank template to create pages from scratch
- That image loading times can be optimized for small images, using a sprite
- How to transition between the pages in your ad
- That objects can be animated on and off the canvas, with actions

Remember, you can use the templates as a foundation to your pages, then customize and enhance them with objects. In the next chapter, we'll look at harnessing a customer's love for our brand with valuable actions and destinations that we can create within our ad.

6
Ad Destinations and Actions

After creating an amazing ad that excites users about our product or brand, we need to channel this and get them to perform an action beneficial to us.

In this chapter, we'll look at:

- Why we shouldn't just redirect the user to our website
- Selling our digital content, such as apps and music
- Taking our store finder to the next level
- Enhancing the structure of our ads
- Socially engaging the user with our brand, using SMS text messaging

Opening external websites

A traditional advertisement on a mobile device consists of a banner, which when tapped takes the user to their mobile browser and often loads a full, cluttered desktop website. Creating an iAd is different, as you have an entire framework to build a mini-application, all housed within a host app. It's possible to create the same, if not better, integrated experiences in our iAd using the iAd Framework and iAd Producer.

Think of your iAd as a microsite that you really don't ever want the user to leave. Let's explore the destinations and user actions we can achieve within our iAd, avoiding having to take users to your main site.

Selling digital products

We can sell digital products, such as songs, movies, or apps, directly in our iAd, without the user having to leave the ad or app they're in. As long as your items are available on the iTunes store, they can be included in an iAd.

 When digital content is downloaded from your ad, you'll receive the same revenue as if it was purchased directly from the store.

Time for action – downloading an app from our ad

Using the **Purchase** template in iAd Producer, we'll add a **Purchase** page into our ad for the addictive, free application `Bouncing Balls`.

We'll continue with our `Coffee Beans` project that we worked on in the last chapter. Open it in iAd Producer.

1. Let's add an extra page to use as our **Purchase** page. From the ad overview, click on the plus icon, found on the lines that show the relationship between the menu and pages, as highlighted in the following screenshot:

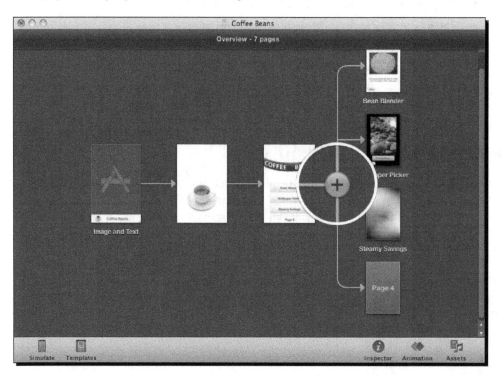

2. Double-click on the newly created page, labeled **Page 4**, to open the template chooser. Select the **Purchase** template, and then double-click on the page again to open it on the editing canvas. You'll see a placeholder product page, similar to those seen in the iOS App Store.

3. If it isn't already open, open the inspector pane, and click anywhere on the canvas to select the store view object that was automatically added to the page by the template. Expand the **Properties** section to reveal the settings we need to configure for this page of our ad.

4. You'll see that we need to provide the **Country** where our item is available, the **Store ID**, and the unique ID iTunes assigns to items, so the template knows which item we want to sell. For now, use 358992973 as the **Store ID** and select your country from the list:

5. You should see the canvas update to show you the **Balance Balls** app. If the item doesn't appear when you select a country, try either **United Kingdom** or **United States**, as the content might not currently be available in your country. We'll look at getting the **Store ID** for your own content from the iTunes Store later.

6. Test the ad on a device and try purchasing the item; you'll be asked to enter your iTunes account password. If you don't want to complete the transaction, tap **cancel** at this step. You'll be unable to download or purchase store items in the iOS Simulator as it isn't permitted to access licensed content.

 Watch out: if you're testing downloading an item that isn't free, you will be charged, even if it's your own product or content.

7. As you can see, there's little that we have to do to create a great, quick, and seamless way of letting users download our content. You'd typically not style this page, as it's consistent with the purchasing experience of the iTunes and App Store. So, leave it as it is and save your iAd project.

What just happened?

We added an extra page to our iAd, using the plus button on the ad canvas in iAd Producer. You can use the plus button to add as many pages as you want to your iAd, but try to keep the total under five to prevent your ad from being overwhelming.

Using an example `Store ID`, we were able to let users of our iAd directly purchase or download an app from the App Store without leaving the ad. The app will download in the background and automatically appear on the device home screen of the user. Now, let's look at adding your own iTunes content to the **Purchase** template.

Time for action – getting iTunes Store IDs

We can get the Store IDs of items required by the **Purchase** template using the built-in store in iTunes:

1. To access the iTunes Store, open iTunes. You'll find iTunes in the `Applications` folder on your Mac. Double-click on the icon to open it.

2. In the sidebar, on the left of iTunes, click on the **iTunes Store** item found under the **Store** heading, shown in the following screenshot:

3. Find the search store text area in the top right of the main bar of iTunes. Enter the content you want to find the ID of, for example, Apple's iBooks app. Press the *Enter* key to search.

4. You'll now see a list of search results; find your item, click on the arrow next to the price, and select **Copy Link**. This will copy the link of your item to your clipboard:

5. Now, we need to paste the link so that we can extract the Store ID from it. Open TextEdit, a text editor that came with your Mac. You should be able to find it in the `Applications` folder. Once opened, you should see a large white text area; right-click on it and choose **Paste**, or use the keyboard shortcut *cmd + V*. You'll see the link (that we just copied) appear. The link is a website URL you're able to share; it will automatically open the iTunes store when it's clicked.

 If you can't select **Paste**, or if something other than the link appeared, go back to iTunes and copy the link again.

6. You'll find the Store ID near the end of the link. Take, for example, `http://itunes.apple.com/gb/app/ibooks/id364709193?mt=8`. In this link, the ID is the string of numbers after `id` and before `?mt=8`, so you would use `364709193` as the Store ID. Try opening the `Coffee Beans` project now and updating the Store ID to the iBooks ID.

7. Now, let's try finding a song; go back to iTunes and search for a song, such as *A beautiful mine* by *RJD2*. From the search results, find the item you want, and copy the link. Paste the link into TextEdit; it should look similar to this: `http://itunes.apple.com/gb/album/a-beautiful-mine/id148031770?i=148032644`.

With songs, you're only able to offer the individual track to purchase, not the entire album, so we need the item ID of the song. The individual song ID is found after `i=`, so for this item it would be `148032644`, not the other id, which is used to identify the entire album.

We can also offer movies to purchase, right in our ad. Copy a link for a movie, for example, *District 9*, and paste it into TextEdit. A movie link will look like `http://itunes.apple.com/gb/movie/district-9/id331251689`. Like the app link, the Store ID for this movie is found after the id text at the end of the link; the ID of this item is `331251689`. Try updating the Store ID in iAd Producer with this ID to see how the purchase template appears for movies and films.

Some content, although visible in your country's iTunes Store; might not appear correctly in iAd Producer or when testing your iAd. Try updating the country to **US** temporarily, to fix this. If you continue to have problems, contact your Apple iTunes store agent or developer support.

8. Finally, books can be included—their ISBN is used as the Store ID—but the book has to be available in the iBook Store. To find a book's Store ID, for example, *Treasure Island*, copy the link and paste it into TextEdit. The link will look similar to `http://itunes.apple.com/gb/book/treasure-island/id370190362?mt=11`, with the Store ID being after `id`, in this case, `370190362`.

What just happened?

We used iTunes and the iTunes Store to find the Store ID of items, which is required by the **Purchase** template in iAd Producer. You can use this technique whenever you need to get the ID of your own items in the store.

Depending on what digital content you have, consider offering it for free or at a discount when promoting it within your ad. Let's tweak our ad as we've inadvertently created a few inconsistencies when we added the **Purchase** page to it.

Time for action – fixing our ad

As the menu template we used for our `Coffee Beans` project automatically updates whenever we add or remove pages, we don't have to do anything to update it. However, there are a few tweaks we'll need to make:

1. Continuing with our `Coffee Beans` project, make sure it is open in iAd Producer. Open the **Purchase** page on the editing canvas.

2. iAd Producer has automatically named our page **Purchase**, which isn't particularly engaging for our user. Without any objects selected, expand the inspector and rename the page in the **Properties** to, say, `Get the app!`. This uses a call to action, requesting and encouraging the user to follow your instruction.

In the following screenshot, you can see the **Properties** section and **Name** field:

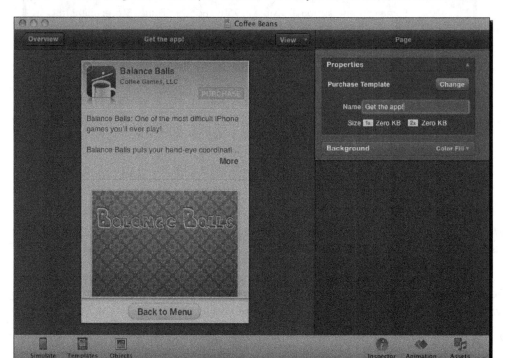

3. Return to the ad overview and open the menu on the canvas. You'll see the text has updated to match the new name for the page, but the styling of the other buttons hasn't been applied to our new menu item. The whole menu object has also been cut off at the bottom of the screen.

4. Click on the menu object and drag it up on the page, so the last button isn't obscured. You may also need to resize the menu by dragging the bottom drag handle to accommodate our additional button.

5. Next, we'll update the style of the button so it matches the others. With the menu selected, double-click on the first button to enter editing mode; then, click on the button again to select it. This can take a few attempts. Once selected, expand the inspector pane if it isn't already and click on **Apply Style to All Buttons**, as shown in the following screenshot. This duplicates the style to all other buttons in the menu so that they match and are consistent:

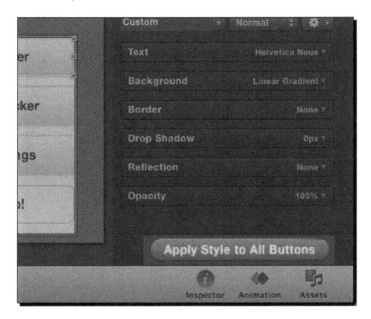

Now that our button matches the others, let's test our ad on a device or in the iOS Simulator.

6. You may have noticed that we can't return from the **Purchase** page as the menu item is missing. It's on the page but hidden behind the purchase object on the page, so we need to send the store item to the back of the page. Open the **Purchase** page on the ad canvas, and click on the purchase object to select it. Right-click and choose **Send to Back**. The menu button should now appear.

7. If you saved a style for your menu items in the last chapter, don't forget to select that style from the style presets list.

8. Unfortunately, the positioning of our menu item interferes with the content of the purchase object, as you can see in the following screenshot. Let's restructure the page to accommodate it:

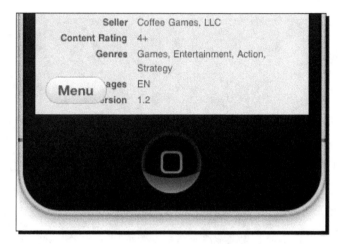

9. By resizing the purchase object, we can have a dedicated area, at the bottom of our iAd, to contain the back button. Click on the purchase object, and drag the bottom drag handle so it's above the **Menu** button.

10. Now center the menu button by dragging it to the middle of the screen. Consider updating the text to `Back to Menu` and resizing the button so it fills more of the space at the bottom of the ad.

11. Change the background of the page to color fill and set it to white; this will separate the scrollable purchase object and the **Back to Menu** button.

12. Reselect the purchase object and add a drop shadow to further separate the two sections of the page.

13. Finally, add a build in and out animation to the button and purchase object. Make the purchase view **Move In From Top** on build in, and **Move Out To Top** for build out. Make the **Menu** button **Move In From Bottom** for the build in and **Build Out To Bottom** for the build out. You can find the build in and out sections in the animations pane, when you have an object selected.

14. Open your iAd in the iOS Simulator or iAd Tester for your device, and check whether we're able to interact as you'd expect. Your final **Purchase** page should look similar to this:

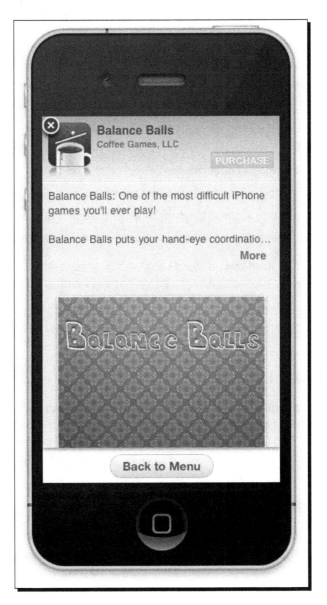

What just happened?

As adding an extra page to our iAd project had caused some styling issues on the main menu and prevented our app navigation from working as intended, we reapplied our button style to the cells and redesigned the **Purchase** page to incorporate a **Back to Menu** button.

Pop quiz – digital downloads

The awareness or revenue you can generate from downloadable content in your iAds can be vast, so let's check whether you're doing it right:

1. How do you get a Store ID, for a digital item, required by the purchase template in iAd Producer?

    a. Just use the name of the item.

    b. Email Apple requesting the ID for your item.

    c. Open iTunes and use the copy link menu item in the store.

    d. Purchase the item and look at our receipt; the ID is there, next to the price.

2. What's the Store ID of this link for a song—`http://itunes.apple.com/gb/album/a-beautiful-mine/id148031770?i=148032644`?

    a. a-beautiful-mine

    b. id148031770

    c. 148031770

    d. 148032644

As you can see, selling digital content, whether music, movies, or apps, is incredibly simple. In three taps, the user has purchased your product and it's on their iOS device. You could also create a free app for your company, offering an even richer experience than your iAd, that persists on the users home screen so they can keep reengaging with your brand.

Advanced store finders

Not all products are digital; sometimes you want to increase the footfall to brick and mortar stores. Earlier, we incorporated a basic store finder into an iAd; now, we'll look at extending this to deliver a fantastic experience to get users to your stores.

Time for action – adding a store finder

We'll add a store finder to our Coffee Beans iAd, so users can find a local store and go buy some great coffee:

1. Open the Coffee Beans project that we've been working on in iAd Producer. We'll start by adding an extra page to our iAd. From the ad overview, use the plus icon to add an extra page to the project. Double-click on the new page to open the template chooser and select **Map**. Double-click on the new page to open it on the ad canvas.

2. The first thing we'll do is add a **custom pin**; this will show on the map for each store near our user. Open the inspector pane and expand the **Properties** section; from the **custom pin** drop-down, select the pin image, for example, **coffee-cup-pin.jpg**. We'll adjust the offset to center the image over the blue location crosshair—change the X and Y offsets until your pin sits on the crosshair. An X Offset of around 8px and a Y Offset of 5px should work well with this image. Your aligned pin should be similar to the following:

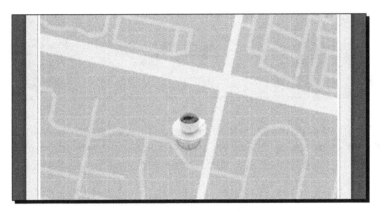

3. If you have a Site ID, enter it now; if not, just use the demo ID that shows the nearest Apple stores.

 Before you submit your iAd to Apple, you'll need to contact them to set up your own Site ID to show your store locations.

4. Now, double-click on the title of your page, the **Location** label, and update the text to something more friendly, say, Find your nearest cup... You should update the background to match the rest of your ad, in this case, to a color fill of *white*.

5. Resize the map area to fill the width of the screen, and maybe add a drop shadow and border of your choosing.

6. Preview your iAd; you'll see we now have a basic store finder in our ad. However, clicking on a pin reveals a plain, default styled details page. Return to iAd Producer and switch to the **Map Details** view, using the toggle at the top of the canvas:

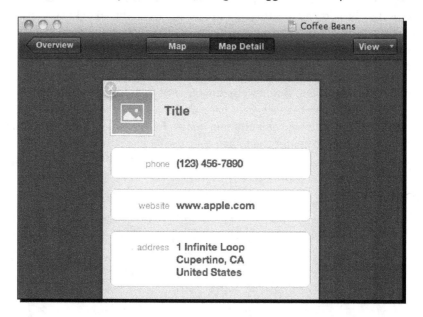

7. By styling this page to match the rest of our ad, we'll create a consistent experience. Set the **Background** to a **Color Fill** and the color to *white*. Add an image to the image placeholder object next to the title; **coffee-cup-small.jpg** works well here.

8. Drag the image **beans 3-dark-roast.jpg** from the **Asset Library** to the canvas. Send it to the back so it's behind all the other objects on the page, and move it so it's at the bottom of the screen.

9. The information area's solid white background does not fit well with our white background or image. We can change the **Background**, **Border**, **Opacity**, and **Drop Shadow**, to improve their style. Click on the first information area, containing the phone number. Then, from the inspector, expand the **Background**, **Border**, **Opacity**, and **Drop Shadow** sections. Set the **Background Color Fill** to a light grey, such as the *Mercury* color from the crayon selector. Make the **Border 2px** wide and change its color to be slightly darker than the background, like *Silver*, from the crayon selector. Change the **Opacity** at the bottom of the inspector to, say, **90%**. This will allow the image to slightly appear through our information areas:

10. With the first information area styled, let's duplicate this style to the other areas, using a style preset. Under the **STYLES** heading, click on the cog button and select **Save**. Enter a name for the style, such as `Map Details Info Area`, and click on **OK**. Now, select the other information areas and apply that style preset to them.

We don't need to update the text in the **Title** text area of the **Map Detail** view, as this is set automatically by the iAd Framework when a user taps to open a store.

Your final page might look something like this:

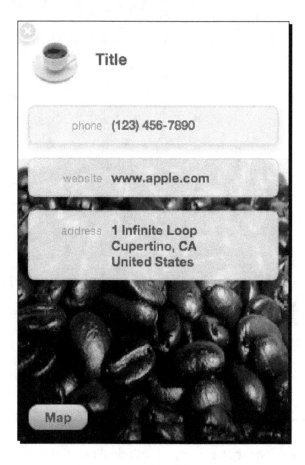

11. Save your ad and test it in the iOS Simulator or on your device.

What just happened?

We added a basic store finder, using the **Map** template, then styled and customized it. After the **Map** page was styled, we changed the plain default store details page by adding a couple of images and restyling the information boxes. Now, finding your stores will almost be as great as being in them!

As our ad becomes more content rich with many pages, we may want to hide certain pages and access them as subpages from other sections of our ad. We'll now look at including hidden pages in our ad.

Time for action – hidden pages

As you can see, we've got too many items in our menu and the first page looks cluttered and messy. Let's make our own custom menu and make our store finder page accessible as a hidden subpage of our ad.

1. We'll be continuing with our coffee beans example; if it isn't already open, open your `Coffee Beans` project in iAd Producer. From the **Overview**, open the **Menu** page on the canvas. You'll see our last menu item; the store finder is cut off the page, as shown in the following screenshot:

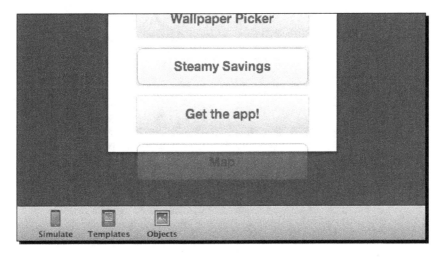

2. We could just move the menu up, but this would produce a cluttered and overwhelming initial screen to show to the user. Instead, we'll create our own navigation menu with button objects and place the map page button in the **Steamy Savings** page, so it's hidden from the main menu.

3. Return to **ad overview** and open the **Steamy Savings** page on the canvas. Before we're able to add anything to this page, we need to temporarily move the `Wipe Clear` object off the canvas to access the page objects. Click on the `Wipe Clear` object and drag it off the main canvas, to the left or right of the page. We'll move it back into place later, once we've edited our page.

4. With the wipe clear off the canvas, select and drag **Voucher Codes** and the **Voucher** area further up the screen towards the coffee cup; this will create some extra room for our **Map** button. If you added it earlier, select the **Present voucher codes in store** text label and delete it, using the *delete* or *backspace* key on your keyboard; we'll replace this with a store finder button.

5. Open the **Objects** library and select **Button**. This will add an empty button to the canvas; resize and move this button so it fits well at the bottom of our ad. Double-click on the button so you can edit the text, and update it to something such as `Find a store now`.

6. With the button selected, expand the **Events** section in the inspector. Change the **Touched Up Inside** drop-down to **Go to Page**, then select **Map**; this will cause the **Map** page to open when the user taps the button:

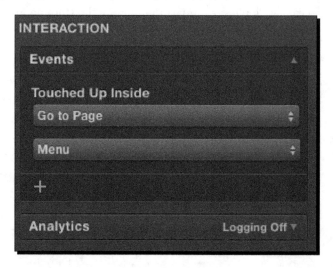

7. Preview your ad and test whether the button works as expected.

8. We'll now want to update our main menu to remove the **Maps** button. Unfortunately, as the menu object is automatically updated when we add new pages, removing the **Maps** button will just cause it to be regenerated next time we modify a page. This means we need to build our own menu out of buttons. There are a few tricks that we can use though that'll make managing our own menu easier. Go back to the ad overview and open the **Menu** page on the canvas.

9. First, we'll save the button style of our menu as a preset so we can quickly apply it to all our own buttons. Single-click on the menu object to select it, then double click to enter the menu item editing mode; finally, click on one of the buttons in the menu to select it. Now, save the style as a preset using the **cog** button, then choose **Save**. Call your preset something like `Main Menu Button`, so you'll know which style to choose later. With the button style saved, we can safely delete our menu object. Click outside of the menu object to exit the menu item editing mode, and then single-click on the menu object to select it. Press the *delete* or *backspace* key to remove the entire object from the canvas.

If the **Save** and **Save As...** items are disabled, try selecting the individual button again; it's often hard to select the right item!

10. As we've no longer got any form of navigation in our **Menu** page, open the **Objects** library and click on the button object to add a new button to our canvas. From the style preset selector, update the style to your menu button style, for example **Main Menu Button**. The button should now look like the one from the menu we deleted; if it doesn't, make sure you have selected the right style.

11. Let's change the button's `Touch Up Inside` event to `Go To Page`. Then, select the page to be `Bean Blender`, the first page of our iAd, with the same technique that we used to add a go-to target for our **store finder** button. Double-click on the button and replace the text with `Bean Blender` so it matches the go-to destination.

12. Next, we'll duplicate this button to save us having to create a new button from scratch. With the button object selected, right-click on it and choose **Copy**, or use the keyboard shortcut *cmd + C*. Now, right-click on the canvas and choose **Paste** from the menu, or use *cmd + V* on the keyboard. Paste the button two more times so you have four buttons on the screen:

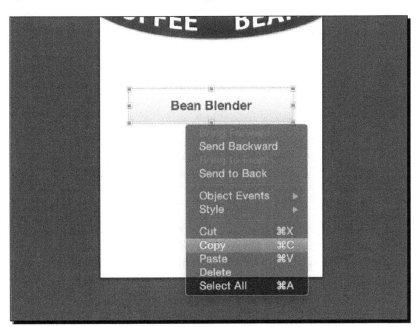

13. Reposition each item so they're equally spaced on the page. Use the yellow guidelines that appear when dragging items near each other to ensure the spacing is correct, as shown in the following screenshot:

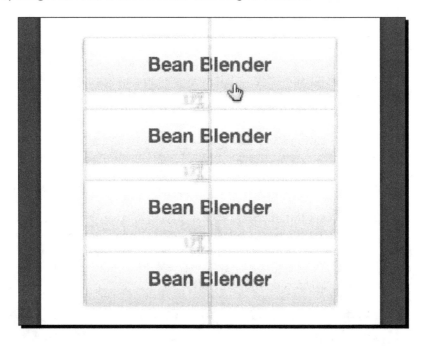

14. Change each item's `Touch Up Inside` event to go to the right page and text, so each page of our ad can be accessed like before. However, don't add a button for the **Maps** page.

 You may have noticed in the ad overview that iAd Producer still shows the **Map** page as being connected to the **Menu** page. This is fine; iAd Producer assumes all of your pages are linked from the core menu page, even when you've changed it.

15. With our custom menu complete, return to **ad overview** and open the **Maps** page. Currently, the button on our **Map** page says **Menu** and returns the user to the menu. However, as this page is now accessed from the **Voucher** page, we'll want to update the button to take them back there. Click on the **Menu** button to select it and then change it to go to **Steamy Savings**. Update the button text to `Back` to tell the user they'll be going back to the previous page they came from, not the menu.

16. Open the **Steamy Savings** page and reposition the `Wipe Clear` object over the page. You might have to right-click the `Wipe Clear` object and choose **Bring to Front** to make sure it's the most forward object on the canvas. Save and preview your iAd.

What just happened?

By building the menu ourselves, we get more control over the page structure of our ad, but lose the convenience of an automatically updating menu object.

Remember: if you're adding any extra pages to your ad, you'll need to go and add another button to the menu that points to that page; similarly, when removing pages, you'll also have to remove the menu item.

Have a go hero

We've made quite a few changes to our ad, so why not try tidying it up? For example, you could do the following:

◆ Add transitions to our new pages to ease the user journey through our ad.

◆ Try adding back in the **build in and out** action animations that we lost when we replaced the menu with a set of buttons.

◆ Check that all buttons have the correct styling applied to them and that tapping them takes you to the right page.

◆ Try adding another page and creating an item on the menu for it.

◆ Test the ad thoroughly, ideally on more than one device. Try to fix any issues that you may find.

Once your ad is looking awesome, save it and show it off to your team, friends, and family. It's a good idea to periodically have a full review and tidy up your ad throughout development, particularly when you're nearing the completion of your iAd.

Sending a message

To generate additional promotion from within our iAd, we can enable pre-composed SMS text messaging and emailing right in our ad, without the user having to leave the ad or app. Encouraging your users to share their passion for your brand or product with a friend in a few simple taps increases the reach of our ad's potential audience substantially.

Time for action – sending the message

Out of the box, iAd Producer doesn't have an object or template that supports sending SMS; however, we can achieve this with the **iAd JS Library**, the framework that powers our iAd. We're able to send an SMS with just four lines of code; don't worry, it's very simple to add this to your ad.

 Remember: iAd Producer is an editor that manages most of the iAd JS library for us, although it currently doesn't support all the available features, so we occasionally have to modify and add some custom code.

1. We'll continue with our `Coffee Beans` project; if it isn't already open, open it now.

2. Let's create a button on the **Menu** page so our users can share our brand with their friends. Open the **Menu** page on the editing canvas and add a button object from the **Objects** library. Change the button text to something like `Tell a friend`, and then position the button on the bottom right of the screen. Change the button's styling. For example, try:

   - Setting the background to a light-to-dark, linear, red gradient
   - Changing the text color to white
   - Adding a border radius to the button so it has rounded edges
   - Including a drop shadow to add a light glow to the button
   - Adjusting the different button states, such as highlighted, so your button changes when tapped
   - You'll probably need to reposition other objects on the page to accommodate the new button

3. You might want to make your button look like the following:

4. When you're happy with the style of the button, it's time to add a tiny bit of code to add our SMS sending functionality of the ad. With the button selected, right-click on it and select **Object Events** | **Touched Up Inside** | **Execute JavaScript**. You can see the menus in the following screenshot:

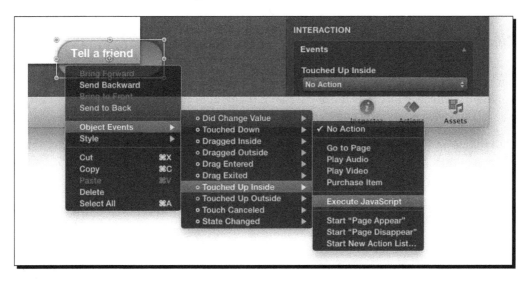

5. You'll see a text window appear on your screen, with some code pre-filled for you; this is simply the set of actions that are run when this event is triggered. In the empty line between `function(event) {` and `};`, type the following lines exactly:

```
window.ad.smsComposer.listener =function(){};
window.ad.smsComposer.toRecipients = [" "];
window.ad.smsComposer.body = "We should have a drink at Coffee
Beans!";
window.ad.smsComposer.presentComposer();
```

Downloading the example code

You can download the example code files for all Packt books you have purchased from your account at `http://www.PacktPub.com`. If you purchased this book elsewhere, you can visit `http://www.PacktPub.com/support` and register to have the files e-mailed directly to you.

6. Save this code file by clicking on **File | Save** from the menu bar, or with *cmd + S* on the keyboard.

7. Return to the iAd Producer main window by closing the code window. Preview your ad on an iOS device; you can't use the iOS Simulator as it doesn't have SMS capabilities. If you don't see the messaging window appear when you tap the button, try repeating these steps and make sure the code matches exactly.

8. Save your iAd project.

What just happened?

We styled a button and added a short piece of custom code. This code is written in JavaScript and called when certain events happen. Object Events are actions that occur on an object; we used **Touched Up Inside** as the event that is triggered when a user lifts their finger off an object. This then causes our code to be executed that in turn opens the SMS window.

With this powerful scripting language, we're able to integrate e-mail, SMS, telephone, and social networking into our advertisements.

Summary

Actions and destinations are goals that are directly beneficial to your brand, whether it's a user socially sharing content with a friend or locating their nearest store with rich mapping. We looked at engaging the user with some of these compelling techniques:

◆ Promoting and buying iTunes store content, such as apps and media, right within our ad, generating additional revenue streams or promotion

◆ Customizing the store finder experience

◆ Hiding certain pages of the ad from the main navigation to offer supplementary content

◆ Sending an SMS text arranging to meet a friend using our first bit of JavaScript code!

We'll learn how to create even further interaction using advanced code later, but first, let's take a look at making ads for the big-screen iPad iAds.

7

Building for the Big Screen

Starting with iOS 4.2, the operating system running on iPhones and iPads, you're able to create rich, fullscreen iAds for the iPad. The iPad's large, 9.7-inch, multi-touch screen gives us an even larger canvas to create immersive and intimate iAds.

In this chapter we'll look at:

- ◆ The differences of an iPad iAd
- ◆ Creating rich, fullscreen banners
- ◆ Including multiple banners in your ad to keep a fresh stream of content in a range of apps
- ◆ Using objects that aren't available in the object library to create custom pages

Creating an iPad iAd

Most of the templates and objects you're familiar with on the iPhone are available on the iPad; however, to create iAds for the iPad, you'll need to start a new project. The iPad screen is substantially larger, and Apple requires you to redesign and plan your ads to take full advantage of this; but we'll be able to share many of the same resources and assets.

If you're using your own assets in the chapter, you'll need the following:

- ◆ A large logo image for the menu screen
- ◆ A background image for your banner, 1024px wide and 66px high
- ◆ A small icon or logo for your banner

- A background image, 1024px wide by 768px high, to be used throughout the pages of your ad

- An image to be used in your splash screen, around 300px wide and 200px high

- Several photographical images to be used in a gallery
- A 2000px wide and 768px high image the user will pan across the screen
- A background for your banner image
- A short, fullscreen movie, 512px wide and 384px high
- A poster image and a snapshot of your movie
- A custom map pin icon, approximately 100px wide and 100px high
- Menu icons, including a back button, for each page of your ad

To recap from earlier when we looked at size limits for our iAd, an iPad iAd has a more lenient limit, as there are more resources that are typically larger than the smaller-screen iPhone ads. Bear in mind these restrictions when creating your resources:

- The banner size is limited to 65 KB.
- Full screen banners (only available on iPad) can be up to 350 KB.
- The **Splash** page has a maximum size of 300 KB.
- As with other ads, the remaining pages don't have a maximum size, but including too many resources will increase your advert's loading time. Try to keep the number of media elements in each page of your iAd to under 20.

When building your iAd, you're able to use the project warnings window to view any issues with your ad, including if you've reached the file size limit. To view your project warnings select **Export | Show Project Warnings** from the menu bar in iAd Producer. Here's an example **Project Report** window showing a project's warnings:

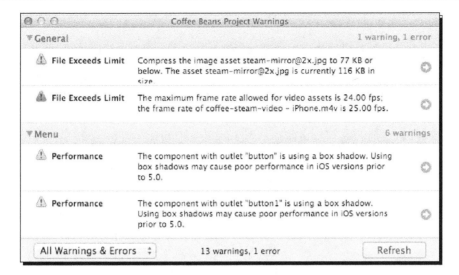

If your assets are too large, consider using the optimization techniques covered in *Chapter 2, Preparing Your Content for Mobile*.

Currently, the iPad doesn't have a retina display, like the iPhone, so you don't need to create your assets at double the resolution; however, remember to work with as high a resolution as possible when creating resources for you iAd. Ensuring you're working with high resolutions means, if Apple do ever release an iPad with a retina display, you won't have to remake all your assets at a higher resolution.

Time for action – setting up an iPad project

Creating an iPad project is just as easy as setting up a new iPhone project. Let's create a placeholder ad that we'll be using throughout this chapter:

1. If you haven't already, open iAd Producer.

2. From the project device selection screen, click on **iPad** and then **Select**:

3. You'll see the same ad overview you're used to working within iPhone projects. The only noticeable changes are the larger and more square placeholder pages in your ad. If you need to find out whether an existing project is iPhone or iPad, select **View** from the menu bar. It will show either iPad or iPhone in the menu drop down.

4. If you're using the example assets for this project, add them to your **Asset Library** now.

5. Choose **File | Save As** from the menu bar, and give your project a memorable name. If you'll be using the example assets of this chapter, use `Cloud 9 - iPad` as the filename. Click on **Save**.

 When naming your files, it's advisable to add the project type to the end of the filename, for example, adding - iPad to iPad projects, to distinguish them from their iPhone counterpart.

What just happened?

Just like you have before, we created a new project in iAd Producer, but this time instead of creating an iPhone project, we selected iPad.

iPad ads are almost identical to their iPhone counterparts, besides the additional screen estate; however, on the iPad, we're able to create fullscreen HTML5 banners.

Time for action – adding a banner to your iPad ad

iPad banners are split into two categories: dynamic banners, like those found on the iPhone, and fullscreen HTML5 banners that are only available on the iPad. We'll look at fullscreen banners next, but first let's create a dynamic banner that works in portrait and landscape:

1. Open your project in iAd Producer; if you're using the example project, open the Cloud 9 - iPad project. From the ad overview, double-click on the banner to open the template chooser. You'll notice that the templates are separated into two categories; for now, select the **Image and Text** banner type. Double-click on the banner again to open it on the editing canvas.

2. By default, iAd Producer scales the banner to 50 percent; however, this scaled-down view can make it difficult to anticipate how our ad will look on the device. Select **View** from the top right of iAd Producer, and then choose **iPad (100%)**. You'll now see the canvas at the correct size; if your Mac screen isn't large enough to show the complete canvas, you'll be able to scroll around to view the entire banner. You might want to resize the iAd Producer window to increase the space available to the canvas. You can do the same by clicking-and-dragging the bottom right of the window outwards:

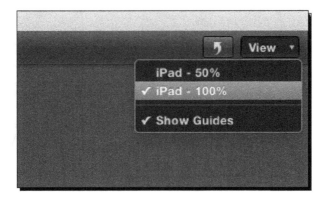

3. Now that we have a placeholder banner, we can customize the elements just like we would on an iPhone project. Let's change the background of the banner to an image of clouds. Open the **Inspector** and expand the **Background** section; now change the type to **Image** and, using the file selector drop-down, select **clouds-banner.jpg** as the background image. You'll see the canvas update to show the background. If you want to close the inspector to make the canvas fit the whole banner then click on the **Inspector** icon again to hide it.

 We're using a background image that is 1024px wide and 66px high, so when the banner is viewed in portrait (768px wide), the background is cropped at the edges. Creating an image that works in both orientations is vital to keep the size of your banner low and lightweight.

4. From **Asset Library**, drag the image **banner-plane.png** to the image placeholder on the canvas. You'll see a fighter jet, complete with shadow, appear on the canvas.

5. By default, the **Image and Text** template just appears on the banner, which isn't very compelling. Let's change the animation of the image so it flies in from the left of the screen. With the image selected, expand the **Actions** pane and add a new action, using the **Slide In** animation. Change the **Delay** to **0.5s** and the **Duration** to **3.5s**. We'll change the **Easing** to **Linear**, as this will prevent the animation from slowing down at the end. Your action settings should look similar to these:

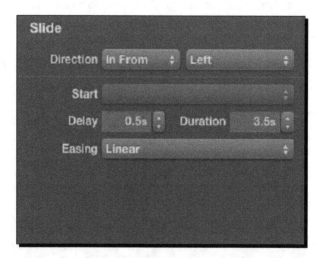

6. Move the image so it's off the canvas, to the right of the banner. This means the slide-in animation will move the image to this point from the left of the screen, so it appears to fly across.

7. With the slick airplane animation capturing the user's attention, let's change the label text to get them to tap to find out more. Double-click on the placeholder label to enter the text editing mode, and change the text to something like `Ever wanted to learn to fly..?`. You might need to resize the label to fit all the text into view. Move the label to the center of the banner. This will stop our banner looking unbalanced once the plane animation has finished. The yellow grid lines should appear to snap the label to the middle of the banner.

8. With the label still selected, open the **Inspector** and change the text color to white. This should make the label stand out more against the cloud background.

9. Keeping the label selected, open the **Actions** pane. Add a **Slide In** action like we did for the plane. This time, change the **Direction** to be from the **Bottom** and update the **Delay** to **4.2s**. This will cause the text to appear after the main flying plane animation has ended.

10. Your banner should look something like the following screenshot:

11. With our banner looking great in portrait view, let's tweak it to work just as well in landscape. Click on the arrow next to the **View** drop-down, at the top right of iAd Producer, to toggle between orientations, or select **View | Landscape** from the menu bar. You might want to hide the inspector pane to reveal more of the canvas.

 Handling orientation is even more important on the iPad, as the device doesn't have a default orientation. App developers are encouraged to support both portrait and landscape.

12. Now that you're in the landscape view for the banner, reposition the label so it's in the center of the canvas. You will notice that the background image has automatically spanned the full width of this wider banner.

13. Save your iAd.

What just happened?

We just created a large iPad banner that works in both portrait and landscape. By using the build in and out animations, we simulated a plane flying across the canvas.

Now preview your iAd (preferably on a device) to view the animation, and test how it looks in both portrait and landscape. If you need to install iAd Tester on your iPad, or want to know how to scale and rotate the simulator, check back to *Chapter 4*, *Making Sure it Works*.

Have a go hero

Once the animation has finished, our banner is a little static; if you want, why not try adding a few tweaks and some polish to keep our banner engaging for the user after the initial animation. You could try the following:

♦ Make the banner more interesting by replacing the label with a multi-label cell, adding some different text to each cell.

♦ Add a shadow to the text, so it stands out in the clouds.

♦ Add an image, `clouds-banner-transparent.png`, to the canvas. Animate this from right to left, linearly, over 15 seconds. This will add even more depth to the animation of your banner.

Now that we've got a great dynamic banner, let's take a look at including a large, immersive, full screen HTML5 banner.

Filling the screen with HTML5 full screen banners

Starting with iOS 4.3, released in March 2011, the iPad is able to display full screen banners. Similar to your splash screen, a full screen banner can only display elements. The user is unable to interact with it, as any touches on your banner will load the rich content of your core ad unit.

HTML5 full screen banners will typically appear in apps such as magazines and games, displaying in between pages or transitioning a user between game levels. We can include multiple banner creatives in an iAd project. This means that the iAd framework, on a user's device, will load the most relevant banner for the user's current experience.

Time for action – providing multiple banner creatives

Any project, either iPhone or iPad, can have multiple banner creatives. It's a great way to accommodate the various situations and apps your iAd will appear in:

1. Open the project `Cloud 9`, in iAd Producer, and double-click on the banner to open it on the editing canvas. You should see the banner that we just added to our ad earlier.

2. In the top left of iAd Producer, next to the **Overview** button, click on the small arrow button, to expand the **banner draw**. This draw shows all the banner creatives currently available in iAd Producer.

3. At the bottom of the banner draw, click on the **+** button to open the template chooser, select any template, and click on **Choose**. This will add a new banner creative to your project:

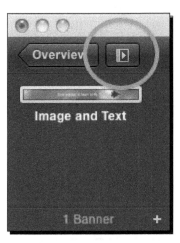

4. To change between banners, simply click on the banner creative thumbnail you want to view, and the canvas will update.

5. Delete the template you just added; we'll add a proper full screen banner next. Click on the banner in the banner drawer to select it, then press the *delete* or *backspace* key on your keyboard to remove it.

What just happened?

Using multiple banners means more apps are able to display your ads. When an application developer is adding iAds into their app, they decide whether to use the dynamic banner or the HTML5 full screen banner. By providing both full screen and dynamic banners in your iAd project, your ad is able to appear in more apps.

You may wonder why this would be beneficial in an iPhone ad, where there is only one banner type, the dynamic banner. If you create an advert with multiple creative banners, the iAd framework will automatically cycle between them. This means users seeing your ad banner multiple times get a different banner, keeping your creative fresh.

 Your advert can have a combination of full screen and dynamic banners, and multiple banners of the same type. If you included multiple similar banners, be sure to update the name in the inspector pane to something identifiable, for each banner.

Time for action – creating an immersive video experience

With full screen HTML5 banners, we're able to capture the user's entire attention by filling the entire screen, giving us a great way to immerse them with our brand. Combining a full screen banner and preroll video will transition the user into our ad, excited to find out about our product:

1. If it isn't already open, open the `Cloud 9` demo in iAd Producer. Double-click on the banner to open the banner on the canvas. Using banner drawer, open the template chooser and select the **Blank** fullscreen template. If you're unsure which template is a standard banner and which is fullscreen, hover your mouse over each one and **Fullscreen** will appear on the correct one.

> You might need to change the view of the canvas to 50 percent so you can see the entire banner.

2. Open the **Inspector** and set the **Name** property to something identifiable, such as `Fullscreen Banner`. Now, we'll set the background image of the page and expand the **Background** section. Change the background to be **Image** and select the file `launch-movie-placeholder.jpg`. By using a background image, our banner will automatically crop depending on the orientation.

3. Just like dynamic banners, our full screen banner needs to work in both orientations. Click on the orientation toggle in the top right of iAd Producer, or choose **View | Landscape**, from the menu bar, to change to landscape view.

4. The placeholder image was designed as 1024px wide and 1024px high; this means it can fill the screen regardless of orientation, with certain parts being cropped or hidden by your iAd.

5. The following screenshot shows the safe region, the middle square that is always available—the areas which are only visible in portrait or landscape, and the corners, which aren't ever visible:

6. By using one image as our placeholder, which works in all orientations, there's no flicker when the device is rotated. This is because we're able to keep the file size and loading time down.

7. Return to the ad overview and double-click on the **Splash** page. From the template chooser, select **Mosaic**. Open the **Splash** page on the ad canvas. Select the mosaic object and update the image property to the video placeholder `launch-movie-placeholder.jpg`.

8. You may have noticed the image is skewed in the wrong ratio. Expand the **Layout** section of the mosaic object and click on **Original Size** to restore the correct proportions to the image.

9. Switch to the **Preroll** page by using the toggle above the canvas. Expand the inspector pane and set the **Video** to **launch-movie - iPhone.mov** and the **Poster Frame** to **launch-movie-placeholder.jpg**.

10. You'll see the canvas update to have our placeholder image for the video. iAd Producer, by default, sets our video to play in full screen mode.

11. Save your iAd and keep it ready to test next.

What just happened?

We created a full screen banner that can adapt to different screen sizes and orientations, and added a compelling immersive video preroll into our ad. A full screen ad can be much more engaging than a dynamic banner, as it captures the entire screen securing the user's attention.

Keep in mind that if you choose to use full screen HTML5 banners, you won't be able to have your ad appear on devices running an older operating system than iOS 4.3. However, all iPads can be upgraded to this OS, so you shouldn't be missing a large audience.

Apple previously allowed the use of video in their fullscreen banners, but removed this due to poor user experience in self-playing video. You can, and should, build up animations on your full screen banner to tempt the user into tapping it.

Despite being full screen, your banner might not always have the full use of the screen, depending on the application it is appearing in. For example, some apps may display your ad within a tab bar and navigation bar, and some full screen games may still show the 20px status bar at the top of the screen. Your iAd will always fill the full width of the screen; only the height can change. Your full screen banner should be tested and tweaked to work in the following boundaries of size:

1. In portrait, your banner could appear as follows:

   ❑ Between 911px to 1024px high

   ❑ Always 768px wide

2. In landscape, your banner could appear as follows:

   ❑ Between 655px to 768px high

   ❑ Always 1024px wide

Fortunately, iAd Tester provides the ability to simulate a variety of potential situations that your ad may appear in.

Time for action – testing full screen banner situations

When your iAd project contains multiple banners, or a full screen banner, iAd Tester provides different options to test each banner, and a variety of situations it may appear in. Let's preview our Cloud 9 ad so far and check out how each of our banners look:

1. Make sure iAd Producer is open, and that the Cloud 9 - iPad project is active.

 If you're using an iPad to test, make sure you're sharing your ads on your local network, or export and copy your ad to your iPad using iTunes. If you can't remember how to test your ad using iAd Producer, we covered sharing your iAd in *Chapter 4, Testing and Debugging*.

2. Open iAd Tester on your iPad or click on the **Simulate** button in iAd Producer to open the iOS Simulator.

3. If you're using iAd Tester on a device, you'll now see all of the projects available; tap your project name. As we've got multiple banners available for this ad, a list of your banners, or creatives, will appear. Let's test the full screen banner; tap **Full Screen** banner from the list.

4. You can now select a simulation for a variety of layouts that your banner could appear in, separated into magazine and game style apps:

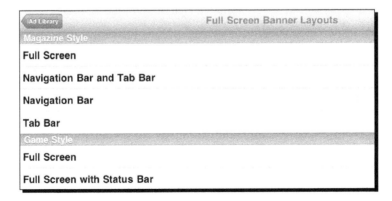

5. Tap the first **Full Screen** item in the list to preview the video in full screen. Try rotating the iPad to see how the banner behaves in each orientation. Once the video has completed, you'll see the placeholder image appear.

6. Tapping anywhere on the banner will open your core ad.

7. To close the banner, tap the close icon in the top left of the screen, at any time.

8. Close the ad and banner, and test the other configurations of your ad.

 The **Navigation Bar and Tab Bar** layout provides the least space for your iAd banner, with only 655px of height available in landscape. Make sure that you test your banners with this style.

9. Return to your list of creatives by closing the current ad (if it's open) and tapping the **Creatives** menu item in the top left of the navigation bar. Open the **Image and Text** banner to see how one or more banners can be accessed from your iAd project.

What just happened?

Using iAd Tester, either on a device or in the iOS Simulator, we tested our iAd's full screen banner. You now know how to select from multiple banner creatives in your ad and can test your full screen banners in a variety of mock situations that they could appear in.

Make sure you're using identifiable names for your pages, so that you can find the banner you want. You can change banner names from the inspector pane. You should try testing your ad with the iPad muted. This way, you can make sure your video makes sense visually, without the audio.

Pop quiz – banners

1. When creating an iAd, why should we include multiple banners?

    a. It's fun to make a lot of banners

    b. Banners are quick to create

    c. If a user doesn't like a certain banner, they can swipe to reveal a different one

    d. Multiple banners means that users seeing our banner several times view a variety of different banners

2. When testing a fullscreen banner, what's the layout that provides the least space for your banner?

   a. Full Screen

   b. Full Screen with Status Bar

   c. Navigation Bar and Tab Bar

   d. Navigation Bar

Have a go hero – improving your banners

With an awesome dynamic banner and rich full screen immersive video, our banners are looking great; consider these few tweaks to make them even better:

- Add an extra dynamic banner to your ad, to have multiple to cycle through
- Create multiple versions of the video using the *save for web* feature in QuickTime, so that the quality and loading size can adapt, depending on the wireless network
- Try improving your full screen banner by layering more objects and using actions to animate them
- Test and tweak your full screen banner in all the situations it may appear in, using iAd Tester

Making massive menus

Unlike the iPhone, where the menu fills a considerable section of the page, we can include a deeper level of interaction with our menu in an iPad ad.

Time for action – combining objects to create a unique menu

We can combine the 3D carousel with buttons, as it's not just limited to images; this means we're able to use buttons that'll act like flying planes for the menu in our ad. In order to combine objects to create a unique menu, follow these steps:

1. We'll be continuing with the `Cloud 9 - iPad` project, so if it isn't already open, open it in iAd Producer.

2. Before we make our menu, let's set up the placeholder pages of our iAd. From the ad overview double-click on the first page item, to open the template chooser. Select the second blank template, a **Blank** landscape page, and click on **Choose**:

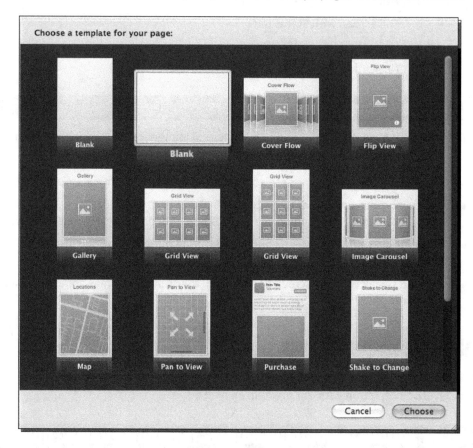

3. Click on the new blank page in the ad overview. Open the **Inspector** and change the name to Test Flight.

4. Repeat this for the other two pages, choose the first **Grid View** template, in landscape, for the next page, and change the name to Making Memories. For the final page, select the **Map** and update the name to Book a flight.

5. With our pages set up, double-click on the menu page and select a wide, landscape, blank page. Double-click on the page again, to open it on the canvas. From the inspector, change the **Background** type to **Image** and select **menu-background.jpg** as your background image. This has the background image and logo combined to save requests and reduce the need for transparent images (which have larger file sizes).

6. Open the object library, from the bottom left of iAd Producer, and add a carousel object to the canvas.

7. With the new carousel object selected, open the inspector pane. Expand the properties section, change the orientation to **Horizontal**, and tick the **Snaps To Cells** box. This will make our carousel scroll left and right instead of up and down and will make sure it always stops on a cell and doesn't get stuck between two.

8. Resize the carousel so it sits underneath the logo and spans the width of the page. It should look a little like the following screenshot:

9. Double-click on the center cell to enter cell editing mode. The rest of the canvas should fade out, and the cell navigator will appear. Click again to select the image placeholder inside the cell. We're going to add a button into our cell instead of an image, so, with the image selected, press the *backspace* or *delete* key on your keyboard to delete the image.

10. Open the object library and add a button to the cell. We want to use an image as our button, so open the inspector pane and change the **Background** type to **Image**. Select **test-flight-button.png** as the image; you'll see the button update with this graphic. Currently, the graphic is cropped and has the button text overlapping it. Try resizing the button to fit the entire image in.

11. You may find the cell isn't large enough to fit the entire button image in. If that's the case, click outside of the cell to exit the cell editing mode, and then click on the carousel again, to select it. From the **Metrics** section of the inspector pane, change the **Cell Length** to a larger number, such as **500px**, and reduce the **Padding** to **30px**. This will increase the size of the cells, so you're able to resize your button to fit the entire image.

12. iAd Producer automatically applies a border to buttons; however, as our button has transparent edges, the border adds an unnecessary frame around the image. In the cell editing mode, and with the button object selected, uncheck the **Border** option.

13. Our image has the text from the button overlapping it, so double-click on the button object to enter the text edit mode; remove all the text by deleting it.

14. Finally, we need to update our button to open the correct page of our ad when tapped. Change the **Go To Page** in the inspector pane's **Event** section to **Test Flight**.

15. We'll use this button as a template for our other cells. Copy the button so we can paste it into another cell.

 To copy an object, right-click the object and choose **Copy** from the context menu, or press *cmd* + *C* on your keyboard, to copy the selected object or item.

16. Using the cell navigator, click on the arrow on the right to move to the next cell. Click on it again so you're two cells away from the button cell that we just created. We'll update the cell in between, later.

17. Delete the image placeholder object currently in the cell, and then paste the button that we just copied.

 To paste an object, right-click on the canvas and select **Paste** from the context menu, or use the keyboard shortcut *cmd* + *V*.

18. We've now got a copy of the button we set up; by copying and pasting the element, we save time by not having to remake the button for each cell. Change the background image of the button to **memories-button.png**. You might need to change the sizing of the button to prevent the image from being cropped. Update the **Go To Page** to **Making Memories**, so the button takes the user to the right page.

19. Move forward again, by two cells, by clicking the cell navigator's right arrow twice. Delete the placeholder image, and then paste the button again, this time replacing the background image of the button with **book-a-flight-button.png** and changing the **Go To Page** of the button to **Book a flight**.

20. We left some cells out when building our carousel; let's add some content to them now. For the carousel to work well, it needs a certain number of cells, or else the angle between each cell is too tight. Go around the remaining cells and update each image placeholder with the image **cartoon-clouds.png**. Try copying and pasting the images, if you want to be able to do it faster.

21. Test your iAd, on a device or in the simulator. You're able to flick the menu around with a cool 3D flying effect. Try tapping one of the menu items to open the relevant page. Your final menu page should look something like the following screenshot:

What just happened?

Using the carousel object, we added buttons with images into the cells, to create an interactive 3D menu that fitted the context of our ad. Like most of the objects in iAd Producer, you're able to remove the placeholder content and adapt the object to create some interesting and unique content.

With this technique, the menu can easily be expanded to add several more pages into our ad, without overwhelming the user.

Have a go hero

Our menu is looking fantastic; change these few things to make it even greater:

- Add button states to the buttons, consider using the same image, and set the button's opacity to 80 percent to give the user feedback to the change in state
- Set animations on the carousel element, so the menu moves in and out from the bottom of the page

Creating a grand gallery

Creating a gallery for the iPad is the same as creating one for the iPhone, except you don't have to worry about having double-resolution graphics, because currently the iPad isn't available with a retina display. You will, however, have to create your images at a larger size than the standard resolution iPhone. In this example, we're using images that are 640px wide and 478px high.

Time for action – making memories in a gallery

Let's add a gallery of images to our ad, using the **Grid** template, that'll show what a typical day with Cloud 9 will be like:

1. Open the Cloud 9 - iPad project in iAd Producer, and double-click on the **Making Memories** page to open it on the canvas. Select the images **cloud-9-example-day-1.jpg** through to **cloud-9-example-day-7.jpg**, and drag them to the grid gallery object on the canvas.

2. The grid gallery will now update to show the images. Change the page's background type to **Image** and select **blue-starburst.jpg**, using the **Background** section of the inspector pane.

3. Change the label currently titled **Grid View** to, say, **Making Memories**. Update the text color to white so it stands out against the rich blue background.

4. At the moment, there's no way for the user to return to the main menu, so let's add a back button. From the object library, select a button to add to the canvas. Change the **Background** type to **Image** and use the image **back-button.png**. You'll need to resize the button object and remove the text so that your button looks correct. Update the **Go To Page** property to open the **Blank Menu Landscape** page.

    You might want to update the name of your menu page; **Blank Menu Landscape** isn't very clear.

5. Copy and paste the back button to the other two pages of your ad, so you've got a universally identifiable way to leave each of your pages.

6. Go back to your **Making Memories** page and test your iAd. Tap an image thumbnail to open the full-size image with a neat 3D animation. The finished page should look like the following screenshot:

What just happened?

We customized our **Grid** template to match the theme of our ad and added our images to it. The **Grid** template offers a high-impact, interactive gallery; all it requires is for you to drag your images to it.

Scrolling content with a scroll view

Unlike the other pages of our ad, let's create an interactive section of our ad using only objects and a blank template.

Time for action – scrolling content in our ad

Let's style the first page of our ad, the blank **Test Flight** page:

1. Make sure the Cloud 9 - iPad project is open in iAd Producer. Double-click on the first page, **Test Flight**, to open it on the canvas.

2. Update the background to be the image **blue-starburst.jpg**, so that it matches the rest of your iAd.

3. Add a scroll view, from the object library, to the canvas. A scroll view is an object that contains a larger view the user can flick to scroll around. It's the core component of the pan to view page template. Using the drag handles, resize the scroll view so it fits the full height and width of the page.

4. Open the **Asset Library**, and drag the image **cloud-scene.jpg** to the scroll view. This will automatically set the background of the scroll view to an image of clouds. Click on the scroll view object to select it and expand the **Layouts** section of the inspector pane. In the **Layouts** section, change the width of the **Content View** to **2000px**; this will allow the scroll view to scroll left and right, to reveal more of the background image:

 The maximum dimension of an image in your iAd project is 2000px by 2000px. Keep this in mind when designing large graphics for scrollable areas. Apple imposes this limit because of the performance limitations on the low-powered devices.

5. Double-click on **Scroll View** to open up the view editing mode. This allows you to add elements to the scroll view that will move around with the view as the user scrolls it. When in the editing mode, you can change the interaction method between selecting objects and panning the view, by selecting either the arrow/ pointer icon or grab/hand icon, respectively:

6. Still in the editing mode, add a new label to the view from the object library. Update the label text to say Want to learn to fly? With our test flight package you can get a taster session in the air for 60 minutes.. No experience necessary!. To fit the entire text in view, resize the label to fit the width of the scroll view. You might need to pan the view across to keep dragging the label to the hidden area of the scroll view. Change the interaction method to pan and drag the scroll view to the reveal the currently off-page area. Switch back to the pointer selection method, and then continue resizing the label. Reposition the label so it starts in the bottom left of the scroll view.

7. Update the text style to match the design of the ad, and its font size to fill the available width provided. Consider using the **Chalkboard SE** font with a **34px** size, and a dark blue shadow.

8. Now let's add one more object to our page, an airplane image that bounces up and down. As iAd Producer doesn't have a constantly animated object available in the object library, we have to use a little trick and copy the image object from the floating **Splash** template. As we've already got our **Splash** page set up and configured in this ad, let's open a new project, copy the animated image object, and paste it back into our main Cloud 9 project. Before continuing, it's recommended to save your project in case something goes wrong in the next steps.

9. Select **File** | **New**, from the menu bar in iAd Producer, or use the keyboard shortcut *cmd + N*. This will open a new iAd Producer window. Select iPad as the project type. Double-click on the **Splash** page from the **Overview** and choose the **Bouncing** template. Double–click on the page again, to open it on the editing canvas. Select and copy the placeholder image object on the page canvas.

10. With the object copied, close this iAd Producer project, using the red close dot in the top left of the window. If asked whether you want to save your untitled project, select **Don't Save**. Your Cloud 9 project should come back into view; if it doesn't, select **Window** | **Cloud 9** from the menu bar.

11. Make sure you're not in the scroll view editing mode, by clicking outside of the main canvas. Paste the object you just copied onto the canvas.

> Copy and paste isn't specific to the project you've currently got selected, so you can use it to share objects between projects.

12. You'll now see the image placeholder appear. Although it looks like a standard image object, this has special properties applied that cause it to bounce, or float up and down. This should work with most of the templates, so you're able to use it whenever a template has an object you'd like to use, that isn't available in the object library.

13. Select the **airplane.png** file for the image. Click on the **Original Size** button in the **Metrics** section of the inspector pane, so the image object is the correct size for the image. Reposition the airplane so it's in the middle of the page.

14. Test your iAd; you'll see you're able to pan the scroll view around to read the text, while the airplane image stays in the center of the screen animating up and down. If you're unable to see the back button, your scroll view object might be overlapping it; right-click on **Scroll View** and select **Send To Back**.

15. Hopefully, your final page should look similar to the following screenshot:

What just happened?

We added content to a scroll view that allows us to include more content that is practical to display on one screen, having the user scroll around to reveal it. Using an object that was available in a template, but not the object library, we copied and pasted it from a **Splash** page to our **Test Flight** page. Sharing objects can be useful for creating iPad and iPhone ads that share the same resources, as you can copy and paste objects and tweak them for the different devices, instead of having to recreate your entire ad from scratch.

Increasing footfall with a store finder

Although most iPads don't have a GPS location-aware chip in them, they're still able to approximate their location when they have a network connection. We can use this to include a store finder page in our large-screen iPad ads.

Time for action – adding the store finder

No ad is complete without a store finder. Let's quickly style the store finder to match the rest of our ad, by changing the background and using a custom pin image:

1. From the `Cloud 9 - iPad` project, open the **Location** page on the editing canvas of iAd Producer.

2. Change the page background to image **blue-starburst.jpg**, and update the page's title label to `Find your nearest center...` Change the font and color to match the rest of the ad; you could save the style of the **Making Memories** title label and apply this throughout your ad to keep a consistent style.

3. Click on the map object to select it, and then set the custom pin to the image **cloud-9-map-pin.png**.

What just happened?

Just as we would for the iPhone, we styled the map with a custom pin and brought the rest of the page style inline with rest of our ad. There aren't any major differences between our iPad map and an iPhone map, except that we used a larger pin image. For example, this image is 100px by 100px, compared to using standard resolution iPhone image of around 30px by 30px.

Have a go hero

Our completed ad is looking pretty awesome, but consider these tweaks to make it even more amazing:

◆ Style the Store finder map details page.

◆ Add animations throughout the ad, to build up the page elements and transition the user smoothly through your iAd.

◆ Add a message to the **Test Flight** page, suggesting that the user scroll, and add extra content to make the page more exciting.

◆ If you're feeling adventurous, why not try redesigning this ad for the smaller iPhone screen? Create a new project and tweak these exercises for the smaller screen. You'll be able to copy and paste many objects to speed up the migration. Don't forget: full screen HTML5 banners aren't available on the iPhone, but you can still have multiple dynamic banner creatives.

Summary

With aviation advertising for the big screen, we created a bold, high-impact ad that looks great on the iPad's large 9.7 inch screen. In this chapter, you learned about:

◆ Creating full screen HTML5 banners for the iPad

◆ Including multiple banner creatives in your iAd

◆ Testing ads with multiple banners, and those with fullscreen HTML5 banners, using iAd Tester

◆ Stealing objects from templates that aren't available in the object library

◆ That there aren't many technical differences between iPad and iPhone ads, but the experience should be tailored to take full advantage of the iPad's rich large multi-touch screen

Now, you're able to create awesome adverts for the iPhone and iPad. In the next chapter, let's take a look at extending their functionality with some simple JavaScript code.

8
Enhancing Our App with Code

iAd Producer manages the HTML, CSS, and JavaScript that power our iAd, meaning we can make a visually impacting ad without any knowledge of these web technologies. We're able to extend the interactivity of our ads by adapting and adding to the JavaScript source code generated by iAd Producer. We'll go through some of the projects that you've been working on and enhance their interactivity with simple and effective tweaks to the JavaScript.

In this chapter, you'll learn about the following:

- ◆ What JavaScript is
- ◆ iAd Producer's code editor
- ◆ Handling events
- ◆ Accessing objects
- ◆ Sending e-mails and SMS
- ◆ Saving calendar events

While this chapter won't make you a JavaScript master, you'll have an understanding of what's happening and be able to apply these snippets and examples to your own amazing iAd projects.

JavaScript

JavaScript, often abbreviated to JS, is a lightweight language created to enhance the interactivity of the web by Brendan Eich of Netscape in 1995. JavaScript uses **objects**, an item that can contain one or more **functions** and **properties.** A function is a list of actions that occurs when called by the user or code, and a property, or variable, is a value that is stored within an object.

If you're already familiar with programming, you'll find that JavaScript was highly influenced by the C language. JavaScript is finding increased use in applications beyond the web browser and is a powerful and useful language to learn.

 Contrary to popular misconceptions, JavaScript doesn't bear a relationship to the Java language. It was initially named Mocha, then LiveScript, and finally changed to JavaScript—a trademark of Sun Microsystems.

Don't worry if you haven't used JavaScript before, we'll go through each exercise step-by-step and explain how the code is interacting with our ad and its components.

The code editor

iAd Producer has a built-in code editor that we'll use to edit our JavaScript code. It is essentially a basic text editor with a few handy tools, such as coloring our code to make it more readable and basic error checking.

Whenever you create a new page in your project, iAd Producer automatically generates a hidden JavaScript file that you can view by selecting **Code** | **Show Code Editor** from the menu bar in the iAd Producer. Each object also has its own JavaScript file that is used to call functions when an event occurs (such as a touch or swipe). To view an object's code, open the editor with the object selected. You can see an example of the code editor in the following screenshot:

```
○ ○ ○                Cloud 9 - iPad - FullscreenBannerDelegate.js
     Edited Code          ⓘ someFunction ⬍                    Add Event Handler ▼

BANNERS                   1  /*
   🌐 Banner.css           2   * Declaring a local variable:
                           3   *    this.someVar = "foo";
   🌐 Banner.js            4   *
   ▼ 📁 Fullscreen Banner   5   * Declaring a global variable:
                           6   *    window.globalVar = "bar";
      📄 FullscreenBanner.js ● 7  *
                           8   */
AD UNIT                    9
   🌐 Global.css          10  function someFunction() {
                          11      var property = 'someValue'; |
   🌐 Global.js           12  }
   🌐 Project.js
   ▶ 📁 Test Flight
   ▶ 📁 Book a flight.
   ▶ 📁 Events
   ▶ 📁 Map Detail
```

Accessing page objects

Whenever we add an object to a page's canvas, we're able to access and edit certain properties of it using some JavaScript code. This allows you to edit properties that aren't available in the iAd Producer interface or change objects in your ad to respond to a user's input.

Time for action – accessing an object

Let's continue using the Cloud 9 - iPad ad that we created in the last chapter. We'll add some tweaks to our **Test Flight** page's scroll view object that wouldn't be possible with the iAd Producer interface:

1. Open the project Cloud 9 - iPad in iAd Producer. If you didn't complete this project, then open the file 8. Store Finder.iadproj in the folder Cloud 9 and then Exercises. This file has the previous exercises completed for you.

2. Double-click on the first page, **Test Flight**, from the ad overview to open it on the canvas. Right-click on the hatched background outside of the canvas and expand the menu item **Page Events | View Did Load | Execute JavaScript**. This will automatically create the required function for this event and open the code editor for this page:

3. In the code editor window, iAd Producer has created a new function for this page that will be called and run when the view appears. The //Code goes here placeholder comment shows you where to put your custom code for this event. Delete the placeholder comment and add the following:

```
//get the scrollView from the canvas
var scrollView = this.outlets.scrollView;
```

 In JavaScript, anything on a line following // is a comment and will be ignored when run. If you want to have a multiline comment, use /* comment goes here */. Comments are useful as they can be used to remind you (or inform other developers working on your code) why you've done things in a certain way. The code editor will turn comments green to distinguish them from the JavaScript.

4. The first line is a comment saying what we're doing, which is retrieving the scroll view object from the page and storing a reference of it in a variable, indicated with `var` and called `scrollView`. Each object on the page is assigned a unique outlet name. To find or modify the outlet value for an object, click and select it from the canvas and open the inspector pane. Expand the **Properties** section and you'll see a text box with the outlet name. You're able to change this to something more memorable, if you have multiple objects of the same type on the page:

5. Now that we have our outlet easily accessible with the `scrollView` variable, we can manipulate it by adjusting its properties. Add the following lines to your function in the code editor:

```
//prevent up & down vertical scrolling
scrollView.verticalScrollEnabled = false;
```

 To disable a property, we use the `false` value, and we use the `true` value to enable it.

6. This will disable the vertical scrolling of our scroll view so it only can be scrolled left and right by the user. As we're preventing vertical scrolling, we should also prevent the vertical scroll bars from appearing:

```
//remove vertical scrollbar
scrollView.showsVerticalScrollIndicator = false;
```

7. By setting the `showsVerticalScrollIndicator` property of our scroll view object to `false`, we disabled the vertical scroll bar from appearing.

8. Your complete code should look similar to the following image in the code editor:

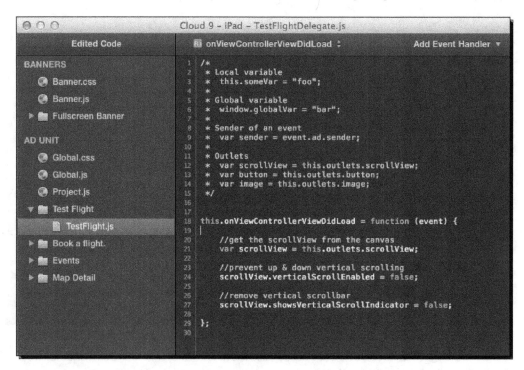

9. Save your project and test the ad in the iOS Simulator or on a device using iAd Tester. You'll notice that the scroll view can no longer be scrolled up and down, only left and right, and a vertical scroll bar does not appear.

What just happened?

We used the `onViewControllerViewDidLoad` event function that is called once the page has completed loading and modified some properties of our scroll view object. iAd Producer doesn't allow certain properties to be accessed, so it can keep its user interface clean and understandable. By hiding advanced functionality from beginners, they make starting out with iAd creation less overwhelming. As you're now an iAd pro, we can take the plunge into JavaScript to create better ads.

Handling user events

Whenever an action on our ad is initiated by the user, or by the system, an event is called. We're able to add a JavaScript function to a variety of events in our ad, such as taps on buttons, device shakes, and orientation changes.

Events are separated into three groups:

♦ **Global Events**: These occur for the entire ad

♦ **Page Events**: These are related to a particular page

♦ **Object Events**: These are specific to one object on a page

For example, the user shaking the device or the ad finishing the loading is a global event, a page loading or appearing is a page event, and a button being touched would be an object event. You can view the event hierarchy here:

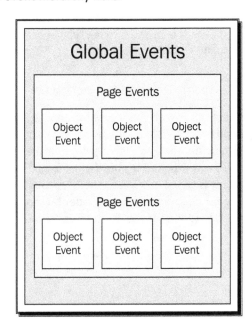

Sending SMS and e-mails

iAd Producer doesn't have an object or template available for sending e-mails or SMS, but the iAd JS framework that powers our iAd has a simple way of presenting the user with an e-mail dialog.

You may remember we briefly touched upon this in *Chapter 6, Ad Destinations and Actions,* when we added the ability to share our ad using SMS. This time, we'll take a deeper look at the code and what is happening at each step and send an e-mail instead.

Time for action – detecting a tap and sending an e-mail

Continuing to enhance our Cloud 9 ad, we'll add a button to our **Book a flight** page that will pre-fill the e-mail component with our booking center's e-mail address.

1. If it isn't already, open the Cloud 9 - iPad project in iAd Producer. Double-click on the **Book a flight** page to open it on the ad canvas. Using the page toggle above the canvas, change to the **Map Details** view.

2. From the object library, add a **Button** to the canvas. Open the inspector and change the outlet name to emailButton.

> When naming outlets, you should start in lowercase and then use camel case; this means each subsequent word after the first should be capitalized. For example, *youShouldCapitalizeEveryFirstLetterOfEachWord.* Doing so makes it easier to read and understand what each outlet does.

3. Update the button text to read Book a flight now!.

4. With the button selected, expand the **inspector** pane and find the **Events** section. The **Touched Up Inside** event will already be selected, but without an action. We use the **Touched Up Inside** event to detect a person releasing their finger from a tap on the object. We use **Touched Up Inside** instead of **Touched Down Inside**, as the **Touch Down** event is called as soon as the user touches on the object. This can create a jarring experience for the user as accidental taps are more likely to occur on touchdown. Change the action for the event to **Execute JavaScript**:

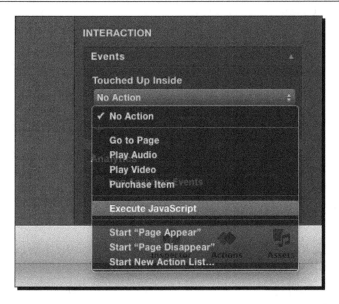

5. The code editor will appear; delete the // Code here placeholder comment
    and add the following:

    ```
    // Set the mail composer listener to an empty function
    window.ad.mailComposer.listener = function(){ };
    ```

6. This sets the **listener** property of our advert's mailComposer object to an empty
    function. Listener's are functions that are called once another action completes;
    for example, our listener is called when an e-mail is successfully sent or if it fails for
    any reason. For now, we're just using an empty function because we don't need to
    handle any sending errors or successes differently. Without an empty function, our
    ad would crash as it would try to find something that doesn't exist.

7. Let's set our recipient e-mail address, which is the e-mail account that will receive
    any bookings. Add the following code after our listener and update your@
    emailaddress.com with your own e-mail address so you're able to test whether it
    works later:

    ```
    // Set our recipient email address for the mail composer
    window.ad.mailComposer.toRecipients = ["you@emailaddress.com"];
    ```

8. Notice the square brackets? They indicate whether anything within them is in an
    array. Think of it as a list of items wrapped within the square brackets. Each item of
    the array is separated by a comma, so if you wanted to include multiple recipients,
    you'd use ["recipientOne@email.com", "recipientTwo@email.com"]
    and so on.

> Although we only passed one item to the recipients, we still had to use an array because that's what the `toRecipients` property expects.

9. With our recipient list set, we can set the `subject` property for our e-mail, while continuing to build up the code in the editor by adding the following:

```
// Set the email subject property
window.ad.mailComposer.subject = "I'd like to book a flight!";
```

10. This simply sets the `subject` property of our ad's mail composer to a **string**—a block of text contained with quotes. We'll pre-fill the body—the main content, of our e-mail:

```
//Set the message body using the mailComposer function
window.ad.mailComposer.setMessageBody( "I'd like to book a
flight..", false  );
```

11. Unlike our other properties, the body text isn't set using the = assignment but by adding values with two brackets. The items contained within these brackets are passed to the `setMessageBody` function of the mail composer. It accepts two arguments, items required by the function, in this case, a string for the body text, and a Boolean value indicating if the body text is an HTML string. A Boolean value is a simple yes or no switch, using `true` or `false` respectively. If we wanted to add HTML web content to our e-mail, we could use `<img src='http://awebsite.com/animage.png' />` as the string and `true` for the Boolean. This would show an image in our e-mail.

> To call or invoke a function, you use the function name followed by `()`. JavaScript functions can also be properties, which is why `window.ad.mailComposer.setMessageBody` needs to be set using values wrapped in (and).

12. With all the required info set for our `mailComposer` property, we can now present the user with the mail composer view. Add this final line of code to the editor:

```
// Show the user the mail composer window
window.ad.mailComposer.presentComposer();
```

This simply calls the mail composer's `presentComposer` function, which tells the iOS device to show the e-mail window and pre-fills it to the values we set.

> Notice how the code is indented in from the left of the screen; each line of code within a function should be indented by four spaces to increase readability. You can use one press of the tab key on your keyboard as a shortcut for this.

What just happened?

As all of this code occurs within the function for the `onTouchUpInside` event of our button, each line is executed step-by-step, with the last step calling a function that shows an e-mail composer with our properties pre-filled in it.

When creating our e-mail, we used arrays, strings, and Boolean values to customize the message composer with our own required content.

The iOS Simulator often won't send e-mails. When you hit send, the message is silently discarded with a success message. To test that your e-mail will reach the recipient, you'll need to test on a device with an e-mail account configured:

Have a go hero

It's great that our users can now get in touch with us without having to leave our ad, so why not try the following:

◆ Send an image in our e-mail; you'll need to have a URL of an image hosted on the web.

◆ Change the mail composer to send SMS. Check out the last exercise in *Chapter 6, Ad Destinations and Actions*, if you need some hints.

◆ Make sure all your lines of code within the function are indented by four spaces/one tab in.

◆ As usual, our ad could do with some styling to update the stock objects we added.

Time for action – adding something extra to our e-mail

While our e-mail contact form is fit for purpose, we can still add some extra polish and neat functionality (just like we've been doing to the visual aspect of our ad). As the **book now** button is on the store details page, let's make our e-mail body include the name of the selected store:

1. Open the `Cloud 9 - iPad` project in iAd Producer and open the **map details view** of the **Book a flight** page on the canvas.

2. We need to get back to the code editor and find the code that we added in the last exercise. With the **book a flight** button selected, click on **Code | Show Code Editor** from the menu bar. This will open the code editor and you can scroll down to find the function `this.onViewTouchUpInside`. When a control only has one function or event added to it, this technique is simple. However, if our control has multiple events, our file can quickly become crowded. To open the code editor directly focused in a function, select the button object, then right-click and choose object events, then **Touched Up Inside,** and finally **Execute JavaScript**. You'll see that events that already have functions assigned have a solid dot next to their name, whereas empty events have an empty circle, as shown in the following screenshot:

3. With the code editor opened and positioned at our event's function, we can modify some of our code to add the store name to the e-mail message's body. Add the following code straight after setting the e-mail subject:

```
//create our message variable
var message = "I'd like to book a flight at " + this.
viewController.annotation.title;
```

4. This creates a variable called `message` that contains the text `I'd like to book a flight at` combined with the text of the title of the map pin's annotation. The `+` is used to join the two strings and we access the text of the maps pin `title` property to construct our message. Now that we have our `message` variable containing the combined string, we need to pass this to the body of our e-mail.

5. To set our new dynamic text in the body of our e-mail, we need to remove the string from the `.setMessageBody` and replace it with our `message` variable. You should update your message body function to match this line:

```
//Set the message body using the mailComposer function
window.ad.mailComposer.setMessageBody(message, false);
```

6. After we update this message body function, this code will set the message body to be the string that we created and stored in the `message` variable.

 Make sure you also remove the quotes, " ", from within the `.setMessageBody` function. Variable names within quotes will cause the variable name, and not the variable value, to appear.

7. Your final updated touchup event function should look like the following screenshot:

```
js Cloud 9 – iPad – MapDetail$emailButtonDelegate.js

    Edited Code          onViewTouchUpInside ⬍                    Add Event Handler ▾

BANNERS                 27
                        28   this.onViewTouchUpInside = function (event) {
   Banner.css           29
                        30       // Set the mail composer listener to an empty function
   Banner.js            31       window.ad.mailComposer.listener = function(){ };
                        32
 ▶ Fullscreen Banner    33       // Set our recipient email address for the mail composer
                        34       window.ad.mailComposer.toRecipients =
AD UNIT                      ["sendMeFanMail@bencollier.net"];
                        35
   Global.css           36       // Set the email subject property
                        37       window.ad.mailComposer.subject = "I'd like to book a Cloud 9
   Global.js                 Flight";
                        38
   Project.js           39       //create our message variable
                        40       var message = "I'd like to book a flight " +
 ▼ Test Flight               this.viewController.annotation.title;
                        41
     TestFlight.js      42       // Set the message body using the mailComposer function
                        43       window.ad.mailComposer.setMessageBody(message, false);
 ▶ Book a flight.       44
                        45       // Show the user the mail composer window
 ▶ Events               46       window.ad.mailComposer.presentComposer();
                        47   };
 ▼ Map Detail           48
```

8. Now test the ad. Open a store details view page and tap the **Book a Flight!** button. You'll see that the main e-mail body text is dynamically set with the title of the store.

> When testing in the simulator, make sure you click on the **Simulate** button from the ad overview, not the store finder canvas. Opening directly from the canvas will cause the ad to crash as it won't load the correct pin data required for the annotation title.

What just happened?

We've made our e-mail more dynamic by adding the current flight center the user is looking at to the message body; this should allow better management of e-mails received by users.

By triggering with the `Touch Up Inside` event of our button, we combined a message string with the dynamic pin annotation property, meaning the body text of our e-mail updates with the name of the store the user is currently viewing.

Have a go hero

If you're feeling comfortable with the JavaScript code we've used so far, you could try extending it further by:

- Adding the address to the message string. Hint: You can access the annotation's address using `this.viewController.annotation.address`.

- Leaving the recipient array empty and creating a `Share with friend` button so a specific store can be shared with a friend. To create an empty array, simply don't add any properties into `[]`.

- Including an additional e-mail address in the recipient array so the e-mail is distributed to two people at your company.

Pop quiz – variables

Variables are a great way to store values in our JavaScript and can help keep our code readable and clear. See if you're able to identify these different variable types and uses:

1. Which of these would be the correct way to declare a variable name `cyril` with the string `the squirrel has lost his nuts`?
    a. var cyril = "the squirrel has lost his nuts";
    b. variable cyril = "the squirrel has lost his nuts";
    c. cyril = "the squirrel has lost his nuts";
    d. "cyril" = the squirrel has lost his nuts;

2. Which of following is the correct way of showing a Boolean value?
    a. yes/no
    b. true/false
    c. on/off
    d. yes/true

Adding a calendar entry

The iAd JavaScript library allows us to add events to the user's calendar; this can let us leave a reminder of certain time sensitive discounts or promotional events.

Time for action – using the calendar

Using our Cloud 9 - iPad project, we'll add an events page with a button that'll add an event to the user's iPad inbuilt calendar:

1. Open the Cloud 9 - iPad project and add a blank page to your ad. Add a button that goes to this page to the main menu carousel. Go back to *Chapter 7, Building for the Big Screen*, if you need a reminder on how to do this. Name the page Events. Use the image **events-button.png** for the button image and place it on one of the placeholder cloud cells, such as **Cell 4**, as shown in the following screenshot:

2. Open the new **Events** page on the ad canvas and add a button to the canvas from the object library. Change the text in the button to read `Add to calendar`.

3. With the button selected, add an `Execute JavaScript` event for when the object is `Touched Up Inside`. Delete the placeholder comment and add the following lines of code:

```
//Convert readable date into milliseconds
   var startDate = Date.parse("Tue, 16 Aug 2011 13:30:00 GMT");
```

4. Using the `Date.parse` function, we convert a human-readable date into a format that JavaScript can understand. JavaScript uses the number of milliseconds since January 1, 1970, 00:00:00 UTC to calculate its date and times.

5. We need to convert the JavaScript time to a format that iAd and iOS can understand. We'll do this using the `Date` function. Add these lines directly after the last two:

```
// Convert milliseconds to a date object
    startDate = new Date(startDate);
```

6. This creates a new `date` object from the millisecond time that JavaScript understands. A `date` object has a range of functions we can use to convert the date into a variety of formats.

> Notice, we didn't include `var` this time before the `startTime` variable name. This is because you only need to declare `var` the first time you create the variable.

7. Using our `date` object that we just created, we can access an ISO date string of our date required by the iAd calendar. Continue adding the following code to our code:

```
//Get the ISO string for the date
var startDateISO = startDate.toISOString();
```

8. This accesses our `startDate` date object and calls its `toISOString` function; we then save this value in the variable `startDateISO`. An ISO date string is an internationalized standard, and used by our iAd to create the calendar dates. We could just cut out these steps and create the ISO date string directly. However, it's better to work with more manageable readable dates. For example, the ISO date for our start time is `2011-08-16T13:30:00.000Z`.

9. With our start date in the right format, we also need to create an end date and time for our event. We'll do this in exactly the same way as our start time, but use a different time in the future. Add the following block of code:

```
// Convert readable date into milliseconds
var endDate = Date.parse("Tue, 16 Aug 2011 20:30:00 GMT");

// Convert milliseconds to a date object
endDate = new Date(endDate);

// Get the ISO string for the date
var endDateISO = endDate.toISOString();
```

10. Exactly as we did for our start time, we now have an ISO date string for the end time of our event.

 To update this for your own event, you'd adjust the start time and end time in the Date.parse() function. Use the preceding examples as a template for your time. To specify different time zones, you can add the offset after the GMT at the end. For example, GMT+0430 would offset the time four and a half hours east of the Greenwich meridian and GMT-400 would offset the time four hours west of GMT and give you USA Eastern Time.

11. With our dates ready, we can now create the event object required by the iAd framework. Add this code to the end of your touch Up Inside event function:

```
// Setup the event object
var theEvent = {
        "description": "Aviation Awards 2011",
        "location": "Brighton, UK",
        "summary": "Acrobatics and airplanes!",
        "start": startDateISO,
        "end": endDateISO
    };
```

12. This object contains a list of properties and values required to create an event. We're able to take the startDateISO and endDateISO values and add them to the start and end properties of our object.

13. Before we're able to display the calendar window, we need to tell our ad where to position the calendar **popover**. A popover is an iPad-specific element that overlays on top of the other user interface objects, and typically appears next to the button that activated it. We need to get the position of our button and adjust it slightly to display the calendar popover in the right place. Assuming your button is near the center of the screen, return to the iAd Producer canvas and select the button object. Open the inspector pane and expand the **Layout** section:

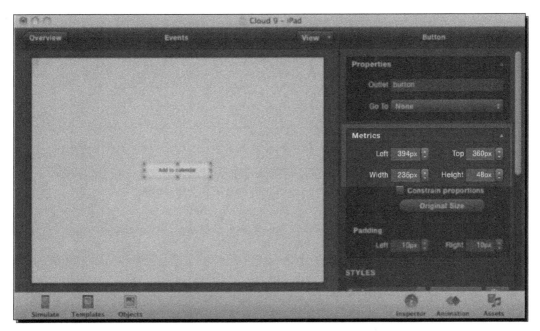

14. We can use these layout metrics to calculate the X and Y positions of our popover. The X position is how far left our popover should show from, and Y is how far from the top of the device screen it should be. To calculate the X position and cause our popover to appear to the right of our button, we take the **Left** value, in this case, above **394** and add it to the **Width**, in this case, **236**, giving a final X value of 630. We want the popover to appear in the center right of the button, so our Y value is calculated by taking the **Top** value, in this example **360**, and adding half of the button **Height**, in this case **24**, giving a final Y value of 384. With these values, we can create our position object and add the following to the function:

```
// On iPad so set the position for the popover
var calPosition = {
    'x':630,
    'y':384
};
```

15. Because we're using integers—number values, instead of strings, we don't need to wrap our position values in quotes.

 As this is only necessary on iPad, we would leave the `calPosition` empty for an iPhone ad because it uses the entire screen when adding a calendar event. Remember, if you move your button, you'll also have to update these values.

16. We'll quickly create an empty listener like we did for our e-mail composer. We don't need any feedback to successful or failed calendar events, so we can just use the following:

```
// Empty listener
var listener = {};
```

17. This will prevent the calendar from not showing because it can't find the listener.

18. With all our objects set up, we can finally tell the iAd framework to show the popover. Add this final line of code to the end of our function:

```
//show the popover
ad.calendar.presentComposer(theEvent, listener, calPosition);
```

19. This tells our advert's calendar to present the event popover and passes it the event object that we created, the empty listener, and the position object for the location of the popover on the screen.

20. Save the project and then test your new button! Your final code should look like the following screenshot:

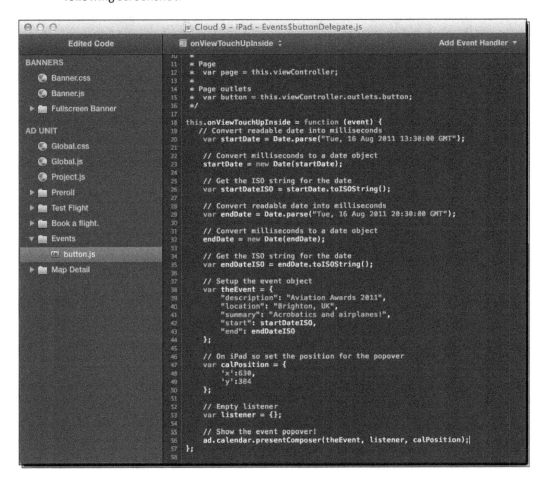

What just happened?

Using the Date object in JavaScript, we converted human-readable dates into a format that our iAd and iOS device could translate into a machine-readable format. By creating two dates, for the start and end time of an event, we then set up an event object that we can pass to the device. This event object holds details of the event along with the start and end time we converted. Finally, as our ad was for the iPad, we had to set up an object defining the X and Y positions on the screen where the popover should appear. Our popover calendar will look a little like the following screenshot:

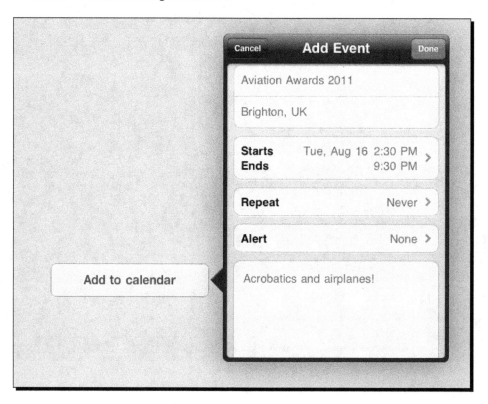

The popover gives the user the chance to edit the event, make the event reoccurring, or add an alarm to remind them. Once the user taps, the event is added to the in-built calendar app on their device, ensuring we keep presence with the user after they've closed our ad.

On the iPhone, we wouldn't need to set a coordinate for the popover and leave the position object empty because the iPhone automatically fills the entire screen with our calendar view.

Have a go hero

A button in the middle of a blank page isn't very compelling and unlikely to inspire our user to add the event to their calendar. Make your page interesting with some images and information about the event, for example, why not try the following:

- Add one or more pictures from past events
- Use labels with details of the event
- Update the background of the page so it matches the rest of our advert
- Don't forget to include a back button so the user can return to the main menu!

Playing audio

iAd Producer has an audio object where the user can tap a play button to hear an audio file included in our ad. This works great for songs and sound bites, but we can also trigger audio clips from JavaScript. As we're using JavaScript to play our audio file, we can use any event in our ad to initiate the audio.

Time for action – controlling an audio player

Let's combine an audio object from the object library with some JavaScript code to make our audio clip play every time the user shakes the device:

1. We'll use our example project `Dino Stores` that we built at the beginning of the book and make the dinosaurs roar each time they shake our **Shake to Change** gallery. Open the project in iAd Producer now. If you haven't completed the project, you can use the `6.Dino Stores - Store Finder` in the `Dino Stores` exercises folder.

2. Open the **Shake to Change** page on the canvas. From the object library, add an audio object to the canvas and position it off screen so the user won't be able to see it.

3. With the object selected, expand the inspector pane and select **roar-noise.m4a** as the audio clip's file, as shown in the following screenshot:

4. Select the shake view object by clicking on the dinosaur image. Right-click on it and select **Object Events | Did Shake | Execute JavaScript**. This will open the code editor and add a placeholder function for this event.

5. When the shake event occurs, we want our audio object to play, so add this JavaScript to the function:

```
this.viewController.outlets.audio.play();
```

6. This simply gets the audio object from our page and calls its `play` function, which surprisingly will make our audio clip play! Make sure the outlet value in the object's inspector is set to `audio`. It should be this by default if it's the only audio object on the page.

7. Close the code editor and test the ad. Navigate to the **Shake to Change** page then shake the device. You'll hear the dinosaurs roar as the pages change.

What just happened?

By adding an audio object to our page, we can access it through JavaScript using its `outlet` property. We moved the audio object off the canvas, so it's included in the page but not visible to the user, and when the shake event of our shake view occurred, we called the `play` function of the audio object. You might notice a delay the first time the device is shaken as the audio loads, but subsequent shakes will cause the audio to play immediately as the device will cache it. To minimize the delay, keep the audio short and optimized, as obviously, smaller files will play quicker than larger ones.

Tweeting with Twitter

When Apple released iOS 5 in the fall of 2011, they included support for tweeting text, links, and images direct from various parts of the operating system. This **Twitter** support has been extended to our iAds and is a great marketing tool due to its sharing reach.

Twitter is a popular micro-blogging service where users can send small, timely updates, limited to 140 characters to people who follow, or subscribe, to them.

Time for action – tweeting the tweet

As not every device will necessarily be running iOS 5, we'll create a check to ensure that the device supports Twitter, and then let the user tweet and share an update about our brand:

1. Open the `Dino Stores` project we used in the last exercise. We'll add a button to the menu screen that'll open up the Twitter dialog. Open the menu page on the canvas and then drag the button from the object library.

2. Position the menu near the bottom of the page and expand it to fill the width. Update the text with a call to action, such as `Tweet a dino fact!`. Your button may look a little like the following screenshot:

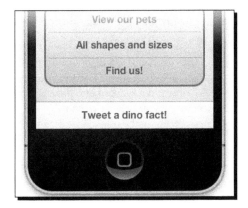

3. Click and select the button, and select **Execute JavaScript** as the **Touched Up Inside** action to create the event and automatically open the code editor.

4. Remove the placeholder comment `//Code here` and replace it with the following code:

```
if (window.ad.twitterComposer) {
        window.ad.twitterComposer.text = 'The longest dinosaur
was Seismosaurus, was as long as five double-decker buses - Dino
Stores';
        window.ad.twitterComposer.URLs = ['http://www.bencollier.
net/'];
        window.ad.twitterComposer.present();
    }
```

5. This checks if the Twitter composer is available and then adds the text and URL that'll compose the tweet. Anything contained in between the curly braces after the `if (window.ad.twitterComposer)` will only run if the Twitter composer object exists. We can now add an `else` block of code that'll run if the Twitter composer is unavailable.

6. Immediately after the code we just added, insert the following:

```
else {
        alert('You need iOS 5 with a Twitter account to send this
tweet');
    }
```

7. This will only run if the earlier check doesn't find the Twitter composer to be available; and will cause an alert to be presented to the user.

8. We can test our ad out, either in the iOS Simulator or on a device. You'll need to make sure your iPhone or iPod is running iOS 5 and that you've configured your Twitter account. When using the simulator, you can change the version of iOS it is running from iAd Producer. From the menu bar, select **Export | Simulator iOS Version | iOS 5.x**. Save your project and click on the **Simulate** button.

 To log in to Twitter on your iOS device or in the simulator, open the **Settings** app and then select **Twitter**. You'll be prompted for your username and password and have the opportunity to create an account, if you haven't already.

9. Clicking on the **Tweet** button will now open up the **Twitter composer** window that we configured:

10. If you see our error alert message appear, make sure you're running iOS 5 with your account configured correctly! You can upgrade your device using iTunes.

What just happened?

Using the Twitter composer, introduced in iOS 5, we tweeted a basic text tweet with a link attached to it. If we tried to access the Twitter composer when our user wasn't on a Twitter-enabled device, our ad would crash. So checking its availability is vital when targeting older versions of iOS.

Have a go hero

If you feel confident with your Twitter code, consider improving it as follows:

- Change the simulator version to a version prior to iOS 5, so you can test the fallback message.

- For the more advanced user, consider hiding the button when the Twitter composer isn't available. We could do this using the page event **viewControllerViewDidAppear**, the `if` statement we used earlier, and setting the `hidden` property of the button outlet to `true`.

The debugger

We're not all perfect, and sometimes we'll make mistakes when writing our JavaScript code; fortunately, iAd Producer has two built-in tools it uses to highlight and discover errors in your code.

Error checking syntax

If you have an error with your code syntax—the rules that define the structure of your code, iAd Producer will prompt you when you try to save that JavaScript file. iAd Producer identifies the line where your error occurs and allows you to save the file anyway (not recommended) or edit it.

General syntactical errors you should check for include:

◆ Forgetting to end a line with a semicolon.

◆ Not separating an object or array values with a comma.

◆ Including a comma on the last item in an array or an object. For example, `['item one', 'item two', last item',]` would be incorrect as there is an extra comma at the end.

◆ Using the incorrect case. JavaScript and its variables are case sensitive, so `thisVariable` and `ThisVARIABLE` are considered two separate values.

◆ Forgetting to close a bracket or brace.

Using the debugger

If your code is syntactically correct but has errors when it's running, the debugger window will appear and highlight the line of code where the error occurred. For example, if we try and access a variable that we haven't assigned a value to, we might find the debugger showing a warning of accessing an undefined function or value.

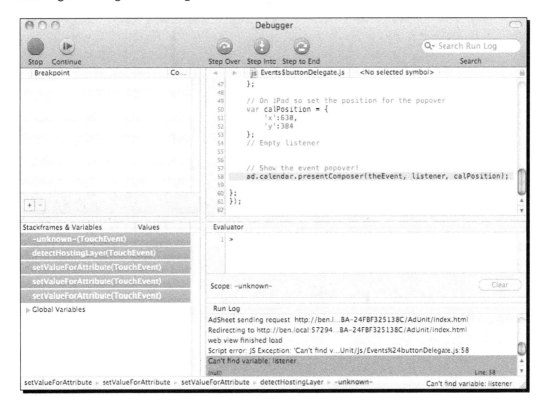

If you're familiar with development, you can set breakpoints to pause your ad at certain parts of your code. To set these, just double-click on the line number of the line you'd like to pause at. You can then use the **continue** button in iAd Producer to resume the execution of the JavaScript.

Coding conventions

When you're writing JavaScript code, you should make sure it complies with some basic rules and best practices used by developers:

- Name the start variables with lowercase by using camel case, which we looked at earlier in the chapter. Variable names should be verbose and relevant to the data they hold.

- Comment your code so it's understandable to you when you revisit the code, and clear for other developers that may look at it in the future.

- End each statement with a semicolon.

- Code within functions should be indented from the edge using the *Tab* key or four spaces. Notice how the second example is more readable and clear:

```
23  // this is wrong!
24
25  function someFunction () {
26  var upClose = false;
27  }
28
29  // this is right!
30
31  function someFunction () {
32      var upClose = false;
33  }
```

Have a go hero

Having learnt some example code snippets, the style that your code should be, and how to identify and fix errors in your code, you could add some enhanced functionality to the other example projects we've created so far. You could:

- Add an audio clip to your shake view in the `Coffee Beans` project

- Add multiple event buttons to the upcoming **Events** page in the `Cloud 9 - iPad` project, each creating calendar events with different times and details

- This should show you how multiple event functions can exist within one page's JavaScript file

 You may want to consider renaming your button outlets when you have multiple buttons on screen. This will make navigating between the functions in your JavaScript file easier.

- Read the Apple documentation to find out the other possibilities of JavaScript in your iAd, available at `http://developer.apple.com`
- Create an entirely new ad for your own product or brand, using a variety of techniques that you've learnt so far

Summary

JavaScript is an incredibly powerful and versatile language, which, coupled with the iAd JS framework, can create some amazingly dynamic and rich ads. In this chapter, we've only brushed upon the potential of expanding our iAds with simple code snippets that have allowed us to:

- Edit values of objects that aren't exposed to us in the iAd Producer inspector pane
- Add events to the user's calendar and continue to remind them of us once they've left our ad
- Send e-mails with dynamic content to let users contact us
- Use the code editor and debugger to catch common errors

With our adverts looking great, having rich interactivity, and giving our users memorable experiences, let's take a look at the logistics of managing a successful iAd campaign.

9

Managing a Successful iAd Campaign

You're able to make an awesome iAd that will amaze your audience on iPhone and iPad. Now you'll need to know how to manage a successful campaign that reaches your target demographic, comes within budget, and has a quantifiable way of measuring success.

In this chapter, we'll look at the skills you'll need to ensure that you get the most out of your iAd campaign, such as the following:

◆ Targeting your ad at specific audiences

◆ Understanding pricing models and costs

◆ Reporting and analytics on a user's interactions within your ad

◆ Taking your ad live and the final pre-submission checks

Finding your audience

With iAd we're able to run campaigns that require the user, or the context your ad appears in, to meet a specific group of criteria so you can target your iAd at your ideal audience.

Finding your target audience can be complicated, as there are many influencing factors on who could be interested in your product or brand.

Your target market may not necessarily be who you'd expect it to be or who you'd like it to be! So, make sure you're aware of whom you should be targeting before you launch your campaign.

If you've got an existing customer base, you can profile them to identify trends and common interests; consider giving customers short surveys and asking them questions, or holding focus groups. Although finding your target market is important, make sure that you don't annoy your existing customer base when trying to glean information from them!

You may want to adapt your market research once you know what targeting options are available to you. Let's take a look at the different types of targeting.

Targeting

With a clear market highlighted, you'll be able to tailor and customize your campaign to maximize its efficiency. This will increase the value of your iAd impressions, by gaining more useful user engagement, and by targeting the relevant demographics that are likely to be interested in your ad and brand. Ads can be targeted with contextual or behavioral data to reach the most likely audience that will be interested and engaged with your iAd.

Contextual advertising

Contextual advertising assumes an advert is relevant because the context it appears in must be of interest to the user as they're viewing or using it. The best example of contextual advertising are sponsored links on websites. They generally analyze the content of a page and try to pick up on the general theme or context by finding common keywords.

The following screenshot shows an example website with advertisements being placed using contextual targeting. When the page loads, it examines the general content of the page and picks out common words and themes, and fetches any ads it thinks might be relevant from the ad network:

You'll find they're often not perfect; for example, a site that mentions rock several times may generate adverts about both AC/DC and the next public convention about the unexpected igneous formations found in South Dakota.

Behavioral targeting

Behavioral targeting analyzes and builds up a profile of users based on their actions, which the advertising network has access to. The user's web journeys can be tracked as they visit different sites or make searches to find trends, which the ad network can then collate and use to make an educated guess of the user's demographic and interests.

Advertising networks especially use behavioral targeting, because they're able to track a user as they navigate between sites on their ad network. For example, if a user goes onto a site about scuba diving, then a hotel site, and finally an airline booking page—it's likely that he is going on holiday. The ad provider then takes this assumption and starts displaying adverts on non-holiday related sites about taking a trip. It uses similar techniques to contextual targeting to highlight the keywords on a page and gauge a common theme.

Advertising networks use controversial **tracking cookies**—a small file saved on your computer to save anonymous session and state data. Cookies are usually used to keep you logged in to websites or remember what's in your shopping cart, but advertisers can use the same technique to anonymously identify a visitor from site to site.

iAd targeting

iAd uses a combination of contextual advertising with behavioral targeting to help you find the most relevant and valuable audience for your iAd. Your ad can specify what categories of apps it will appear in or target the user's general preference of app categories.

Thanks to Apple's profiling of a user with their iTunes store account and device information, we're able to target our campaigns with the following user behaviors and information:

- Demographics
- Application preferences
- Music passions
- Movie, TV, and audiobook genre interests
- Location
- Device (iPhone, iPad, and iPod touch)
- Network (Wi-Fi and 3G)

With demographics, you're able to target by groups of people, with the ability to filter users by age, sex, and other information, anonymously available on their iTunes profiles. Location is ideal when you don't have a global brand presence because you're able to target by country or region. If you're selling digital goods within your app, you should only target countries where you app or content is available.

Application preferences use the download history of a user to estimate what category of apps they're interested in. This, combined with music, movie, TV interests, and some assumptions, can be a great way of finding users that match your ideal customer.

You'll have to liaise with your iAd Agent to set up and tweak your campaign and contact them early to discuss and get their feedback on the standard targeting they will be able to provide for your campaign.

Pricing models

With television and radio advertising, we're unsure about how engaged a viewer or listener is with our campaign; their attention could be (and often is) elsewhere. With iAd, we're almost guaranteed the user is immersed with our content, as they've opted to interact with it. This makes the cost per engagement with iAd more valuable. Typically, you'll find that you pay more for advertisements that target more popular demographics, but how this is measured and charged to you depends on the pricing model used.

Mobile advertising follows an advertising model similar to the Internet channels that you may be familiar with. If you aren't, or want a refresher, we'll take a look at the current models and a world of acronyms.

Cost per Millie (CPM)

Cost per Millie (CPM) is where you pay for impressions of your advertisement. Millie is Latin for thousand, therefore CPM is what it costs to show your ad banner or link to 1000 viewers.

 CPM is often confused with Cost per Million. Make sure you don't confuse it or else your campaign will appear much cheaper than it is! Sometimes CPM is referred to as CPI or Cost Per Impression.

CPM is the most common pricing model in advertising, because it is easily mapped to traditional print or TV advertising, in which copies sold or ratings would be used to determine the effective number of eyeballs viewing the ad. **Eyeballs** is the term coined by the advertising industry for viewers of their advertisements. With iAd, we refer to people interacting with our ads as users, because they're more important and engaged than a basic viewer, thanks to iAd's compelling ads. With CPM, you're paying to show the viewer your banner, regardless of whether they decide to click or tap on it.

We can calculate the cost per impression of our ad by taking the CPM price and dividing it by 1000. For example, a campaign with a CPM which costs $20 would represent a fee of $0.02 every time a user views your ad's banner.

Pay per Click (PPC)

I'm sure in time we'll call this pay per tap, but in this model, you pay whenever a user clicks the link to your website or taps the banner of your ad. The **Cost per Click (CPC)** is the average of how much each click (or tap) will cost you. No matter how many impressions your banner receives, you only have to pay whenever your banner is tapped and your ad opened. Paying per click can be more valuable than CPM, as you only have to pay when a user shows an interest and taps your banner to begin engaging with your brand.

There are two sub-pricing models with pay per click, either flat rate or bid-based.

Flat rate PPC

Flat rate pay per click uses a preagreed rate between the advertiser (you) and the publisher (say, Apple). With flat rate, you'll know exactly how much every tap of your banner will cost you.

For example, if your PPC rate is $1.50, and 1000 users tap your banner, you'll have to pay $1500, regardless of how many impressions your banner receives.

Bid PPC

With **Bid pay per click**, you partake in a bidding war with other advertisers for the banner slot. You decide the maximum you're willing to pay per click, and the publishing network picks the highest bidder more often when displaying banners. You still only have to pay when a user clicks your banner, not per impression.

If you're willing to pay more per click, then the ad network is more likely to show your banner over a competing banner. You'll usually only pay a little over the bidder below you, instead of your maximum bid price.

With a maximum bid of $2 per click, receiving 1000 clicks could cost anything from $10 to $2000.

Bid pay per click can be cost effective when you're targeting niche markets that have few competing advertisers in them.

Cost per Action (CPA)

Cost per Action(CPA) is similar to PPC, but this time, you're paying for a conversion or action from the user. This could be paying to get more fans on Facebook, more followers on Twitter, or sign-ups to your mailing list.

For example, if you're willing to pay $0.50 every time a user downloads your $2.99 app from your ad, achieving 1000 sales would cost you $500.

iAd's pricing model

iAd uses a mixed model, where you pay for a set number of impressions and additionally pay per tap/click for opening your ad. This is effectively a flat rate PPC combined with a CPM.

You can expect to pay a CPM of around $10, that's $0.01 per banner impression, and a PPC of approximately $2.00. To get details on pricing and minimum campaign commitments contact Apple at `http://advertising.apple.com`, as prices significantly vary from campaign to campaign and the scale of your brand.

With iAd for Developers, the scheme from Apple where they provide the basic iAd to advertise an app available on the App Store, Apple usually operates an exclusive CPC model. Only paying for clicks and not impressions reduces the barrier of entry and the CPC is approximately $0.25. However, you're unable to modify the iAd Developer ad template beyond the banner so your ads will lack such a compelling experience compared to your iAd Producer ads.

Measuring success

iAd Producer has an inbuilt analytic logging system, which by default, monitors and captures anonymous user data. This data is sent to the iAd Network, where Apple collates it to generate rich reports that you can access to monitor the engagement and success of your ad.

By default, iAd Producer enables logging on live ads, but we're able to view the raw data of our development ads and tweak it to provide an even deeper analysis of our iAd project.

Time for action – viewing the logs

When we're developing our ad, we're able to view what logs will be sent to the iAd Network using a couple of lines of JavaScript. To view the logs, follow the ensuing steps:

1. Open an existing project in iAd Producer. In this example, we'll be using the Dino Stores iPhone iAd that we'd been working on earlier in this book.

2. We need to enable certain objects and pages for analytic events. This means our analytics only contains the meaningful data we choose. Open the **Menu** page on the ad canvas and expand the inspector pane. Click on **Analytics** to expand it and tick the **Log Analytics Events** box. The **Log ID** is auto-generated from the page name. So, if you've been giving your pages meaningful names, you probably won't have to change it. You can see the **Analytics** section in the following screenshot:

3. The **Analytics** section of the inspector pane also appears when you've selected an individual object, so you're able to make certain objects active within a page to generate logging events.

4. Return to the ad overview and select **Code | Project Events**, followed by **Execute JavaScript**, and finally, **adDidFinishLaunching**, from the menu bar. This will open the code editor with a placeholder function. Replace the //code here comment with the following line:

```
iAd.Analytics.sharedObject.logsToConsole = true;
```

5. This tells the iAd's built-in analytics to show up in the debugging console, so that we can preview what kind of data is being logged.

6. Open the **Debugger** window by choosing **Code | Show Debugger**, from the menu bar.

7. Open the ad in the iOS Simulator by clicking on the **Simulate** button in the main iAd Producer window.

8. Bring the iAd Producer **Debugger** window into focus and look at the **Run Log** pane, as you interact with your advert. You might want to reposition the iOS Simulator and the **Debugger** window, so that you're able to see both at once, as highlighted in the following screenshot:

9. We can see the logs here; for example, look at the following log snippet:

```
iAd Content: [ANALYTICS]: {"v":"1.4.1","1324329243506":{"an":"tran
sition","at":"view","as":"Menu"}}
```

10. This shows the event of the `Menu view` controller appearing. Don't worry that this isn't particularly readable. This is the data sent to Apple, who will process and collate it into more understandable information.

11. Now go through the rest of your iAd project, enabling analytics for any remaining objects and all the pages that you'd like to track. Typically, you'd want to log as many events as you can. Try interacting with different objects and seeing the events that they generate.

Make sure that you disable this logging before taking your ad live. Once live, your ad will always submit this logging data. This flag merely causes the logs to appear in the debugger. Each time a log appears in the debugger, there's a small performance cost, which is why we should remove unnecessary logs before submission. To disable the logging either remove the code that we added or change the `true` to `false`.

What just happened?

Using the default logging in iAd Producer, we previewed the information that Apple records and sends to the iAd Network for us to view later. This high level of event logging means that we can gain insights into the most interesting and popular sections of our ad and brand.

Customizing the logs

While the default logging provided by iAd Producer is comprehensive and useful, we're able to modify its behavior to better suit our ad. For example, out-of-the-box iAd Producer won't log our custom event functions, but that's easy to fix.

Time for action – customizing the logs

We'll customize our log messages to ensure that they're logical and understandable when we later come to analyze them. In order to customize the logs, follow the ensuing steps:

1. We'll need an iAd Producer project that contains custom events. For this exercise, let's use the `Coffee Beans` ad that we made earlier.

2. Select an object that has custom events set, for example, the **Tell a Friend** button on the menu page of our Coffee Beans project. Open the inspector pane, and expand the **Properties** and **Analytics** sections. Update the **Outlet** name to something meaningful, such as tellAFriend.

 Notice that we're using the camel case naming convention for the outlet name. Because outlets are exposed in JavaScript, we should follow the same conventions as if we were writing JavaScript directly.

3. Now, tick the box **Log Events**, to enable logging for this object:

4. You'll need to do this for every custom object that you want to track data for. Turn on the logging to console analytics option (just as we did in the previous exercise), and you'll see the events for the button appear in the debugger:

```
[ANALYTICS]: {"v":1.4,"1310344477450":{"s":"12","n":"controlTouchU
pInside","t":"iAd.Button","as":"tellAFriend","an":"tap","at":"gest
ure"}}
```

5. Here, we can see the `controlTouchUpInside` event being called.

> Because the iOS Simulator doesn't support the smsComposer function, we may need to add the following line to our `touchUpInside` event:
>
> ```
> //Feature detect to stop an ad crash
> in simulator & iPod touch
>
> If (window.ad.smsComposer ===
> undefined) return;
> ```

What just happened?

We enabled the analytics logging of a custom object that we added to our canvas. iAd Producer doesn't do this by default, so make sure you check whether each interactive object you want to generate logs for has this checked. We modified the ID used in the logs to a value, which will be more understandable and useful when it reaches the iAd Network and appears in the reports.

With this vast amount of data being collected and processed, it can be difficult to separate and identify common areas. Fortunately, we can group our iAd analytics into sections.

Time for action – using sections

iAd Producer lets us segment our analytics into sections, to make it easier to separate the results. You're able to do this without having to modify any JavaScript:

1. Open the project that you'd like to set up sections for in iAd Producer. We'll continue with the `Coffee Beans` ad we used in the last exercise.

2. From the ad overview, click on a page, such as **Wallpaper Picker**, and expand the **Analytics** section of the inspector pane. Click on the **Section** drop-down menu, and then select **Manage Sections**.

3. Click on the **+** button near the bottom left of the pop-over menu that appears, and enter the text for your section, say Downloadable Content.

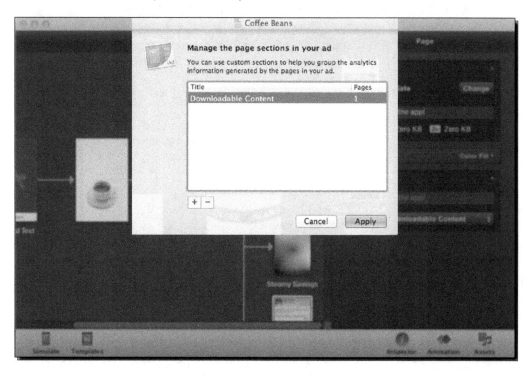

4. Choose **Apply** to close the menu. Now, reselect the drop-down for **Section** and set the section to **Downloadable Content**, for the selected page.

3. Select another related page, say Get the App, from the ad overview, and also set its section to **Downloadable Content**.

> You don't need to apply a section to every page, only to those you want to group when analyzing in the reports.

5. Turn on the logging (see the last exercise) and open your page in the iOS Simulator. You'll notice that any logs generated by the page, including object-specific events, will be grouped in the section you set up:

```
[ANALYTICS]: {"v":1.4,"1310510020556":{"s":"8","n":"viewController
ViewDidAppear","t":"iAP.ViewController","as":"GetTheApp","an":"tra
nsition","at":"view","k":"Downloadable Content"}}
```

6. Notice that the **Downloadable Content** section now appears in the request sent to the iAd Network.

What just happened?

Using the **Sections** field in the **Analytics** options of iAd Producer, we set up a section for our downloadable content on two of our ad's pages. This means any analytics logging generated by these pages, such as it coming into view or the user interacting with the content, will be filterable in the iAd reporting interface. While sections might not seem necessary or too powerful in smaller ads, when you start pushing the boundaries of iAd Producer with hidden navigation and advanced page structures, it'll quickly become vital.

This data is collected and collated by Apple and is available in reports. You'll need to contact your iAd Account Manager for information on how to access this. By grouping data into sections, analyzing the popular and engaging parts of your ad can be made much easier. You can map trends, and tweak and update your ad and campaign to match these responses. For example, if you notice more people using your store finder than your e-mail sharing feature, you could put more emphasis on the store finder or even consider opening additional stores in popular areas.

Pop quiz– naming your ad's sections

Choosing a good analytics naming convention is vital, because once you've decided on a pattern, changing it can be problematic, as you won't be able to map it against existing data. See if you can decide the best naming conventions. Remember these are only suggestions, and there isn't strictly a right answer!

1. You have a store finder page and a gallery in your ad; would you:

    a. Do nothing; there are only two pages in the ad, so no sections are needed.

    b. Name the store finder section `Contacting Us` and the gallery `Galleries`.

    c. Categorize both pages under a **Sub-Pages** section.

    d. Add a **Shops** and an **Images** section.

2. Take our `Coffee Beans` example project that we worked on earlier. It has an informative page about coffee, a wallpaper picker, an interactive coupon, a store finder, and an in-ad app download. How could you group these with sections?

    a. Give each page a section so they're easy to separate and identify.

    b. There are so many pages that trying to group them would be pointless.

    c. Use `User Actions` for any pages that is the user actioning on our product, such as the store finder or downloading an in-ad app, and `Information` for informative pages like the process of roasting a coffee bean.

    d. Separate pages by their content type; for example, group the coffee bean process and wallpaper picker into an `Image Rich` section and the map into a `Mapping` section.

Have a go hero – analytics

Analytics are vital for measuring the success of your iAd campaign, so make sure that you include them as part of your strategy. You should:

◆   Try out analytics in other ads that you've made.

◆   See what analytics are being produced for each of your ad's pages. You may find the need to rename objects and pages, so that they make more sense when processing them later. You'll find that the default names provided by iAd Producer aren't incredibly useful.

 Make sure object and page names will be understandable outside of the ad; for example, name a button for sharing your ad `tellAFriend` instead of `button1`.

◆   Add `custom` sections to pages of your ads to group similar data together. Take the time to think about your sections, as this feature can be a valuable tool.

Going live

With your ad looking amazing, and a clear understanding of the pricing model and how much your ad will cost to run, we're able to take the final steps to take our iAd live on the iAd Network.

Whenever you're testing an ad using iAd Producer's local sharing, you're previewing the development code, which differs from the optimized code used by ads served by the iAd Network. In rare cases, optimizing code can introduce bugs, so it's a great idea to use the optimized export option as a final test before uploading your ad to the iAd test server.

To export an optimized version of your ad, select **Export | Export to Disk (Optimized)**, from the iAd Producer menu bar. If you can't remember how to export and transfer your optimized ads to your device, refer back to *Chapter 4, Making Sure It Works*.

Here, we can see the unoptimized, exported source code of one of our project's map views:

```
js Bookaflight$mapViewDelegate.js

   js BookaflightSmapViewDelegate.js

 1  iAP.EventDelegate.registerViewEventDelegate('mapView', 'Bookaflight',
    function() {
 2  this.onDidReceiveResponseData = function (event) {
 3
 4      var mapElement, collection, nodes, node, annotations, savedValues,
    len, i;
 5
 6      mapElement = event.ad.sender.mapElement;
 7      collection =
    event.ad.responseXML.getElementsByTagName('StoreLocations')[0];
 8      nodes = collection.childNodes;
 9
10      // Check for nodes:
11      if (!nodes) {
12          return;
13      }
14
15      // Collect an array of iAP.MapAnnotations:
16      annotations = [];
17      for (i=0, len = nodes.length; i<len; i+=1) {
18
19          // Use an XML node of type 'Element':
20          node = nodes[i];
21          if (node.nodeType !== 1) {
22              continue;
```

When you export an optimized version of your ad iAd Producer, uses several techniques to reduce the size of your ad and increase the efficiency of your iAd, such as:

◆ **Removing unnecessary whitespace**: While the spaces in your code make it more readable, they waste bandwidth when transferring your ad wirelessly to the user.

◆ **Changing variable names to single characters**: Again, just like with whitespace, using readable names isn't required by machines, so we can reduce the bytes sent to the user by replacing them with shorter names. For example, `myLongVariableName` would get renamed to `a`, saving approximately 17 bytes whenever your ad is transferred.

◆ **Combining files**: Fetching each file from the iAd Network has an extra overhead, while the device and servers communicate with each other. Your optimized ads combine several files into one to reduce this.

You may remember that we used an **image sprite,** in an earlier chapter, to reduce the requests to the server by combining lots of images into one large image, then only showing the required parts at any time.

◆ **Creating a manifest file**: A manifest file is part of the HTML5 spec and tells the device which files to prefetch and cache, to ensure that your ad transitions smoothly from page to page, without the user having to wait for additional content to load. The caching should improve the experience for users on intermitted connections, as the iAd framework will try to download resources whenever a connection is available.

Here, we can see the optimized source code for our project's map page, after these techniques have been applied:

```
js BookaflightDelegate.js

◀  ▶   js BookaflightDelegate.js   ▲▼
 1  iAP.EventDelegate.registerViewEventDelegate("mapView","Bookaflight",functio
    n(){this.onDidReceiveResponseData=function(a){var
    j,f,b,d,g,c,h,e;j=a.ad.sender.mapElement;f=a.ad.responseXML.getElementsByTa
    gName("StoreLocations")[0];b=f.childNodes;if(!b){return}
    g=[];for(e=0,h=b.length;e<h;e+=1){d=b[e];if(d.nodeType!==1){continue}
    c={};Array.prototype.map.call(d.childNodes,function(i){if(i.nodeType!==1)
    {return}if(i.childNodes.length===0){return}
    c[i.nodeName]=i.childNodes[0].nodeValue});if(c.street&&c.city)
    {c.address=c.street+" "+c.city;if(c.state){c.address+=", "+c.state}
    if(c.zip){c.address+=" "+c.zip}}
    c.listener=this;c.customPinImage=this.pinImage;c.xOffset=this.pinOffsetX;c.
    yOffset=this.pinOffsetY;if(c.name&&(!c.title)){c.title=c.name}if(c.title!
    =null){g.push(iAP.MapAnnotation(c))}}
    j.addAnnotations(g)};this.onAnnotationCalloutTapped=function(c){var
    b=c.ad.sender;var
    a=b.mapElement.getAnnotationById(c.ad.annotationId);iAd.ViewController.inst
    ances.MapDetail.annotation=a;this.viewController.transitionToViewController
    WithID("MapDetail")}});
```

It's important to validate your ad before submission. This will highlight any issues with assets or content, within your iAd. To validate your ad, you'll need to select **Export | Show Project Warnings**. We looked at fixing any issues in *Chapter 4, Making Sure It Works*; check back there if your project has any warnings that you're unsure about.

After you've tested and validated your ad, the next step is to submit the ad to the iAd Network for approval and publication. To submit your ad to the iAd Network, you'll need to contact your iAd Agent to activate your account for live submissions and provide you with submission instructions.

Once you have committed to your iAd campaign, you should contact Apple to begin setting up your iAd account and get more information about the costs, estimated impressions, and clicks your campaign should be expected to generate.

Have a go hero – test submission

Take one of your existing projects and simulate taking it live. You could:

◆ Fix up and validation warnings

◆ Run your images through the optimization process once more, in case any got skipped as you developed your ad

◆ Optimize images multiple times, without risking degradation in quality, because we're using lossless optimization techniques

◆ Export and test the optimized version of your ad

◆ Test this on as many devices and different iOS versions as you may want to check performance on

◆ Liaise with your iAd Agent to enable your account for the iAd Test Server

◆ You should test using a variety of network connections to ensure your media content adapts correctly, depending on available bandwidth

 The iAd Test Server gives you a real-world testing environment, which mimics the live servers Apple will use to distribute your final ad.

◆ Get the ad signed off with your management team to highlight any issues they may have with the campaign

Tracking the campaign

Once you have gone live, you'll need to analyze the reports generated by the analytics, along with the cost of your campaign. Campaign costs are the combined CPC and CPM from your ad. Apple shows you these broken down on a day-to-day basis.

Here's an example report for a campaign that has been running for three days:

Day	Ad Spend	Impressions	Clicks	CTR
08/16	$345	351,512	31,328	8.91%
08/17	$500	483,332	51,889	10.73%
08/18	$489	411,515	48,947	11.89%

Ad Spend is the combined CPC and CPM cost for a day. You're able to set a limit for the maximum daily amount that you're willing to spend. Once your daily limit has been reached, your ads won't be delivered by the network until the next calendar day.

Impressions and **Clicks** are the number of times your banner appears in an app and the number of user's that have clicked your banner to explore the core ad experience, respectively.

Click-Through Rate (CTR) can be calculated by working out the percentage of impressions that resulted in the user tapping your banner and viewing your ad. If you have a low CTR, say under 5 percent, you should consider making your banner more compelling, to entice more users to tap it, or tuning your ads targeting to reach a market more interested audience.

As with most aspects of your live campaign, your iAd Account Agent is your key contact to advise and help you adapt your ad strategy for optimal success on the iAd Network.

Summary

Now, not only can you make amazing ads, you can make sure they're successful by:

- Finding and targeting the right audience
- Tracking the users of your ad and highlighting popular sections
- Ensuring your ad is optimized for the iAd Network
- Evaluating costs and maximizing your campaign efficiency

With the skills to make, manage, and monitor a successful campaign, you're now an iAd master! Good luck! As you've learned the rich interactive nature of iAds that can create unobtrusive revenue streams within applications, let's take a look at adding them into your own apps.

10
Adding iAds into Your App

Now that we've seen how awesome iAds can be for your brand, we'll take a look at adding them into your existing application to add an additional revenue stream.

In this chapter, you'll learn how to:

- ◆ Set up an empty placeholder iPhone application, in case you don't currently have an app and its source code
- ◆ Add the iAd banner view to an application
- ◆ Update the banner to handle device rotations
- ◆ Hide the banner when no adverts are available

If you haven't created an iPhone application before or don't have experience with iOS development, don't worry; we'll give you the full code required to add this into an app. In fact, you're able to add the basic iAd banner into an app without any programming experience at all. With that said, the less adventurous may prefer to pass this information onto their app development team.

Setting up the base project

If you've not already got an application but would still like to try adding iAd into an app, we can make a quick single-screen placeholder iPhone project that'll be ready to have a banner added to it.

We'll be using Xcode; we installed this in *Chapter 4, Making Sure it Works*, when we set up the iOS Simulator, so you should have it available (if not, then jump back and set it up now).

If you don't want to set up the demo app, you can find the completed placeholder project with the book assets in the `iAd Demo App` folder.

Time for action – a placeholder app

Using Xcode and its inbuilt interface builder and the drag-and-drop UI designer, we'll make a single screen iPhone application with some mock components to simulate an app:

1. Open Xcode. If you haven't used it before, you can find it in the `Applications` folder, which is in the `Developer` folder on the root directory of your Mac.

This differs from the `Applications` folder that iAd Producer is in. If you can't find Xcode, then use the search function in finder to locate it.

2. Xcode will open the **Welcome to Xcode** window. From here, select **Create a New Xcode Project**. When asked to choose a project type, click on **View Based Application | Continue**.

3. You'll need to enter a **Product Name** (this is what you want to call your application) and a **Company Identifier** (this is usually your website URL reversed). For example, use `Demo iAd App` as the name and `com.examplecompany` as the identifier.

_4._ Ensure that the **Device Family** is **iPhone** and deselect **Include Unit Tests**. When your Xcode window looks similar to the following screenshot, click on the **Next** button:

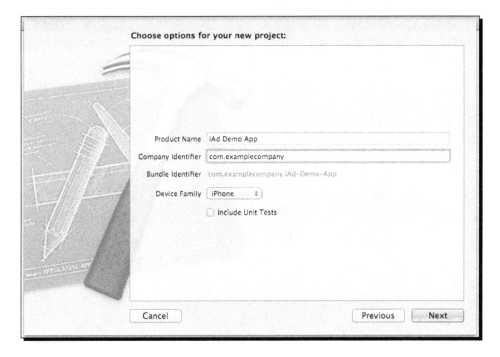

_5._ Choose a location to save your project and the associated files and then click on **Create**.

_6._ Wait while Xcode sets up your project. It will create several files and folders within the directory you chose to save the project. Once the Xcode window has loaded, locate the file `iAd_Demo_AppViewController.xib` from the Xcode project navigator. The project navigator is a pane located to the left of Xcode. If you can't see it, select **View | Navigation | Show Project Navigator** in the Xcode menu bar.

7. This opens the XIB file—think of this file as a page in your iAd. It'll open in the Xcode interface builder. The interface builder is like the canvas in iAd Producer; you're able to drop objects from a library to build up your page. To add an object to our canvas, known as a view, open the object library by selecting **View | Activities | Object Library**. A pane will expand on the right of Xcode and you'll find the object library located at the bottom of it:

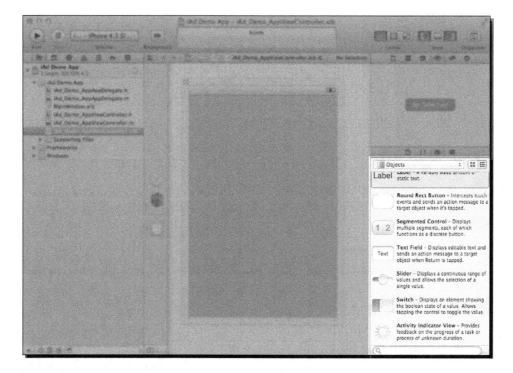

8. Here we can see a list of available user interface components, which we can add to our view. Find a label and drag it onto the view.

You'll notice that many of these controls are just like iAd Producer. That's because Apple has tried to keep parity between many of the objects on iOS to reduce the barrier of entry and the learning curve.

9. Double-click on the label to edit its text. Change the text to something like Apps With iAd Rock! and then click outside the label to exit the editing mode. If you want to change the style of your label, you can use the attributes inspector, which behaves similarly to the properties and styles in iAd Producer. You can find the attribute inspector above the object library. Add a few more objects, such as a button, a switch, a slider, and a text field. Position these on the view, but leave space near the bottom. This is where our banner will appear later.

10. Your view could look something like this:

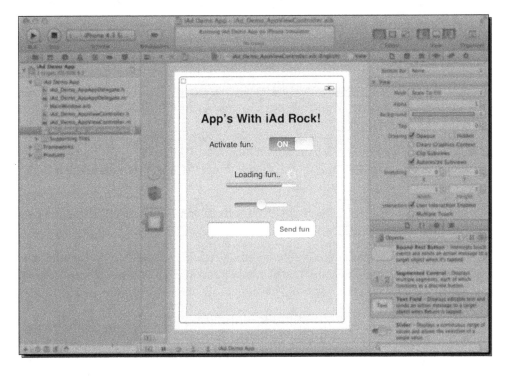

11. Really, it doesn't matter how you make this page look; it's just so we have some context when we add our banner in the next exercise.

12. Finally, we can run our app in the simulator. Select the **Run** button (with a play icon) from the top left of Xcode and the simulator should open. You should be able to toggle the switch and move the sliders around. Whenever you run a project, Xcode builds the app and automatically saves all the files.

What just happened?

We created a view-based application from the Xcode templates that gives us a single view app with a blank view to which we're able to add objects. We added some objects to the view so we have some content available when we run the app. With our view layout complete in the interface builder of Xcode, we simulated the app to see how it behaved.

Testing the iAd on the device requires you to register it with Apple to provision and enable it for development. This requires an active paid developer membership, which we signed up to in *Chapter 1, Getting Started with iAd*, to gain access to iAd Producer.

Time for action – running on the device

If you haven't configured your device for development, we can use Xcode's organizer tool to log in to the Apple provisioning portal and set up the required certificates and register your device:

1. Open Xcode, if it isn't already. Select **Window** | **Organizer** from the menu bar. This will open the organizer that allows us to manage our iOS devices, their provisioning, and app submissions.

2. Now plug an iOS device in, such as an iPhone or iPad. If it's syncing with iTunes, wait for it to finish. Make sure that the **device** tab of the organizer is selected and find your device in the list to the left.

3. Select the device and click on the **Use for Development** button to allow it to be set up for development.

4. Once the device has been configured locally, select the **+ Add to Portal** button to contact the Apple developer portal that will set up your device. Enter the **Username** and **Password** for your Apple ID/developer account:

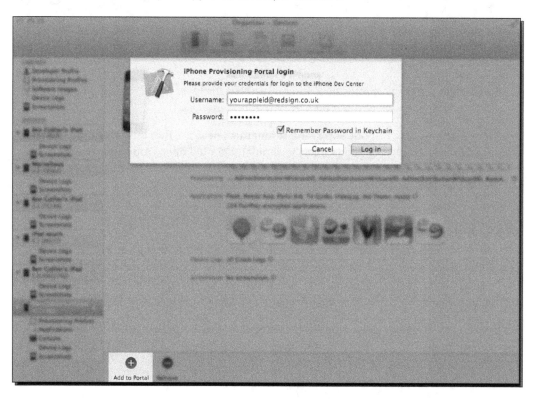

5. The organizer will now talk to Apple and enable Xcode on your device to interact. Once this has completed, your Mac will be able to send builds to the device.

6. Close the organizer window and change the device **Scheme** to `Your Device Name` from the drop-down selector next to the **Run** and **Stop** buttons. Xcode will build your app and you should see it running on your device shortly after.

What just happened?

Xcode automatically added your device to the provisioning portal, which you can view and manage at `http://developer.apple.com`. When adding a device to the portal, Xcode carries out the following steps:

◆ Submits the **Unique Device Identifier** (**UDID**) to the Apple provisioning portal.

◆ Adds the device to your registered devices list, which is linked to your developer account. Each account can add up to 100 devices.

◆ Creates and installs certificates on your behalf, which are used to secure the builds so only you can make them.

◆ Generates and sets up a development **provisioning profile**—this tells the device if it's allowed to run an app or not. A provisioning profile contains a list of UDIDs for each device, which is entitled to run the associated app.

 You'll need to repeat this process for each device that you want to test on and it's specific to the Mac user account. If you switch machines, you'll need to reconfigure Xcode and follow these steps again.

With our demo app in place and running on the simulator and device, we can add our first iAd banner to it!

Adding the banner to your view

We're able to add the iAd banner to a view of your app using the interface builder. It's a simple drag-and-drop to get the basic banner functionality.

Time for action – adding the banner

We'll add an iAd banner into the placeholder app that we built in the last exercise. If you want to use your own app make sure you're familiar with the interface builder in Xcode. Follow these steps in order to add the banner:

1. Open your project, or our demo project in Xcode.

2. From the file list, open the file `iAd_Demo_AppViewController.xib`, if it isn't already. This will launch the interface builder. From the object library, drag the **Ad BannerView** object to the main view. The object library contains a large amount of items that can make it hard to navigate. You can use the search text area underneath it to filter results. Searching for a banner reveals any banner-related objects. In the following screenshot, you can see a search for **banner**:

3. Reposition your banner view so it snaps into place at the bottom center of the screen.

4. Apple recommends putting your banner at the top or bottom of your app and making sure it is static; putting it in scrollable views or lists limits the on-screen time of the banner, which will severely impact the revenue generated by your campaign. Try to run your app using the **Run** button or the keyboard shortcut *cmd + r*. You'll find that the app crashes before it's able to start up. This is due to there being a dependency of the banner view that we'll need to include. An iAd banner requires the iAd framework to be included with our application.

5. To add the iAd framework, click on the name of your project in the project navigator pane on the left of Xcode. If you're using the demo project, this will be `iAd Demo Project` and can be found at the very top of the project navigator. This will open the info of your project in the main Xcode window. Select your project name under **TARGETS** and change the tab to **Build Phases**.

6. Expand the **Link Binaries With Libraries** section and click on the **+** button at the bottom of the section to open the library/framework picker. Search for `iAd` and select **iAd.framework**. Then click on **add**.

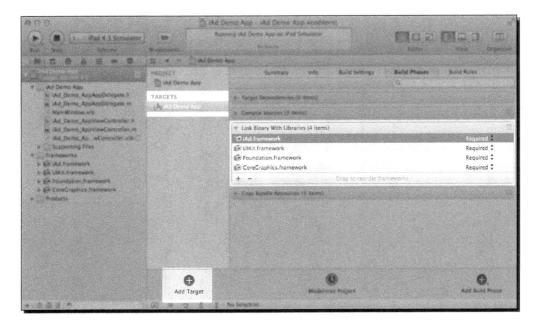

7. From the project navigator file list, drag the **iAd.framework** file to the `Frameworks` folder. You don't have to do this step, but it helps keep your project tidy.

8. Run your app. You should see the test banner appear after a few seconds. Try tapping it to open the demo advertisement.

9. Great work! Your project now successfully has an iAd in it!

What just happened?

We just added the Ad BannerView object to our app's view and positioned it at the bottom center of the screen. Using the build phases, a list of steps called when building and running the app, we added the iAd framework to be sure it's available in our app. We had to add the `iAd.framework` to our app's project or else the banner view wouldn't be able to access the correct components and cause the app to crash.

When an app is in debug or development mode, the iAd Network automatically serves a test advertisement. This is to prevent **click fraud**, where artificial clicks (or taps) are generated to cheat the system and falsely increase revenue:

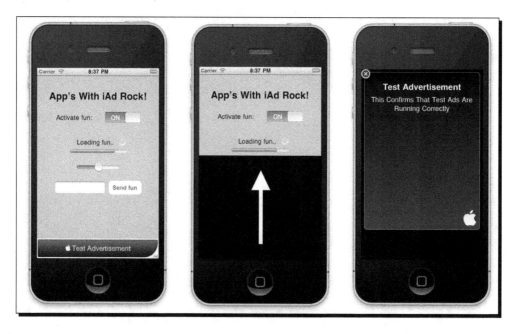

Before you submit your application to the App Store, we need to enable our ads for production. We'll do this in the next chapter, but first let's look at improving our banner experience within the app.

Handling orientation changes

You may remember that when we built banners in iAd Producer, we checked whether they worked in both portrait and landscape; however, currently, our demo app only works in portrait. Making sure your app displays banners in any orientation will ensure that you get maximum exposure and revenue from the iAd Network.

Time for action – you spin me right round

If you're using the demo app, then let's enable all the possible orientations. Make sure our banner adjusts itself accordingly:

1. Open the demo app in Xcode. If you're using your own app that already supports multiple orientations, skip ahead to step 4.

2. To enable our app to know it should spin the view when the device is rotated, we need to modify a simple bit of Objective C. Open the file `iAd_Demo_AppViewController.m` from the project navigator; you'll see the code appear on screen. Find the method `(BOOL) shouldAutorotateToInterfaceOrientation`, which should be near the end of the function. This is called by the device when it's rotated and we're able to tell it when it should and shouldn't update the view. Find the following line:

```
return (interfaceOrientation == UIInterfaceOrientationPortrait);
```

3. At the moment, it checks if the rotation orientation is portrait, and returns `YES` if it is and `NO` if it isn't. We're able to override this check and always say `YES`; change the line to read:

```
return YES;
```

4. This will mean the app will allow the view to rotate to any possible orientation.

5. Run the app and try rotating it; you'll see that the view rotates but it gets cropped in landscape and the banner view isn't visible. For now, we'll ignore the rest of the cropped content but adjust our banner to be in view regardless.

6. Open your view's XIB file in the interface builder. If you're continuing with the demo app, it'll be `iAd_Demo_AppViewController.xib`. Click on the ad banner view at the bottom of the view to select it. From the menu bar, select **View | Utilities | Show Size Inspector**.

7. This opens the size inspector that lets us modify the layout information of the banner view. The size inspector is a pane on the right of Xcode, above the object library.

8. Find the **Autosizing** box and click on the top red double-t beam shape to disable it. Then enable the bottom one with a click. Your auto-sizing settings should look like the following screenshot:

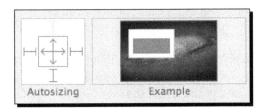

9. This means the banner's position will be set from the bottom of the screen instead of the top, so it'll always be attached to the bottom of the view no matter the height.

10. Test the ad again. The banner now sits at the bottom of the screen no matter what the orientation, but it's not dynamically updating to fill the screen correctly. We need to make the banner view accessible to our code so we can inform it when a rotation occurs. This works similarly to the outlets in iAd Producer.

11. Open the file `iAd_Demo_AppViewController.h` from the project navigator. This will open the code editor in Xcode. After `#import <UIKit/UIKit.h>`, add the following code:

```
#import <iAd/iAd.h>
```

12. This tells the file that we'll be using the iAd framework so it should import it. Now in-between `@interface iAd_Demo_AppViewController : UIViewController` and `@end`, add the following code:

```
{
ADBannerView *bannerView;
}
@property(nonatomic, strong) IBOutlet ADBannerView *bannerView;
```

13. This creates a variable called `bannerView`, which will be accessible from our code. The `IBOutlet` tells the interface builder that the `bannerView` is available as an outlet.

14. Change the code editor to the file `iAd_Demo_AppViewController.m` and after `@implementation iAd_Demo_AppViewController`, add the following code on a new line:

```
@synthesize bannerView;
```

15. This will allow us to access the `bannerView`'s properties.

> You might find that Xcode tries to help you write the code with auto completion and suggestions. In order to confirm that you want it to use a suggestion, press the *tab* key.

16. With our outlet in place, we can connect to it in the interface builder. Open `iAd_Demo_AppViewController.xib` and right-click on the **File's Owner** icon—a wireframe cube found to the left of the interface builder. Click-and-drag the circle, after the **bannerView** outlet in the overlaid list, and drag to the **AdBannerView** on the main view, as shown in the following screenshot:

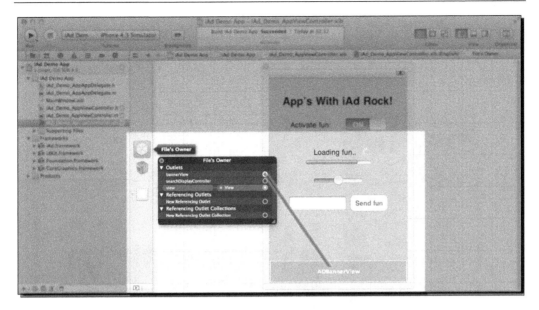

17. This links the outlet we made in our code with the banner on the interface builder view. Now we can access our banner in the code and can inform the banner when a rotation occurs. Before the @end line near the bottom of the file, add the following block of code:

```
(void)willRotateToInterfaceOrientation:(UIInterfaceOrientation)
toInterfaceOrientation duration:(NSTimeInterval)duration
{
    if(UIInterfaceOrientationIsLandscape(toInterfaceOrientation))
        bannerView.currentContentSizeIdentifier
=ADBannerContentSizeIdentifierLandscape;
    else
        bannerView.currentContentSizeIdentifier =
ADBannerContentSizeIdentifierPortrait;
}
```

18. You may find auto complete useful when adding this code. We're taking the `willRotateToInterfaceOrientation` method that is called by the device just before the rotation occurs. We then check the orientation it's going to rotate to and update the `contentSizeIdentifier` property of our banner to that new orientation.

19. Run the app and test by rotating the device; the banner will now update to fill the screen and display a landscape ad.

What just happened?

We improved the experience and potential revenue of our app by tweaking the banner view to work. Your banner should dynamically update the banner creative, no matter what orientation the device is in:

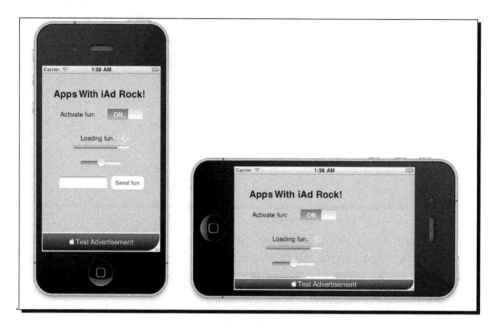

By making the banner view accessible from the code, we're now able to add several more enhancements to our app, such as hiding the view when no ads are available or providing fallback content.

Pop quiz

Xcode and Objective C can be a little overwhelming at first, but once you grasp the basics, you'll notice the similarities it has with iAd Producer. See what you've learnt by trying these questions:

1. To make an object in the interface builder accessible from the code, would you?

    a. Declare an IBOutlet in your code and then connect the outlet in the interface builder

    b. Rename the item in the interface builder and then use that in the code

    c. Just write the code and the interface builder will add the item

    d. Access the views items as [UIView objectAtIndex:0], depending on their location on the page

2. If an iAd banner is crashing our app, what is the most common cause?

    a. No adverts are available

    b. The ad downloaded is too large for the OS to cope

    c. There's no Internet connection

    d. The project is missing the iAd framework

Handling no available ads

Your app will encounter scenarios where the iAd Network is unable to serve an ad. This could be due to poor network coverage or iAd not yet being available in the country of a user. We should gracefully handle this by making sure that we don't display an empty banner and bringing the banner back into view if one becomes available.

Time for action – ban the banner

With a few small tweaks to our view and code, we can animate our banner on and off the screen, depending on the availability of ads:

1. Open the demo project, or your own project containing an Ad Banner View, in Xcode. Open the main controller file for your view, for example, iAd_Demo_ AppViewController.m.

2. Lets' assume that an ad is always going to fail and move the banner out of view as soon as the app comes into view. We'll then wait for the successful message from the iAd Network and bring it into view. Add this following code around line 30:

```
- (void)viewWillAppear:(BOOL)animated
{
    CGRect frame = self.view.bounds;
    CGPoint bannerOrigin =CGPointMake(CGRectGetMinX(frame),
CGRectGetMaxY(frame));
    bannerView.frame = CGRectMake(bannerView.bounds.origin.x,
bannerOrigin.y, bannerView.frame.size.width, bannerView.frame.
size.height);
}
```

3. This takes the frame of the banner and sets the y value to be the height of the current view, which repositions it off screen. Try running your app; you'll see that the banner never appears, even though it's likely the one loaded, because the banner never gets back in place when an ad loads successfully.

4. We'll now use the `delegate` methods of the iAd banner to handle the success and failure responses of the ad. A delegate is a way of interacting and receiving events or messages from an object; in our case, we can implement the banner's delegate in our code so it notifies us of changes. Let's update the code, so the banner knows what it should use for its delegate. In the `viewWillAppear` method we modified a few steps back, add the following to the end of the method:

```
bannerView.delegate = self;
```

5. After adding this, you should see a yellow warning icon appear next to the line number. Click on this to reveal the warning:

6. This warning tells us that although we've set the delegate of the banner view to be the current file (by saying `self`), it currently wouldn't be able to handle its role. Switch files to `iAd_Demo_AppViewController.h`, which is known as the header file, and find `UIViewController`. Update it to say the following:

```
UIViewController<ADBannerViewDelegate>
```

7. This tells our view controller class that it can respond to requests from an Ad Banner View's delegate. With our delegate in place and our view controller able to respond to it, we can now add the successful and failure methods that will handle the ad. Before the `@end` of your `iAd_Demo_AppViewController.m` file, add the following:

```
#pragma mark ADBannerViewDelegate methods
```

8. This isn't required, but it helps separate the sections of our code and highlights where the `delegate` methods start from.

9. After our `pragma mark` line, we can add the delegate methods. Starting with the code to bring the banner back into view once an ad has successfully loaded. Add this method immediately after your `pragma mark` line:

```
- (void) bannerViewDidLoadAd: (ADBannerView *) banner
{
    CGRect frame = self.view.bounds;
    CGPoint bannerOrigin =CGPointMake(CGRectGetMinX(frame),
CGRectGetMaxY(frame));
    bannerOrigin.y -= bannerView.bounds.size.height;

    // Animate into view
    [UIView animateWithDuration:2.0f
        animations:^{
            bannerView.frame = CGRectMake(bannerView.bounds.
origin.x, bannerOrigin.y, bannerView.frame.size.width, bannerView.
frame.size.height);
        }];
}
```

10. Here we've added the method `bannerViewDidLoadAd`, which is a delegate method of the banner. When the iAd Network successfully delivers an ad, it calls this code. We then take the banner's frame and adjust it to bring it back into view, with the added tweak of animating the change so that the banner will move in from the bottom of the view. Run the ad and you'll see the banner appear.

 Sometimes the iAd Network doesn't deliver an advert to simulate a failure. If you find a banner hasn't appeared, try closing and re-opening your app to trigger another ad.

11. With our banner animating in, let's make sure it can also animate out if there's a problem downloading an ad. Once the banner is visible, it'll circulate between various creatives, so we shouldn't just assume once we have one ad that we'll continue to receive a stream of them. Similar to the `bannerViewDidLoadAd` delegate method, we can use the `didFailToReceiveAdWithError` method when we're unable to get an ad. Use this method with the following code, placing it beneath the code we added in the last step:

```
(void)bannerView:(ADBannerView *)banner didFailToReceiveAdWithError:(NSError *)error
{
    CGRect frame = self.view.bounds;
    CGPoint bannerOrigin =CGPointMake(CGRectGetMinX(frame),
CGRectGetMaxY(frame));
    // Animate into view
    [UIView animateWithDuration:2.0f
        animations:^{
            bannerView.frame = CGRectMake(bannerView.bounds.
origin.x, bannerOrigin.y, bannerView.frame.size.width, bannerView.
frame.size.height);
    }];
}
```

12. You may notice that this code is almost identical to when we receive an ad; except, now we're not subtracting the height of the banner from the frame, so it is offscreen. In the next exercise, we'll look at optimizing our code by not duplicating it.

13. If you patiently watch your app, it'll eventually fail to download a banner and you should see the current banner slide out of view.

What just happened?

We added some code to the `viewWillAppear` method, which is called whenever the view is about to become visible. This code hides the empty banner off screen to make more space available for additional components. Using delegates, we set up the view to respond to messages from the iAd Network and animate the banner on and off the screen, depending on the availability of ads.

Have a go hero

Our app is looking great with our banner appearing in our app and correctly resizing on rotation, and displaying or hiding itself when ads become available. If you're finding these steps simple, then try these more advanced tasks:

- Update the **Autosizing** properties of the items in the placeholder app, so they don't get cropped in landscape.

- If you're comfortable with iPhone development, consider grouping all of your content into a view separate from the banner. This can then be a sibling of the banner view and it's layout can be resized, dependent on a banner's availability.

- If you have your own app, try sharing one banner object between all the pages in your app for efficiency.

- Create an iPad project and add a full screen banner into it. For reference, use: `http://developer.apple.com/library/ios/#documentation/ UserExperience/Conceptual/iAd_Guide/Full-ScreenAdvertisements/ Full-ScreenAdvertisements.html`.

- Try the next *Time for Action* section, where, for the more adventurous, we'll tidy up the code!

- Read more about the fundamentals of Objective C at `http:// developer.apple.com/library/mac/#documentation/Cocoa/ Conceptual/CocoaFundamentals/CommunicatingWithObjects/ CommunicateWithObjects.html`.

Time for action – clean the code

When you begin to duplicate code, you're increasing the efforts required to maintain your app, because you have to go through every instance and change it. In our last exercise, we have three similar blocks of code that we can combine into one method that intelligently handles the situations. This function will handle the hiding and displaying of our ad, depending on the banner's availability. Continuing with our demo app, complete the following steps to clean up the code:

1. Before the delegate methods of the banner, and before the `pragma mark`, create an empty method by adding this code:

```
-(void) adjustBannerVisibility
{
}
```

2. We'll need to add the following to the header file, `iAd_Demo_ AppViewController.h`, before the `@end` statement in the file add to tell the project that this new method is available:

```
-(void) adjustBannerVisibility;
```

3. This will suppress any warnings from Xcode about unknown methods. Now return back to the main file—`iAd_Demo_AppViewController.m`.

4. We can now build the function of this method up. It's going to replace and manage the showing and hiding of the banner. Add the following content inside the method:

```
CGRect frame = self.view.bounds;
CGPoint bannerOrigin =CGPointMake(CGRectGetMinX(frame),
CGRectGetMaxY(frame));
    // check if the banner is loaded
    if(bannerView.bannerLoaded) {
        // bring banner into view
        bannerOrigin.y -= bannerView.bounds.size.height;
    }


    // Animate into view
    [UIView animateWithDuration:2.0
        animations:^{
            bannerView.frame = CGRectMake(bannerView.bounds.
origin.x, bannerOrigin.y, bannerView.frame.size.width, bannerView.
frame.size.height);
    }];
```

5. This works the same the previous banner code, but in the one method. The `bannerView.bannerLoaded` checks if we have a banner loaded and then adjusts the offset accordingly.

6. Currently, we're adjusting the banner in the `viewWillAppear`, `didFailToReceiveAdWithError`, and `bannerViewDidLoadAd` methods. Go through each of these methods, and replace the banner frame code with our new method. You can call our method by using the following line of code:

```
[self adjustBannerVisibility];
```

 Make sure you don't remove the `banner.delegate = self;` from the `viewWillAppear` method. This will stop your banner from ever appearing!

For example your `bannerViewDidLoad` method should now look like the following:

```
-(void)bannerViewDidLoadAd:(ADBannerView *)banner
{
    [self adjustBannerVisibility];
}
```

7. As with any change, test your app and make sure the new code works as expected!

What just happened?

By combining several methods into one method, we reduce the risk for failure in our code due to a mistake, and can update our code in one central place without having to duplicate any changes. The app is now much tidier. Deleting code is really satisfying because it means less work in the future!

Summary

In this chapter, we used iAd to provide a simple, well recognized, and immersive banner and ad experience to your app users. To make the banners work elegantly in our app and to maximize revenue opportunities we:

◆ Created a placeholder app to test the iAd functionality

◆ Placed our banner in a static location, using the interface builder

◆ Handled displaying the banner only when it had content

◆ Optimized our code to increase its maintainability

With great visibility of our ads and handling the occasions where no ads are available, we should be able to generate a healthy best-possible revenue stream from our app. Before we can start cashing the checks, we need to activate our application for live ads and look at how we can track the revenue; all coming up in the final chapter!

11

Tracking Revenue and Fallbacks

With iAd banners appearing in your app, you'll want to know how to track the revenue they're generating and how to display alternative banners when the user is offline or the iAd Network is unavailable.

In this final chapter, we'll cover the following topics:

- ◆ Accepting the iAd Network contract
- ◆ Activating your live ads in submitted applications
- ◆ Measuring your income and the terminology used in mobile display advertising
- ◆ Falling back to other ad networks when an iAd isn't available

With this final set of key skills, you'll soon be a mobile advertising master.

Enabling live ads

By default, the iAd Network delivers test advertisements to your app when you've added an iAd banner to one of your views. Apple requires you to activate your application in iTunes Connect before they will serve live, revenue-generating adverts to your app.

Accepting the contract

Enabling live ads for the first time requires you to set up and accept the iAd Network Contract; you may already have this enabled, but if you haven't or are unsure, follow the next exercise to check and sign up.

Time for action – signing the dotted line

If you don't have any applications currently using iAd, the chances are you've not requested and activated the iAd Network Contract with Apple. It's a few simple steps to request this contract, and as long as you accept the terms and conditions, you'll be able to begin generating revenue with the iAd Network.

1. Log in to iTunes Connect by opening `https://itunesconnect.apple.com` in your browser. Your username and password will be the same as your Apple ID we used in *Chapter 1, Getting Started with iAd*, when signing up for the Apple iOS Developer Program.

2. Once logged in, select **Manage My Applications** from the list of options at the lower half of the page. If you haven't yet created an application in iTunes Connect, select **Add New Application** and follow the steps.

> If you're unsure of the application submission process, Apple has a guide for developers available at `http://itunesconnect.apple.com/docs/iTunesConnect_DeveloperGuide.pdf` that covers the process of submitting an application. You're able to manually accept the iAd Network Contract from the Contracts, Tax, and **Banking** section in iTunes Connect.

3. When an application is available in iTunes Connect, select it by clicking its icon. This will open the application summary page; from here, select **Setup iAd Network**. If you've not agreed to the iAd Network Contract, you'll be prompted to sign before continuing.

4. Click on the link to the **iAd Network** contract to open up the available contracts page. Find the **iAd Network** contract, highlighted in the following screenshot, and select **Request**:

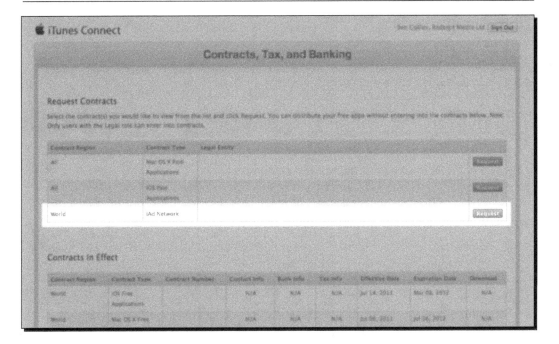

5. Read and accept the terms and conditions. Apple will e-mail you the contract as a PDF, but it'll be active immediately. Before you're able to begin receiving payments for your ads, you'll need to set up your contact info, bank info, and tax info—you'll find these in the **Contracts in Progress** section.

6. You've now accepted the iAd Contract and the iAd Network can begin delivering the money-making banners to your iAd-enabled apps!

What just happened?

Apple won't allow us to display live adverts within our apps before we've entered a contractual agreement with them. Make sure you read the terms and conditions, as they lay out the rules of the agreement, including payment terms and Apple's rights to revoke access to the iAd Network, if your app doesn't meet certain guidelines. As mentioned, your apps will begin to make money once you've submitted an iAd-enabled app, but you won't be able to collect your earnings until you've set up your contact info, bank info, and tax info.

Enabling your ads

Although you've added the iAd banner in your application and accepted the iAd Contract, you would want to display live ads on each app and generate revenue; and this individually needs to be activated and iAd-enabled.

Time for action – enabling ads

With an active iAd Contract with Apple we're able to begin serving live iAd campaigns on a per-app basis. To enable ads, follow the ensuing steps:

1. Log in to iTunes Connect using your Apple ID. Select **Manage Your Applications**. Find and open the application you'd like to enable ads for.

2. From the right-hand menu, select **Set Up iAd Network**, as shown in the following screenshot:

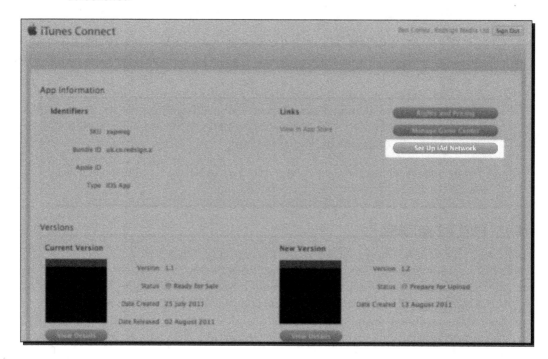

3. Select whether your primary audience is for under 17 year olds. Apple currently doesn't deliver ads to apps targeted at minors. Click on the **Enable iAd** switch then click on **Save**.

To view this screen, your app must be in an editable state. This means you've prepared the details in iTunes Connect for an update or a new app, but haven't yet uploaded the app binary or clicked the **Ready to Upload** button.

4.   Your app is now iAd enabled! Any future binaries you submit for this application will display live ads, once available in the App Store.

What just happened?

As real iAds only appear in non-development apps submitted to the App Store, you have to enable your app before submission because activating your app for iAd only enables it for future uploads. This means you risk test advertisements being delivered in your live app, which by their very nature don't generate any revenue! Once enabled, the only way to stop the delivery of ads to your application is to submit an app update without any banner views. You can't remove your app from the iAd Network from iTunes Connect.

Apple limits live banners from appearing in your development apps to prevent falsely earning revenue while testing your app, and to stop taps being exploited with **click fraud**. Click fraud is when taps or clicks are artificially generated to falsely increase revenue from the iAd Network.

Monitoring your income

Similar to tracking your own iAd campaign, displaying and monitoring the ads in your app requires you to understand the metrics and terminology. The key terms used that we'll be looking at when monitoring income are:

- Revenue
- Impressions
- Requests
- Fill-rate
- eCPM
- Click-through rate

Revenue

This is the key metric—how much money your apps are making! Apple splits their earnings from ads 60/40 in your favor; so for every $100 they generate, you'll receive $60 of it. The revenue shown is your actual take home earnings. Revenue is calculated from a mixture of impressions and clicks the banners in your app receive.

Apple transfers your generated income to you by check or bank transfer once your accumulated revenue reaches a certain threshold.

Impressions

An **impression** is when a banner is loaded and appears in your application. Therefore, the impressions shown are the total amount of banners that have appeared in your app for a given time period.

Requests

Each time your app requests a new banner from the iAd Network to display within your app, this is logged by Apple as a **request**. Each use of your app by a user will typically result in many requests, as the banners in your app will only be displayed for a set period of time before being cycled with fresh content.

Fill-rate

The **fill-rate** is the percentage of requests sent from your app that are successfully filled and return an ad for display. The higher the fill-rate, the better because it means your app is displaying as many ads as possible. A low fill-rate can occur when your app is used heavily in markets that are not yet in the iAd Network.

 To find out the countries and territories currently served by the iAd Network, visit `http://developer.apple.com/iad/`.

If your fill-rate is zero percent, consider contacting Apple; occasionally they can disable ad delivery if they have concerns about the content of your app or don't have any advertisers currently offering ads for your app's genre.

eCPM

eCPM, or effective cost per mille (thousand), is your revenue divided by how many thousand impressions of banners your app shows. It allows you to extrapolate your earnings if the usage of your app, therefore the impressions, were to increase.

If your combined revenue from impressions and clicks is at $2000, and your app's banner impressions are 100 thousand, then your eCPM would be $20. This means for every 1000 impressions, your average earnings would be $20. You can then estimate your earnings; say your app receives 200 thousand impressions, then you'd likely earn 200 multiplied by $20, or $4000.

Click-through rate

The **click-through rate** is the percentage of banner views that result in the user clicking, or tapping it to reveal the core ad unit. Clicks generate more revenue than simple impressions, so having a high click-through rate is ideal. If your click through rate is low, it could be due to the positioning of your banner not being easily accessible to users of your app. Make sure your banner view is added and visible throughout your app, either at the top or the bottom of the screen.

Time for action – analysing earnings

The iAd Network provides a rich visual interface with data and graphs for you to track your app's earnings. You'll need an active app that is live on the store and generating revenue to continue.

1. Sign in to iTunes Connect by visiting `http://itunesconnect.apple.com` and using your Apple ID. From the available options, select **iAd Network**.

 This will only be available once you have a live app using the iAd Network; follow the steps in the last exercise to enable an app for live iAds.

2. After successfully signing in, you'll be shown a summary of all your iAd-enabled apps' earnings for the last seven days and 24 hours. For example, look at the following screenshot:

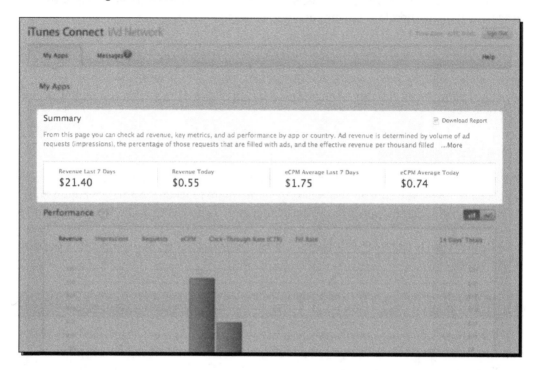

3. Beneath the summary, you'll find a bar chart showing the revenue of your app over the last 14 days; you're able to change between various performance metrics by clicking on the name of the metric found above the graph. You can use these graphs to find patterns and trends in your earnings, such as highlighting which days bring the best revenue or mapping earnings to external promotions, driving people to your app:

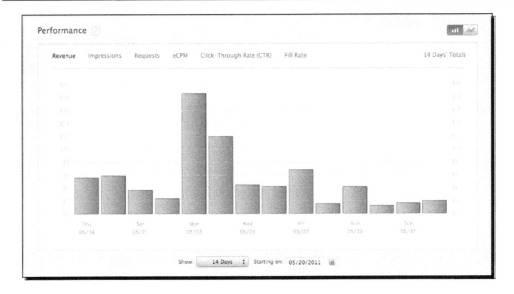

4. Try changing the duration and dates of the graph for your earnings by adjusting the controls found directly under the graph.

5. To view the breakdown of your individual apps, scroll to the bottom of the window to the area shown in the following screenshot. From here, you'll be able to select an application and see the data filtered for it.

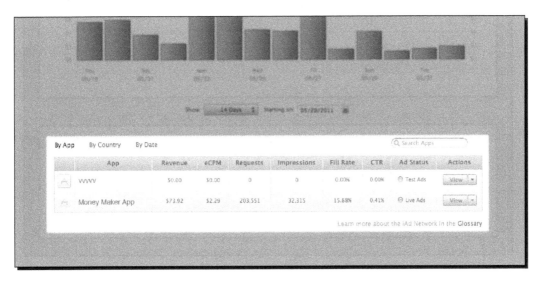

What just happened?

By logging into the iTunes Connect management portal and viewing our iAd earnings, we're able to view summaries, graphs, and accumulated or per-app earnings. This data is typically updated every 24 hours, so keep that in mind when tracking your earnings.

Pop quiz – earning learnings

Being able to track your revenue and predict future earnings can be vital in determining the longevity and profitability of your iAd-enabled apps. Try to answer these questions:

1. If your app has a low click-through rate, what should you do?

   a. Check if you've enabled live banners for all your apps with banners

   b. Add two banners to your app so accidental taps are more likely

   c. Promote your app in countries that are in the iAd Network list

   d. Ensure your banner appears throughout your app, in the recommended position at the top or bottom of your views

2. What is a request?

   a. When the core ad unit is loaded after a tap on a banner

   b. A request occurs when your app first loads and buffers all the ads

   c. When your app asks the iAd Network for a banner to display

   d. The number of times a banner is shown

3. As fill-rate is the percentage of requests from your app that result in an ad showing, how would you calculate it?

   a. Impressions divided by requests

   b. 100 divided by the number of requests, multiplied by the impressions

   c. 100 divided by the number of impressions, multiplied by the total requests

   d. The click-through rate multiplied by 100

Fallbacks

There are occasions when the iAd Network will be unavailable or unable to serve an advert to your application. Ads may be unavailable in your app for many reasons, including:

- The user having no active Internet connection
- The iAd network not currently being available in the country of some of your users
- No available banner and ad creatives in the iAd inventory being targeted for a user or your app's demographic

In these circumstances, no banners or ads will appear in your app. If advertising is the key income for your application, you'll want to provide a fallback advert or revenue stream.

Time for action – adding another ad

As the iAd framework notifies us when no adverts are available, we can use this delegate method to display an alternative banner, namely, a simple image.

1. We'll continue with our demo iAd app that we created in the last chapter; open it in Xcode now. For our banner, we'll use an image that is the same size as an iAd banner, 320px wide and 50px high, but we'll also require a high-resolution, double-sized image for retina displays. In the `iAd Demo App` folder included with the book resources, locate the images `Banner@2x.png` and `Banner.png` to the project navigator, that is, to the left of Xcode.

   Unlike iAd Producer, Xcode doesn't automatically produce our low-resolution images from the high-resolution versions. We need to create one image at 640px by 100px and then save another version at half the size. You can use **Preview** to edit, resize, and save each banner. Name your high-resolution image with `@2x` in the filename before the file extension.

2. With our images available in our project, we'll add them to our view. Select the **iAd_Demo_AppViewController.xib** view to open it in the interface builder. From the object library, find the image view object. Don't forget about the search functionality in the object library if you're unable to locate it. Drag an **Image View** to the view and resize and position it to sit over the current iAd banner view.

3. From the **Attribute Inspector**, set the **Image** property of the image view to **Banner. png**. It should be available from the drop-down list that shows all available images in the project. We don't use our `@2x` image here because the app will automatically load this when the device has a retina display, providing the filenames are the same:

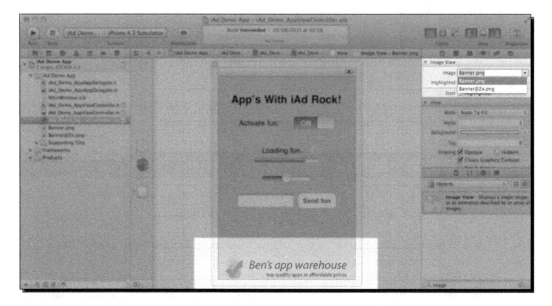

4. You'll see the mock banner image appear on the view. With this in place, we need to update the application code to hide and show the correct banner, dependent on iAd availability.

5. Before we're able to access our fallback banner from our code, we need to add it as an outlet. Select and open the header file `iAd_Demo_AppViewController.h` in the code editor; we have to add a reference to our image view that we can use as an outlet. After the first `ADBannerView *bannerView;`, add the following on a new line:

```
UIImageView   *imageView;
```

6. An image view added in the interface builder is used as reference as `UIImageView` with UI at the beginning because it's a user interface object.

7. After the `@property` where we declare the banner view as an outlet, add the following line of code:

```
@property(nonatomic, strong) IBOutlet UIImageView *imageView;
```

This will let us link the image view in the interface builder with the code.

8. Finally, before we can connect our image view, open the main code file, `iAd_Demo_ AppViewController.m`. Then, after `@synthesize bannerView;`, we need to synthesize our image view by adding the following:

```
@synthesize imageView;
```

9. Return to the view in the interface builder and connect the outlet `imageView` from the **File's Owner** to the image view on the view, as demonstrated in the following screenshot:

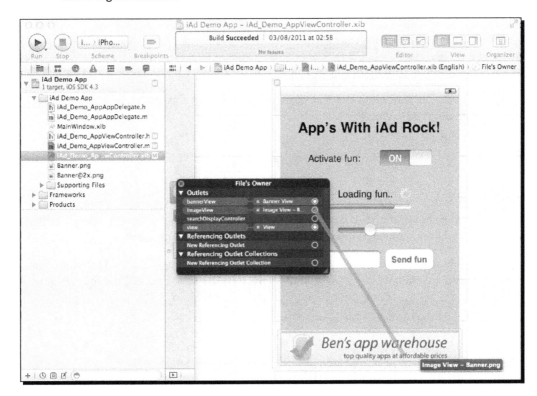

 Refer to the previous chapter, if you need a reminder on connecting outlets in Xcode.

10. With the view's outlet connected, we're able to reposition the mock-banner, depending on the iAd's banner availability. Go back to the main file for the view to open it in the code editor. Find the method `adjustBannerVisibility` around line 71. This is called and executed whenever we need to adjust the positioning of our banners, so it is the ideal method to use. Duplicate (by copying and pasting) the line that contains `CGPoint bannerOrigin` and rename `bannerOrigin` to `fallbackBannerOrigin`, so it now reads as follows:

```
    CGPoint bannerOrigin = CGPointMake(CGRectGetMinX(frame),
CGRectGetMaxY(frame));
    CGPoint fallbackBannerOrigin = CGPointMake(CGRectGetMinX(fra
me), CGRectGetMaxY(frame));
```

11. This will give us two frames to adjust, one for the banner and one for the fallback.

12. Find the `if` statement that checks whether a banner has loaded and add the following code after it:

```
    else {
        fallbackBannerOrigin.y -= imageView.bounds.size.height;
    }
```

13. This code will only be executed when the `if` statement is false, so when a banner view isn't available, this block will run. Similar to our banner view frame, we adjust the fallback banner frame by its height to bring it back into view.

14. Finally, we'll add the changes to the frame in our animation block and find the line where we animate our banner view frame into the view and add the following:

```
    imageView.frame = CGRectMake(imageView.bounds.origin.x,
fallbackBannerOrigin.y, imageView.frame.size.width, imageView.
frame.size.height);
```

15. The final method should look like the following code snippet:

```
-(void) adjustBannerVisibility
{
    CGRect frame = self.view.bounds;
    CGPoint bannerOrigin = CGPointMake(CGRectGetMinX(frame),
CGRectGetMaxY(frame));
    CGPoint fallbackBannerOrigin = CGPointMake(CGRectGetMinX(fra
me), CGRectGetMaxY(frame));
    // check if the banner is loaded
    if (bannerView.bannerLoaded) {
        // bring banner into view
        bannerOrigin.y -= bannerView.bounds.size.height;
    }
```

```
      else {
          fallbackBannerOrigin.y -= imageView.bounds.size.height;
      }
      // Animate the frames view
      [UIView animateWithDuration:2.0f
                      animations:^{
                          bannerView.frame = CGRectMake(bannerView.
      bounds.origin.x, bannerOrigin.y, bannerView.frame.size.width,
      bannerView.frame.size.height);
                          imageView.frame = CGRectMake(imageView.
      bounds.origin.x, fallbackBannerOrigin.y, imageView.frame.size.
      width, imageView.frame.size.height);
                      }];
  }
```

16. Run your app. You should see the fallback banner appear and then swap with a live iAd if a banner from the iAd Network is available. Try turning off your Internet connection to force the fallback to come into effect.

What just happened?

Although this is a very rudimentary banner system, it allows you to continue to generate some revenue when the iAd Network isn't available. By adding an image view to the app's main view with an outlet, we're able to reference it from our code. With our fallback image accessible, we modified the `adjustBannerVisibility` method to hide or show our image dependent on the availability of an iAd banner, using the `bannerLoaded` property of our banner view.

You could use this banner for your own promotion, potentially of other apps, or sell the space to others wanting to advertise within your application. You can use your fill-rate and requests to estimate how many times this fallback banner has appeared. However, this won't accommodate for when your users are offline.

Have a go hero

Our image-based banner provides a suitable fallback when the iAd Network is unavailable. If you're comfortable with iOS development and want to improve the banner fallback and its profitability, consider these tweaks:

◆ Replace the image view with an alternative image when the device changes to a landscape orientation.

◆ Use the image views outlet and the rotation method to update the file used for the image.

- Download your banners from a remote server so you can update them with new advertisements.

- Enable the banner to be clickable and open up an external webpage.

- Add an alternative ad network's banner view in place of our custom image. Many people use AdMob—`http://www.admob.com/` from Google. However, there are many smaller providers available.

Summary

By tracking revenue and providing fallback content, you're monitoring and improving the financial success of your app. In this final chapter, you've done the following:

- Accepted the Apple iAd Contract that is required to display live adverts in your apps

- Activated live ads in each of your apps

- Learnt the terminology used for tracking revenue

- Viewed the revenue your apps are generating

- Displayed fallback banner content when the iAd Network is unavailable

With these skills, you're fully able to embrace iAd, as both an advertiser and ad publisher. Good luck!

Pop Quiz Answers

Chapter 2, Preparing Your Content

Why do we optimize our images with software like ImageOptim?	Answer: C As images can often contain unnecessary data, optimizing them reduces the file size so they download quicker to the user of our iAd.
What tool should you use in Preview to remove a solid block of color to make part of an image transparent?	Answer: B Instant Alpha is correct; it's called this because alpha is often used as a term for the level of transparency an image has.
Which image format should you use whenever you can?	Answer: A You should use JPEGs whenever you can; they're able to be compressed to keep their file size down.
When would you need to use a PNG image?	Answer: B You'd use a PNG when you have a transparent 'see through' section of an image, as JPEG doesn't support transparency. Other times you'd use PNG, including for images with text or crisp line art, and images with large blocks of color.

What audio format should you convert your sound files to?	Answer: B m4a audio files use AAC, which iOS devices are able to decode quickly and efficiently.
What does the 'reference movie' created by QuickTime do?	Answer: C The reference movie selects the optimal version of your video depending on the user's bandwidth. This ensures users on high bandwidth connections see the best quality video available, and users on slower networks don't spend needless time waiting for content to load.

Chapter 3, Making Your iAd

Why should we tweak our iAd banner to look good in portrait and landscape?	Answer: B & D Trick question! Apple requires each iAd to work in portrait and landscape so it looks great in any orientation. Supporting both situations means our iAd can appear in any app containing an iAd banner.
What is a radial gradient?	Answer: C A radial gradient is a transition between two or more colored circles; we use them in iAd Producer as they can generate a great lightweight effect without any images.
Where would you go to find media you've imported into your iAd?	Answer: D The Asset Library contains all the assets you've imported into your iAd Producer project. To add media to your asset library just drag them to the asset library, or choose File then Import Assets from the menu bar.
What is the name for a text box that changes between multiple values?	Answer: A Whilst the other names are more exciting, the multi-label object consists of several cells which transition between each other.

Appendix

Chapter 4, Making Sure it Works

| What did we have to install to use the iOS Simulator? | Answer: A

Both Xcode and the iOS SDK were installed at the same time to give us access to the simulator. Xcode is the tool used by developers to build iOS and Mac apps that are available on the App Store. |
|---|---|
| How do you do a pinch gesture using the iOS Simulator? | Answer: D

Holding down 'ctrl' brings up two touch points on the screen; you can then click and drag to simulate two fingers pinching or de-pinching the screen. |
| If you wanted to test the buttons in your iAd, which is the best to use? | Answer: B

The inaccuracy of touch based inputs can only be tested using real fingers, so on device testing is vital to make sure buttons and touch areas are large enough to be tapped with ease. Whenever you touch the screen of your iOS device, it performs thousands of calculations to determine the center of the touch, which can't be simulated with a mouse click. |
| You've changed the animation of one of your elements and want to see how it looks; which method would you use? | Answer: A, then B, then C.

Besides the canvas, all of these are able to show you how the animation will look; however, testing on a device is the only way to know how well they will perform. The iAd Testing Server shouldn't be used for this kind of testing; you should only use this for final checks before launching your iAd. |
| You've imported some extra assets and want to check they've been scaled correctly; which of these would you use? | Answer: A, B, and D

When importing assets, it is useful to check iAd Producer has scaled them as you'd expect for high resolution retina and standard resolution displays. Graphics can be previewed in either retina or standard resolution in all testing methods except in Safari, although only a true retina device will show you exactly how the images will look. |

Chapter 5, Templates and Objects

If you want a blank menu template with navigation, what should you do?	Answer:D
How do you know what styles are saved when creating a style preset?	Answer:D Whenever you save a style preset, you're shown an editable checklist of the styles that will be stored with the preset.
What styling should you apply to a highlighted, or tapped, button?	Answer: A You should invert the normal button gradient to create a depressed, pushed in feel, mimicking a real button.
What color should be applied to a button in the normal, or default state?	Answer: B Your normal button state should be light at the top and dark at the bottom. This pops the button out from the screen and makes it look realistic.
Why might you want to prevent the transition between your splash page and preroll video?	Answer: B If your splash page matches the first frame of your video, then you should remove the transitions to prevent a flicker between the two. Specifically, the preroll shouldn't have its transition set to none.
When does the **Page Disappear** action start?	Answer: C The build out animation always occurs before the page disappear transition.

Chapter 6, iAd Destinations

How do you get a Store ID, for a digital item, required by the purchase template in iAd Producer?	Answer: C To get the Store ID we search for an item using the iTunes Store in the iTunes app, then click **copy link** in the menu next to the price. We can then get the ID from the link.
What's the Store ID of this link for a song - `http://itunes.apple.com/gb/album/a-beautiful-mine/id148031770?i=148032644?`	Answer: D As you can only purchase songs, not albums, in iAds, the Store ID for song links is the last bit, after `i=`. iAd Producer will show an error when you try to use an ID which isn't correct.

Chapter 7, Building for the Big Screen

When creating an iAd, why should we include multiple banners?	Answer: D Including multiple banner creatives means users seeing your ad several times get an updating stream of banners, keeping your iAd looking fresh and interesting.
When does the **Page Disappear** action start?	Answer: C The Navigation Bar and Tab Bar layout type leaves your fullscreen banner in landscape with 655 pixels of available height. Therefore this is the layout which is often most likely to cause issues with your iAd.

Chapter 8, Creating Interactive Ads

Which of these would be the correct way to declare a variable name `cyril` with the string `the squirrel has lost his nuts`?	Answer: B If your splash page matches the first frame of your video, then you should remove the transitions to prevent a flicker between the two. Specifically, the preroll shouldn't have its transition set to none.
Which of following are the correct way of showing a Boolean value?	Answer: B Boolean values are defined with either true or false, which can be used to show on or off states in a variable or used to set properties of certain controls.

Chapter 9, Managing a Successful iAd Campaign

You have a store finder page and a gallery in your ad; would you:	Answer: B Although it could be tempting to include no sections on a small ad, remember, you may want to modify and tweak the ad later. Say you add another gallery or an email contact form; you've now able to use the analytics you captured from earlier versions of your ad.
Give each page a section so they're easy to separate and identify.	Answer: C Giving each page a section would defeat the point of using sections as pages and their events are already grouped and collated. Equally, ignoring sections would be a mistake as there are some clear correlation between our pages. Ultimately, sections come down to your overall analytics strategy and personal preference - just make sure they make sense.

Chapter 10, Adding iAds into Your App

To make an object in interface builder accessible from the code would you:	Answer: A We need to declare our outlet in both our header and main file, and then connect it to the file owner in interface builder. You are able to add objects to your view programmatically from the code, but they'll only appear at runtime and won't show up in interface builder.
If an iAd banner is crashing our app, what is the most common cause:	Answer:D Although not the only cause of crashes, it's likely you've forgotten to add the iAd framework to your projects build phase.

Chapter 11: Tracking Revenue and Fallbacks

If your app has a low click through rate, what should you do:	Answer: D As click through rate is the percentage of impressions that result in the user clicking your banner view, it's likely a low value could be caused by poor positioning of your banner. You should only ever show one banner so increasing the amount of banners won't increase your click-through rate and could result in your iAd Contract being revoked.
What is a request?	Answer: C Providing the user is online, every request for an iAd banner within your app will be registered and tracked in the iAd Network.
As fill rate is the percentage of requests from your app that result in an ad showing, how would you calculate it?	Answer: B The fill rate is calculated by working out the percentage of requests to the network that are fulfilled with a banner being returned. If your app sends 2000 requests, and receives 1000 banners, your fill rate is 50% because 100 divided by 2000, multiplied by 1000 is 50.

Index

O

object events 225
Objective C 287
objects
  about 154-158
  adding 150-153
  combining, to create unique menu 205-209
onTouchUpInside event 229
onViewControllerViewDidLoad event function
    225
Opacity style section 148
orientation 19
  changes, handling 278-281
Original Size button 215
Original Size option 154
outlet property 243

P

padding 139
page events 225
page objects
  accessing 221-224
pages
  creating 138-141
  notable page templates, highlighting 142
Pan to View template 143
placeholder app
  about 270-273
  Xcode used 270, 271
play function 243
PNG 30
popover 237
portal
  device, adding 274, 275
poster frame 128
pragma mark line 285
prerollin videos
  using 128-132
Preroll page 202
presentComposer function 229
Present voucher codes in store, text label 181
Preview
  about 30
  using, for image cropping 30-32

Preview tool 35
pricing models 254
project
  device, running on 274, 275
properties
  about 220
  section 129, 131, 167
provisioning profile 275
Purchase page 166
Purchase template 167

Q

QuickTime 42
QuickTime X 42

R

Rectangular Selection tool 33
Retina display 18
reveal transition 14
Roast Flavors
  URL 154
root view 15
rotating template 133

S

Safari
  testing in 87, 88
screenshots
  recording 121, 123
  taking 120
scroll view
  used, for scrolling content 212-216
section, from image
  cropping 33-35
sections
  using 261-263
setMessageBody function 228
shakes 19
Shake to Change template, core ad pages
  using 79, 80
Shake view object 154
showsVerticalScrollIndicator property 224
slide transition 13

Thank you for buying
iAd Production Beginner's Guide

About Packt Publishing

Packt, pronounced 'packed', published its first book "Mastering phpMyAdmin for Effective MySQL Management" in April 2004 and subsequently continued to specialize in publishing highly focused books on specific technologies and solutions.

Our books and publications share the experiences of your fellow IT professionals in adapting and customizing today's systems, applications, and frameworks. Our solution-based books give you the knowledge and power to customize the software and technologies you're using to get the job done. Packt books are more specific and less general than the IT books you have seen in the past. Our unique business model allows us to bring you more focused information, giving you more of what you need to know, and less of what you don't.

Packt is a modern, yet unique publishing company, which focuses on producing quality, cutting-edge books for communities of developers, administrators, and newbies alike. For more information, please visit our website: www.PacktPub.com.

Writing for Packt

We welcome all inquiries from people who are interested in authoring. Book proposals should be sent to author@packtpub.com. If your book idea is still at an early stage and you would like to discuss it first before writing a formal book proposal, contact us; one of our commissioning editors will get in touch with you.

We're not just looking for published authors; if you have strong technical skills but no writing experience, our experienced editors can help you develop a writing career, or simply get some additional reward for your expertise.

PUBLISHING

iPhone User Interface Cookbook

ISBN: 978-1-84969-114-7   Paperback: 262 pages

A concise dissection of Apple's iOS user interface design principles

1. Learn how to build an intuitive interface for your future iOS application

2. Avoid app rejection with detailed insight into how to best abide by Apple's interface guidelines

3. Written for designers new to iOS, who may be unfamiliar with Objective-C or coding an interface

4. Chapters cover a variety of subjects, from standard interface elements to optimizing custom game interfaces

iOS 5 Essentials

ISBN: 978-1-84969-226-7   Paperback: 300 pages

Harness iOS 5's new powerful features to create stunning applications

1. Integrate iCloud, Twitter and AirPlay into your applications

2. Lots of step-by-step examples, images and diagrams to get you up to speed in no time with helpful hints along the way.

3. Each chapter explains iOS 5's new features in-depth, whilst providing you with enough practical examples to help incorporate these features in your apps

4. From the author of Xcode 4 iOS development.

Please check **www.PacktPub.com** for information on our titles

www.ingramcontent.com/pod-product-compliance
Lightning Source LLC
LaVergne TN
LVHW062305060326
832902LV00013B/2055